GATHERINGS

A WEST TEXAS
COLLECTION OF RECIPES

CREDITS

This cookbook is a collection of our favorite recipes,
which are not necessarily original recipes.

Published by: Favorite Recipes® Press
P. O. Box 305142
Nashville, Tennessee 37230

Library of Congress Number: 92-28196
ISBN: 0-87197-349-9

First Printing: 1992   12,500 copies

FOREWORD

Caprock Girl Scout Council is proud to celebrate the 80th Anniversary of the Girl Scouts of the United States of America with this cookbook, *Gatherings*. Since 1956, the girls and the adults who have led them have come together from the 18 counties of our council to learn and enjoy the greatest of our land and history.

From the ranches of Dickens, Bailey, Cochran and Parmer and the farms of Motley, Briscoe and Crosby our Girl Scout families have sent these recipes to you. Your Girl Scout neighbors in Lynn, Terry and Yoakum counties dug through mamas' cookbooks to pick the best of their treasured favorites. Long distance calls from Lubbock, Hockley and Lamb drew in a few famous friends that have moved on but know where home is. Long remembered Sunday dinners in Garza, Castro, Swisher, Hale and Floyd are the reason for the one-of-a-kind delights.

For 35 years we have gathered to teach the family values that the people of Caprock hold dear. Girl Scouting and its promise "to try to serve God and country and to help people at all times" will continue to help girls ages 5 to 17 learn how to make these values come alive in their own lives.

GATHERINGS

"We Gather Together to Ask the Lord's Blessings" is sung on Sundays and as a woman turns the chicken for dinner.

We gather the grain before the rain comes, as the rain gathers to feed the roots which feed the flock.

We gather in front of the post office or at the mall to catch up on neighbors...and who's hurt...or who's out of town.

Family and dear friends gather to christen a new baby and taste the casseroles brought to celebrate the new day.

We gather to plow our neighbor's fields or harvest his crop when he is taken sick or gone to tend someone dear.

We gather our children to hear stories of Aunt Hank when she first saw the Caprock, and of Quanah Parker.

We gather at the big kitchen table as mama makes tortillas and puts on a pot of beans.

We gather as Black and Brown and White and Yellow to vote and hope for tomorrow's dream . . . .

Myra G. Burris

ACKNOWLEDGEMENTS

The Caprock Girl Scout Council of West Texas wishes to express its appreciation to those individuals who have assisted with the collection of recipes in the cookbook, *Gatherings*.

COOKBOOK COMMITTEE

Jan Kennedy, Editor
Susan McDonald,
    Marketing Director
Debbie Bergen
Debbie Greenwood
Sylvia Gonzalez

Andrea Hernandez
Nelda Merriott
Ann Owens
Lee Ruth Krieg, Council President
Myra G. Burris, Executive Director

COMMUNITY COOKBOOK COLLECTORS

Kay Alexander
Rhonda Bentley
Lynn Buxkemper
Pat Cruse
Cathy Davis
Linda Duckworth
Georgia Mae Ericson
Brenda Farr
Mrs. J. W. Gardenhire
Suzzie Hubble
Carol Huggins

Sheila Keefer
Shelly Livingston
Janet McBee
Cleo Nugent
Dee Dee Riley
Cathy Self
Ramona Thiel
Paula Thrasher
Barbara Todd
Kristy White
Joyce Williams

We also acknowledge the dedication of the Council Staff and Board of Directors for their enthusiasm and support of *Gatherings* and Girl Scouts throughout the eighteen counties.

BOARD OF DIRECTORS

Lee Ruth Krieg, President
Sylvia Martinez, 1st Vice-President
Lynn Buxkemper, 2nd
   Vice-President

Mickey Hall, 3rd Vice-President
Sue Looney, Board Secretary
Darrell Calvert, Treasurer

MEMBERS-AT-LARGE

Alice L. Chavez
Vivian Cockrell
Georgia Mae Ericson
David Garza
Kathy Gilbreath
Debbie Greenwood
Dorothy Griffin
Lillie Hart
Pat Henry

Sam Hill
Sheila Jolivette
Donald Park
Floyd Price
Dede Sava
Larry Valdez
Carlos Vigil
Myrt Wilder
Richard Zartman

STAFF

Myra G. Burris, Executive Director
Penny Morin, Director of
   Membership Services
Diana Phillips, Director of Fund
   Development and PR
Kathy Hunt, Director of Program
Debbie Martin, Field Executive/
   PR Coordinator
Renee Parker, Field Executive/
   PR Coordinator
Janice Sutton, Field Executive/
   PR Coordinator

Sylvia Pena, Community
   Development Director
George Moore, Camp Ranger
Joyce Nash, Business Manager
Maria V. Cavazos, Secretary
Debi Schulz, Secretary
Opal Barker, Receptionist
Yolonda Kelly, Resident Camp
   Director
Anne Glover, Registrar

Special thanks to Myra Burris for her support and enthusiasm for the cookbook and for her beautiful sketches.

CONTRIBUTORS

VIP CONTRIBUTORS

A special note of thanks to these very important people who donated their favorite recipes to *Gatherings*:

First Lady Barbara Bush
Senator John T. Montford
Former First Lady Nancy Reagan
Waylon Jennings

Alair, Karen
Alexander, Hazel
Alexander, Kay
Allen, Alice
Allen, Patsy
Amen, Cathy
Amerson, Barbara
Amerson, Jessie
Anderson, Judy
Babb, Barbara
Banks, Lana
Beach, Martha
Beecher, Kate
Bell, Betty
Bentley, Rhonda
Bentley, Shonda
Bergen, Debbie
Bergen, Helen
Blackmon, Joan
Blake, Mrs. R. W.
Blankenship, Natalie
Blevins, Angel
Blevins, Camille
Blevins, Jaquita
Blevins, Tabatha
Blodgett, Karen
Bobbett, Gladys
Bock, Kathy
Bolden, Joline
Bolyard, Tami

Bonilla, Irma
Bowman, Judy
Bramlet, Annabel
Brown, Dianne
Bryson, N. A.
Burress, Shirley
Burris, Myra G.
Burt, Connie
Busby, Lauren
Butler, Sandy
Buxkemper, Lynn
Byers, Pansy
Caceres, Mary Lou
Cain, Charlotte
Carr, Kathy J.
Cavazos, Maria V.
Chadwick, Colleen
Chambers, Ginny
Childress, Una
Chisholm, Maurine
Clayton, Myrtle
Cloud, Darla
Coker, Barbara
Coleman, Susan
Connell, Elizabeth
Cook, JoAnn
Cook, Lisa
Cook, Welda
Corbin, Mrs. Kilmer
Corley, Paula

Cowley, Janis
Cox, Carrie Lynn
Cox, Terri
Cruse, Pat
Curry, Betty
Curtis, Kathy
Daniel, Monda
Davis, Jane
DeAnda, Josie
Dennis, Betty
Dobmeier, Ann Marie
Dominquez, Connie
Donovan, Hazel
Duckworth, Linda
Duckworth, Shelia
Dykes, Sharon
Efird, Ruth
Ericson, Georgia Mae
Estrada, Megan Ashley
Falbo, Nell
Farr, Brenda
Farris, Mrs. T. Kinder
Fields, Roger
Florez, Ophelia
Flusche, Joanne
Forbes, Sue
Galloway, Debbie
Garcia, Margie P.
Gardenhire, Mary Frances
Geissler, Phyllis
Gentry, Janet
Glover, Anne S.
Goen, Guy H.
Gonzalez, Sylvia
Gonzalez, Vanessa
Greenwood, Debbie
Gross, Christine
Gross, Jim
Haberer, Debbie
Haberer, Sue
Hale, Zelma
Hall, Mickey
Hall, Sygale
Hampton, Gladys
Hatch, Suzanne
Hatchel, Caroline
Hausmann, Bettye
Hendrix, Mary Edna
Henry, Pat
Hernandez, Monica
Hight, Dahlia

Hightower, Christy
Hill, Johnnie
Hoho, Beulah
Hubble, Suzzie
Huffaker, Linda
Huggins, Carol
Hunt, Kathy
Hunter, Mrs. Roland
Jakobsmeier, Margie
James, Magoline
Johnston, Joan
Johnston, Marie
Johnston, Naomi
Jones, Barbara June
Jones, Dell
Jones, Jane Prince
Jones, Windy
Keesee, Sheriff D.L. "Sonny"
Kellar, Jenna V.
Kelley, Leta
Kelly, Yolonda
Kennedy, Jan
Kern, Julia
Kirby, Mrs. Billie
Krieg, Lee Ruth
Kyle, Betty Anne
LaMaster, Zita
Lattimore, Mrs. James
Leal, Lori
Lee, Myrtle
Leicht, Margaret Mary
Lepard, Kay
Lewis, Mern
Lewis, Camille
Lewis, Sara
Lientz, Janice
Linn, Abisué
Livingston, Shelly
Longoria, Laura
Lovelady, Debbie
Lowe, Carrie
Mallett, Connie
Martin, Billie
Martin, Connie
Martin, Debbie
Martin, Valerie
Martinez, Charity
Mason, Darla
McAllister, Laverne
McAllister, Mildred
McDonald, Susan

McCulley, Jane B.
Merriott, Nelda
Miles, Mickey Ann
Miller, Laquita
Miller, Vickie
Mills, Frankie
Mims, Beth
Moorhouse, Linda
Moore, Beth A.
Moore, George
Morin, Penny
Moses, Debi
Moses, Pat
Murdock, Wanda
Nash, Joyce
Nichols, TyAnn
Noble, Ann
O'Hair, Jeanette
Ontiveros, Connie
Orman, Debbie
Otken, Helen
Owens, Ann
Owens, Tammy
Paez, Rosa
Parish, Betty
Parish, Gwen
Parish, Jenna
Parker, Brenda
Parker, Nicole
Pellham, Jennifer
Pena, Sylvia
Phillips, Diana
Porter, Joan Thompson
Pounds, Judy
Pratas, Cyndi
Pylant, Lola
Quarles, Angela
Quarles, Linda
Rackler, Joann
Ramos, Tina
Ray, Tammy
Redman, Phyllis
Richards, Doris
Russell, Alarah
Salsky, DeAnn
Sandman, Mrs. Ben
Scott, Betty
Simmons, Berta
Smith, Latina
Steffens, Debbie

Stephens, Carolyn
Stephenson, Leigh Anne
Stewart, Joann
Stolle, LaVerne
Stroud, Karla
Struve, Minnie H.
Suttle, Imogene
Sutton, Janice
Tatum, Carrie
Tharp, Marlana
Thompson, Anne
Thompson, Linda
Thompson, Lorene
Threet, Gail
Tobias, Carol
Torres-Naron, Ruth
Townsen, Kristi
Tucker, Shirley
Tullis, Meredith
Turner, Amanda
Turner, Holly
Tyson, Rita
Urrutia, Stella
Vandiver, Doris
Vandiver, Lyn
Verden, Evelyn
Vernon, Doreen
Vessels, Patsy
Wagnon, Betty
Waits, Lelloine
Watkins, Susan
Webster, Mary Beth McKibben
White, Judy
White, Lydia
White, Sherry
Wiles, Debbie
Wiles, Holly
Williams, Gary
Williams, Joyce W.
Williams, Mercedes
Wilson, Joni Lynch
Wilson, Louisa
Wilson, Paula
Wilson, Renee
Wolf, Dawn
Wood, Jan
Woods, Thresa
Wright, Mrs. Eldon
Young, Richard

SPECIAL THANKS

JOE DON BUCKNER
Photographer

Joe Don Buckner was born in Lockney, Texas, and moved to Lubbock when he was five years old. He attended Lubbock Christian University, South Plains College and Texas Tech University.

Joe Don became a professional photographer at the age of sixteen. He has owned and operated a commercial and portrait studio and has worked for many years as a photo journalist.

Currently, Joe Don is the Photo Manager of the *Lubbock Avalanche-Journal*. He is the recipient of several awards from the Associated Press for feature and color photography.

ROBERT ALDEN SHIVE
Poet

Robert Shive is a 4th generation Texan who was reared in Coahoma, Texas, a town founded and named by his great grandfather. Rob was educated at Howard College and Texas Tech University. Shive has been writing poetry for 20 years and writes frequently about his favorite subject, the people and state of Texas. The poet finished his first book entitled *Drylander* in 1988. He is currently working on his second collection of poetry, *Dust Devils*. Shive currently resides and works in Lubbock, Texas, where he is employed as Director of Admissions and Student Affairs for the School of Allied Health at Texas Tech University Health Service Center.

CONTENTS

NUTRITIONAL GUIDELINES

The editors have attempted to present these family recipes in a form that allows approximate nutritional values to be computed. Persons with dietary or health problems or whose diets require close monitoring should not rely solely on the nutritional information provided. They should consult their physicians or a registered dietitian for specific information.

Abbreviations for Nutritional Analysis

Cal — Calories	Dietary Fiber — Fiber	Sod — Sodium
Prot — Protein	T Fat — Total Fat	gr — gram
Carbo — Carbohydrates	Chol — Cholesterol	mg — milligrams

Nutritional information for these recipes is computed from information derived from many sources, including materials supplied by the United States Department of Agriculture, computer databanks and journals in which the information is assumed to be in the public domain. However, many specialty items, new products and processed foods may not be available from these sources or may vary from the average values used in these analyses. More information on new and/or specific products may be obtained by reading the nutrient labels. Unless otherwise specified, the nutritional analysis of these recipes is based on all measurements being level.

- **Artificial sweeteners** vary in use and strength so should be used "to taste," using the recipe ingredients as a guideline. Sweeteners using aspartame (NutraSweet and Equal) should not be used as a sweetener in recipes involving prolonged heating which reduces the sweet taste. For further information, refer to package information.
- **Alcoholic ingredients** have been analyzed for the basic ingredients, although cooking causes the evaporation of alcohol thus decreasing caloric content.
- **Buttermilk, sour cream** and **yogurt** are types available commercially.
- **Cake mixes** which are prepared using package directions include 3 eggs and ½ cup oil.
- **Chicken**, cooked for boning and chopping, has been roasted; this method yields the lowest caloric values.
- **Cottage cheese** is cream-style with 4.2% creaming mixture. Dry-curd cottage cheese has no creaming mixture.
- **Eggs** are all large. To avoid raw eggs that may carry salmonella as in eggnog or 6-week muffin batter, use an equivalent amount of commercial egg substitute.
- **Flour** is unsifted all-purpose flour.
- **Garnishes**, serving suggestions and other optional additions and variations are not included in the analysis.
- **Margarine** and **butter** are regular, not whipped or presoftened.
- **Milk** is whole milk, 3.5% butterfat. Lowfat milk is 1% butterfat. Evaporated milk is whole milk with 60% of the water removed.
- **Oil** is any type of vegetable cooking oil. Shortening is hydrogenated vegetable shortening.
- **Salt** and other ingredients to taste as noted in the ingredients have not been included in the nutritional analysis.
- If a choice of ingredients has been given, the nutritional analysis information reflects the first option. If a choice of amounts has been given, the nutritional analysis reflects the greater amount.

Appetizers & Beverages

Bailey County

Magic sands,

XIT, the YL.

Blackwater Draw,

the Pecos and Northern.

Peter James Bailey, citizens,

this is your piece of Texas,

your mark is made.

R.S.

CHEESE BALL

16 ounces cream cheese, softened
10 ounces extra-sharp Cheddar
  cheese, shredded
1 4-ounce jar pimentos, chopped

1 4-ounce can green chilies, chopped
1/4 teaspoon onion salt
1/8 teaspoon garlic salt
1/2 cup cracker crumbs

Combine cream cheese, cheese, pimentos, chilies, onion salt and garlic salt in bowl; mix well. Shape into large ball. Roll in cracker crumbs. Chill thoroughly. Let stand to come to room temperature. Yield: 65 servings.

Approx Per Serving: Cal 46; Prot 2 g; Carbo 1 g; Fiber <1 g;
    T Fat 4 g; 77% Calories from Fat; Chol 12 mg; Sod 79 mg.

Janice Lientz, New Deal

CHEESE ROLLS

16 ounces cream cheese, softened
1 cup shredded Cheddar cheese
1 2-ounce jar dried beef, chopped

1 green bell pepper, chopped
1/2 cup finely chopped pecans

Mix first 4 ingredients in bowl. Shape into 2 grapefruit-sized balls. Roll in pecans. Chill until serving time. Serve with crackers. Yield: 50 servings.

Approx Per Serving: Cal 51; Prot 2 g; Carbo 1 g; Fiber <1 g;
    T Fat 5 g; 83% Calories from Fat; Chol 14 mg; Sod 80 mg.

Jenna V. Kellar, Earth

CRAB MEAT SPREAD

1 6-ounce can crab meat
1 envelope unflavored gelatin
1 10-ounce can cream of mushroom
  soup

8 ounces cream cheese, softened
1 cup chopped celery
1 cup chopped green onions
1 cup mayonnaise

Drain crab meat, reserving 3 tablespoons liquid. Soften gelatin in reserved liquid. Combine with soup in saucepan. Cook until heated through. Stir in cream cheese. Add celery, green onions and mayonnaise; mix well. Spoon into fish mold. Chill until set. Unmold onto serving plate. Serve with crackers. Yield: 60 servings.

Approx Per Serving: Cal 48; Prot 1 g; Carbo 1 g; Fiber <1 g;
    T Fat 5 g; 85% Calories from Fat; Chol 9 mg; Sod 82 mg.

Lelloine Waits, Abernathy

Ham Log Appetizer Spread

1 cup deviled ham
8 ounces cream cheese, softened
3 tablespoons finely chopped green
  bell pepper
2 tablespoons finely chopped onion
2 tablespoons finely chopped pimento

1 tablespoon prepared horseradish
1 teaspoon Worcestershire sauce
1/8 teaspoon freshly ground pepper
1/2 cup finely chopped chives
3 tablespoons salad seasoning

Combine deviled ham, cream cheese, green pepper, onion, pimento, horseradish, Worcestershire sauce and pepper in bowl; mix well. Divide mixture into halves. Spoon onto waxed paper. Roll into 3 to 4-inch logs. Chill, wrapped, for several hours or overnight. Mix chives and salad seasoning on waxed paper. Roll chilled logs in chive mixture, coating generously. Serve with crackers. Yield: 50 servings.

Approx Per Serving: Cal 32; Prot 1 g; Carbo <1 g; Fiber <1 g;
  T Fat 3 g; 82% Calories from Fat; Chol 8 mg; Sod 179 mg.

Mary Beth McKibben Webster, O'Donnell

Shrimp Butter

3/4 cup butter, softened
8 ounces cream cheese, softened
Juice of 1 lemon

1 1/2 onions, minced
2 4-ounce cans shrimp, crumbled
1/4 cup chopped fresh parsley

Mix butter, cream cheese, lemon juice and onions in bowl. Add shrimp; mix well. Roll in parsley. Chill, covered with plastic, for 24 to 48 hours. Yield: 50 servings.

Approx Per Serving: Cal 47; Prot 1 g; Carbo 1 g; Fiber <1 g;
  T Fat 4 g; 84% Calories from Fat; Chol 19 mg; Sod 141 mg.

Christy Hightower, Lubbock

Fruit Dip

8 ounces cream cheese, softened

1 7-ounce jar marshmallow creme

Combine cream cheese and marshmallow creme in bowl; mix well. Serve with apples, bananas, grapes, peaches, strawberries or other favorite fruit. Yield: 30 servings.

Approx Per Serving: Cal 47; Prot 1 g; Carbo 6 g; Fiber 0 g;
  T Fat 3 g; 49% Calories from Fat; Chol 8 mg; Sod 26 mg.

Lyn Vandiver, Muleshoe

TANGY FRUIT DIP

1 envelope whipped topping mix
1 teaspoon presweetened orange
    drink mix

1 11-ounce can mandarin oranges,
    well drained

Prepare whipped topping using package directions. Stir in drink mix. Add mandarin oranges; mix well. Serve with apple, pear, pineapple or orange slices.
Yield: 50 servings.

Approx Per Serving: Cal 10; Prot <1 g; Carbo 2 g; Fiber 0 g;
    T Fat <1 g; 34% Calories from Fat; Chol <1 mg; Sod 3 mg.

Jan Kennedy, Lubbock

SOMBRERO DIP

1 pound ground beef
1/4 cup chopped onion
1/2 cup picante sauce
1 tablespoon chili powder
1 teaspoon salt

1 16-ounce can kidney beans
1 cup shredded Cheddar cheese
1/4 cup chopped onion
1/2 cup chopped black olives

Brown ground beef and 1/4 cup onion in skillet. Stir in picante sauce, chili powder and salt. Process undrained kidney beans in blender. Stir into ground beef mixture. Spoon into slow cooker. Top with cheese, 1/4 cup onion and black olives. Heat on Low until serving time. Yield: 65 servings.

Approx Per Serving: Cal 31; Prot 2 g; Carbo 1 g; Fiber 1 g;
    T Fat 2 g; 55% Calories from Fat; Chol 6 mg; Sod 93 mg.

Janet Gentry, Lubbock

SOUTHWESTERN DIP

11 ounces cream cheese, softened

1 8-ounce jar picante sauce

Combine cream cheese and picante sauce in bowl; beat with wire whisk or electric mixer. Chill until serving time. Serve with tortilla chips. May substitute light cream cheese for cream cheese. Yield: 40 servings.

Approx Per Serving: Cal 30; Prot 1 g; Carbo 1 g; Fiber <1 g;
    T Fat 3 g; 82% Calories from Fat; Chol 9 mg; Sod 55 mg.

You may double or reduce this recipe easily.

Debbie Lovelady, Muleshoe

SPINACH AND PIMENTO DIP

2   10-ounce packages frozen chopped
   spinach
1 cup sour cream
1   4-ounce jar pimentos, chopped
3 green onions, chopped

1 envelope vegetable soup mix
1   8-ounce can water chestnuts,
   chopped
1   16-ounce loaf Hawaiian bread

Cook spinach using package directions; drain. Combine spinach, sour cream, pimentos, green onions, soup mix and water chestnuts in bowl; mix well. Chill overnight. Scoop out center of loaf to form shell; cut center into pieces. Spoon dip into bread shell. Serve with bread pieces. Yield: 80 servings.

Approx Per Serving: Cal 29; Prot 1 g; Carbo 4 g; Fiber <1 g;
    T Fat 1 g; 33% Calories from Fat; Chol 1 mg; Sod 73 mg.

Welda Cook, Earth

SPINACH AND LEEK DIP

1   10-ounce package frozen chopped
   spinach, thawed
1 cup sour cream
1 cup mayonnaise
1 envelope leek-onion soup mix

1   8-ounce can water chestnuts, finely
   chopped
Mrs. Dash seasoning to taste
1   12-ounce loaf French bread, cut
   into pieces

Squeeze moisture from spinach. Combine with sour cream, mayonnaise, soup mix, water chestnuts and seasoning in bowl; mix well. Serve with bread pieces. Yield: 65 servings.

Approx Per Serving: Cal 50; Prot 1 g; Carbo 4 g; Fiber <1 g;
    T Fat 4 g; 65% Calories from Fat; Chol 4 mg; Sod 65 mg.

Windy Jones, Lockney

THREE-LAYER DIP

5 avocadoes, mashed	1 envelope taco mix
2 tablespoons green chili salsa	1 16-ounce can refried beans
2 tablespoons lemon juice	2 tomatoes, cut into wedges
2 tablespoons mayonnaise	1 cup chopped olives
Salt and pepper to taste	1/2 cup chopped onion
2 cups sour cream	1 cup shredded Cheddar cheese

Combine avocadoes, salsa, lemon juice, mayonnaise, salt and pepper in small bowl; mix well. Mix sour cream and taco mix in medium bowl. Layer beans, sour cream mixture and avocado mixture in shallow serving dish. Top with tomatoes, olives and onion. Sprinkle with cheese. Yield: 80 servings.

Approx Per Serving: Cal 54; Prot 1 g; Carbo 3 g; Fiber 2 g;
    T Fat 4 g; 70% Calories from Fat; Chol 4 mg; Sod 100 mg.

Lola Pylant, Muleshoe

BLACK BEAN SALSA

1/2 cup chopped red onion	4 plum tomatoes, chopped
1/2 cup chopped green bell pepper	1 large jalapeño pepper, chopped
1 clove of garlic, crushed	2 tablespoons chopped cilantro
2 tablespoons oil	3 tablespoons fresh lime juice
1 16-ounce can black beans	1 1/2 teaspoons hot pepper sauce
1/2 teaspoon salt	1 teaspoon grated lime rind

Sauté onion, green pepper and garlic in oil in skillet until tender. Add beans, salt, tomatoes, jalapeño pepper, cilantro, lime juice and pepper sauce; mix well. Top with lime rind. Serve hot or cold. Yield: 50 servings.

Approx Per Serving: Cal 16; Prot 1 g; Carbo 2 g; Fiber <1 g;
    T Fat 1 g; 32% Calories from Fat; Chol 0 mg; Sod 58 mg.

Christy Hightower, Lubbock

SALSA

2 green jalapeño peppers
1 clove of garlic
½ teaspoon salt

1 16-ounce can whole peeled
   tomatoes
½ teaspoon dill pickle juice

Remove stems from peppers; prick peppers with toothpick. Cook in cast-iron skillet until lightly browned. Combine with garlic and salt in blender container. Process until pulverized. Add tomatoes. Process just until tomatoes are chunky. Pour into 1-quart saucepan. Add pickle juice. Bring to a light boil over medium heat. Yield: 30 servings.

Approx Per Serving: Cal 4; Prot <1 g; Carbo 1 g; Fiber <1 g;
   T Fat <1 g; 9% Calories from Fat; Chol 0 mg; Sod 60 mg.

Ruth Torres-Naron, Abernathy

SWEET ONION SALSA

1 16-ounce can whole tomatoes,
   chopped into small pieces
2 jalapeño peppers, finely chopped
1 large sweet onion, chopped

1 4-ounce can chopped green chilies
Juice of ½ lemon
Garlic powder to taste
Salt and pepper to taste

Combine all ingredients in bowl; mix well. Store in refrigerator. Yield: 65 servings.

Approx Per Serving: Cal 3; Prot <1 g; Carbo 1 g; Fiber <1 g;
   T Fat <1 g; 7% Calories from Fat; Chol 0 mg; Sod 24 mg.

Berta Simmons, Lubbock

ARMADILLO EGGS

2 cups baking mix
2 pounds sausage
1 8-ounce can jalapeño peppers
1 cup Monterey Jack cheese, chopped

2 eggs, beaten
1 8-ounce package Shake'n Bake
   oven-fry for pork

Mix baking mix and sausage in bowl. Remove stems and seeds from peppers; rinse. Stuff peppers with cheese. Pat sausage mixture around peppers into egg shapes. Dip into beaten eggs. Roll in Shake'n Bake. Place on large baking sheet. Bake at 350 degrees for 30 to 45 minutes or until browned. Cut into bite-sized pieces. Yield: 12 servings.

Approx Per Serving: Cal 350; Prot 14 g; Carbo 29 g; Fiber 1 g;
   T Fat 20 g; 51% Calories from Fat; Chol 73 mg; Sod 1500 mg.

Shelly Livingston, Wilson

CHEESE APPETIZERS

8 ounces cream cheese, softened
1 cup sour cream
1½ cups shredded Cheddar cheese
1 4-ounce can chopped green chilies, drained

1 4-ounce jar pimentos, drained
1 2-ounce can chopped olives
1 teaspoon garlic salt
1 12-count package flour tortillas

Combine first 7 ingredients in bowl; mix well. Spread mixture on each tortilla; roll up. Chill for 1 hour. Cut into pieces. Yield: 50 servings.

Approx Per Serving: Cal 68; Prot 2 g; Carbo 5 g; Fiber <1 g;
    T Fat 5 g; 59% Calories from Fat; Chol 11 mg; Sod 135 mg.

Shelia Duckworth, Olton

CHEESE COOKIES

8 ounces New York State cheese, shredded
1 cup butter, softened
2 cups flour

2 cups crisp rice cereal
¾ teaspoon salt
½ teaspoon red pepper

Mix cheese and butter in bowl. Add flour, cereal, salt and red pepper; mix well. Shape into walnut-sized balls; flatten. Place on ungreased baking sheet. Bake at 325 degrees for 10 to 15 minutes or until light brown. Cool on baking sheet for several minutes. Remove to wire rack to cool completely. Yield: 80 servings.

Approx Per Serving: Cal 46; Prot 1 g; Carbo 3 g; Fiber <1 g;
    T Fat 3 g; 64% Calories from Fat; Chol 9 mg; Sod 66 mg.

Anne S. Glover, Lubbock

ROAST BEEF AND CREAM CHEESE ROLLS

2 8-count cans crescent rolls
1 6-ounce can deviled roast beef
8 ounces cream cheese, softened

1 onion, chopped
Garlic salt, salt and pepper to taste
1 green bell pepper, chopped

Spread roll dough on lightly floured surface. Beat roast beef and cream cheese in mixer bowl. Add next 4 ingredients; mix well. Stir in green pepper. Spread over roll dough. Roll up. Freeze until firm. Cut into thin slices. Place on baking sheet. Bake at 350 degrees for 8 minutes or until light brown. Yield: 45 servings.

Approx Per Serving: Cal 68; Prot 2 g; Carbo 4 g; Fiber <1 g;
    T Fat 5 g; 65% Calories from Fat; Chol 8 mg; Sod 143 mg.

Phyllis Geissler, Earth

CRAB MEAT-STUFFED MUSHROOMS

12 ounces fresh mushrooms
1/4 cup melted butter
1   7-ounce can crab meat, drained,
   flaked
2 tablespoons soft bread crumbs
2 eggs, lightly beaten
2 tablespoons mayonnaise

2 tablespoons chopped chives
1 teaspoon lemon juice
1/8 teaspoon ground whole pepper
2 tablespoons melted butter
2 tablespoons soft bread crumbs
2 tablespoons melted butter

Remove stems from mushrooms. Brush caps with 1/4 cup melted butter. Arrange in greased 8x10-inch baking dish. Combine crab meat, 2 tablespoons bread crumbs, eggs, mayonnaise, chives, lemon juice, pepper and 2 tablespoons melted butter in bowl; mix well. Fill mushroom caps with crab meat mixture. Mix 2 tablespoons bread crumbs and 2 tablespoons melted butter in bowl. Sprinkle over stuffing. Bake at 375 degrees for 15 minutes. Serve hot. Yield: 12 servings.

Approx Per Serving: Cal 123; Prot 5 g; Carbo 2 g; Fiber 1 g;
   T Fat 11 g; 77% Calories from Fat; Chol 72 mg; Sod 150 mg.

This recipe was shared by a gourmet friend in Fairbanks, Alaska.

Colleen Chadwick, Plainview

HAM PINWHEEL APPETIZERS

8 ounces cream cheese, softened
1/4 teaspoon dry mustard
1/4 teaspoon paprika
1/8 teaspoon salt
1/8 teaspoon pepper
Tabasco sauce to taste

1 teaspoon Worcestershire sauce
1/4 teaspoon soy sauce
2 teaspoons dried chopped chives
2 tablespoons mayonnaise
1 tablespoon chopped almonds
5 slices sandwich ham

Combine cream cheese, dry mustard, paprika, salt, pepper, Tabasco sauce, Worcestershire sauce, soy sauce, chives, mayonnaise and almonds in bowl; mix well. Spread on ham slices. Roll up; secure with wooden toothpicks. Freeze until firm. Cut into slices while frozen or when slightly thawed. Yield: 20 servings.

Approx Per Serving: Cal 63; Prot 3 g; Carbo <1 g; Fiber <1 g;
   T Fat 6 g; 80% Calories from Fat; Chol 17 mg; Sod 156 mg.

Mary Beth McKibben Webster, O'Donnell

CREAM CHEESE ROLL-UPS

12 ounces cream cheese, softened
1 16-ounce can crushed pineapple, drained
1 egg yolk
1 tablespoon sugar
1 teaspoon vanilla extract

20 slices mixed-grain bread, crusts trimmed
3/4 cup melted margarine
1 1/2 cups sugar
1 tablespoon cinnamon

Mix cream cheese, pineapple, egg yolk, 1 tablespoon sugar and vanilla in bowl. Spread on bread slices. Roll up each slice; dip in melted margarine. Roll in mixture of 1 1/2 cups sugar and cinnamon. Place on baking sheet. Bake at 350 degrees for 10 to 12 minutes or until brown. Cool thoroughly. Cut each roll into 4 pieces. Chill until serving time. Yield: 40 servings.

Approx Per Serving: Cal 121; Prot 2 g; Carbo 14 g; Fiber 1 g;
    T Fat 7 g; 50% Calories from Fat; Chol 15 mg; Sod 104 mg.

This is a good recipe to use as a finger food dessert.

Dianne Brown, Muleshoe

HAM ROLL-UPS

1 10-ounce package frozen chopped spinach
2 cups cooked rice
1/2 cup chopped onion
1/2 teaspoon dry mustard
2 eggs

25 slices boiled ham
1 10-ounce can cream of mushroom soup
1/2 cup sour cream
1/4 cup grated Parmesan cheese

Cook spinach using package directions; drain and press dry. Combine spinach, rice, onion, dry mustard and eggs in bowl; mix well. Place 1 1/2 tablespoons spinach mixture on each ham slice; roll up. Place seam side down in 9x13-inch baking dish. Mix soup and sour cream in bowl. Pour over ham slices. Sprinkle with cheese. Bake at 350 degrees for 20 to 25 minutes or until heated through. May substitute cream of celery soup for cream of mushroom soup and sharp Cheddar cheese for Parmesan cheese. Yield: 15 servings.

Approx Per Serving: Cal 164; Prot 15 g; Carbo 10 g; Fiber 1 g;
    T Fat 7 g; 38% Calories from Fat; Chol 59 mg; Sod 835 mg.

Betty Anne Kyle, Lubbock

Tortilla Roll-Ups

8 ounces Cheddar cheese, shredded
4 ounces mozzarella cheese, shredded
8 ounces cream cheese, softened
1½ cups sour cream
1 4-ounce can green chilies

1 4-ounce can sliced black olives
Green onions to taste
Chopped jalapeño peppers to taste
6 large flour tortillas

Combine Cheddar cheese, mozzarella cheese, cream cheese, sour cream, chilies, olives, green onions and peppers in bowl; mix well. Spread on tortillas; roll up. Chill, wrapped in waxed paper, overnight. Cut into pieces. Place on baking sheet. Bake at 350 degrees for 30 minutes or until heated through. Yield: 50 servings.

Approx Per Serving: Cal 80; Prot 3 g; Carbo 4 g; Fiber <1 g;
    T Fat 6 g; 66% Calories from Fat; Chol 15 mg; Sod 113 mg.

JoAnn Cook, Wilson

Green Chili Snacks

1 8-count can crescent rolls
3 ounces cream cheese, softened
½ cup shredded Cheddar cheese

3 tablespoons chopped green chilies
2 tablespoons minced onion
5 drops of Tabasco sauce

Separate roll dough into 4 rectangles, pressing and sealing perforations. Combine remaining ingredients in bowl; mix well. Spread over rectangles. Roll up as for jelly rolls. Cut each roll into 10 slices. Place cut side down on greased baking sheet. Bake at 375 degrees for 12 to 15 minutes or until brown. Yield: 40 servings.

Approx Per Serving: Cal 33; Prot 1 g; Carbo 2 g; Fiber <1 g;
    T Fat 2 g; 62% Calories from Fat; Chol 4 mg; Sod 66 mg.

Latina Smith, Morton

Sausage-Cheese Balls

1 pound pork sausage
1 pound shredded longhorn cheese

4 cups baking mix

Combine sausage, cheese and baking mix in bowl; mix well. Shape into small balls. Place on greased baking sheet. Bake at 350 degrees for 10 minutes or until light brown. Yield: 100 servings.

Approx Per Serving: Cal 48; Prot 2 g; Carbo 3 g; Fiber 0 g;
    T Fat 3 g; 55% Calories from Fat; Chol 7 mg; Sod 119 mg.

Beth A. Moore, Lubbock

SAUSAGE PINWHEELS

1 pound sausage
2 cups flour
1/2 teaspoon salt
2 teaspoons baking powder

2 teaspoons sugar
2 tablespoons cornmeal
1/4 cup shortening
13 tablespoons milk

Cook sausage in skillet until light brown; drain. Combine next 5 ingredients in bowl. Cut in shortening. Add milk; mix as for biscuits. Divide dough into halves. Roll each half into rectangle on lightly floured surface. Spread with sausage. Roll up as for jelly rolls. Chill thoroughly. Cut each roll into 1/4-inch slices. Place on large baking sheet. Bake at 400 degrees for 15 to 20 minutes or until brown. Yield: 35 servings.

Approx Per Serving: Cal 68; Prot 2 g; Carbo 6 g; Fiber <1 g;
    T Fat 4 g; 49% Calories from Fat; Chol 6 mg; Sod 131 mg.

Rita Tyson, Morton

TEXAS CAVIAR

1 large tomato, chopped
1 large green bell pepper, chopped
1 15-ounce can black-eyed peas

1 15-ounce can white hominy
1 medium onion, chopped
1 cup Italian salad dressing

Combine first 5 ingredients in large bowl; mix well. Pour salad dressing over all. Marinate, covered, in refrigerator overnight. Yield: 75 servings.

Approx Per Serving: Cal 23; Prot <1 g; Carbo 2 g; Fiber <1 g;
    T Fat 2 g; 64% Calories from Fat; Chol 0 mg; Sod 49 mg.

Monica Hernandez, Lubbock

CAJUN PARTY MIX

1/4 cup margarine
1 tablespoon parsley flakes
1 teaspoon celery salt
1 teaspoon garlic powder
1/2 teaspoon cayenne pepper

4 to 8 drops of Tabasco sauce
8 cups Crispix cereal
1 3-ounce can French-fried onions,
    chopped

Melt margarine in open roasting pan in 250-degree oven. Stir in next 5 ingredients. Add cereal; stir until well coated. Bake for 45 minutes, stirring 3 times. Stir in onions. Cool on paper towels. Store in airtight container. Yield: 100 servings.

Approx Per Serving: Cal 18; Prot <1 g; Carbo 2 g; Fiber <1 g;
    T Fat 1 g; 42% Calories from Fat; Chol 0 mg; Sod 44 mg.

Lee Ruth Krieg, Lubbock

THE NUTSNACKER

1¼ cups whole almonds
8 ounces cream cheese, softened
½ cup mayonnaise
6 slices bacon, crisp-fried, crumbled

1 tablespoon chopped green onion
½ teaspoon dillweed
⅛ teaspoon pepper

Spread almonds in single layer in shallow pan. Bake at 300 degrees for 15 minutes or just until almonds change color, stirring frequently. Mix cream cheese and mayonnaise in bowl. Add bacon, green onion, dillweed and pepper; mix well. Chill, covered, for several hours to overnight. Form into 2 pine cone shapes. Place on serving platter. Press almonds into cheese mixture at slight angle and in rows, overlapping rows until all cheese mixture is covered. Garnish with pine sprigs. Serve with a variety of crackers. Yield: 25 servings.

Approx Per Serving: Cal 114; Prot 3 g; Carbo 2 g; Fiber 1 g;
    T Fat 11 g; 85% Calories from Fat; Chol 14 mg; Sod 77 mg.

This is a special treat at our house during Christmas time.

Lynn Buxkemper, Slaton

VEGGIE PIZZA

2 8-count cans crescent rolls
8 ounces cream cheese, softened
½ cup mayonnaise
½ cup sour cream
1 envelope ranch salad dressing mix

½ cup chopped carrot
½ cup chopped green onions
½ cup chopped broccoli
½ cup chopped mushrooms
1 cup shredded Cheddar cheese

Spread dough on ungreased baking sheet. Prick with fork. Bake at 375 degrees for 20 minutes. Cool for 15 minutes. Mix cream cheese, mayonnaise, sour cream and salad dressing mix in bowl. Spread over crust. Sprinkle with vegetables and cheese. Chill until serving time. May substitute or add other vegetables of your choice. Yield: 10 servings.

Approx Per Serving: Cal 439; Prot 8 g; Carbo 26 g; Fiber <1 g;
    T Fat 34 g; 69% Calories from Fat; Chol 48 mg; Sod 863 mg.

Linda Huffaker, Tahoka

COUNTY LINE COMMUNITY PUNCH

1 46-ounce can pineapple juice	8 cups water
2 envelopes lemon-flavored drink mix	2 cups sugar
1 6-ounce can frozen lemonade	1 quart ginger ale
concentrate, thawed	

Combine pineapple juice, drink mix, lemonade concentrate, water, sugar and ginger ale in large container; mix well. May add food coloring if desired. Yield: 25 servings.

Approx Per Serving: Cal 117; Prot <1 g; Carbo 30 g; Fiber <1 g;
    T Fat <1 g; 0% Calories from Fat; Chol 0 mg; Sod 4 mg.

This community recipe is over 35 years old.

Amanda Turner, Anton

FRENCH COFFEE PUNCH

1 quart vanilla ice cream	1 cup cold water
1 quart chocolate ice cream	8 cups boiling water
1 cup instant coffee granules	2 cups sugar

Place vanilla and chocolate ice cream in punch bowl. Dissolve instant coffee granules in 1 cup cold water in small bowl. Combine with boiling water in large bowl. Add sugar, stirring until dissolved. Add enough water to measure 1 gallon. Pour into punch bowl, stirring until ice cream is melted. May add 2 cups whipped cream and 1 cup rum. Yield: 45 servings.

Approx Per Serving: Cal 84; Prot 1 g; Carbo 15 g; Fiber <1 g;
    T Fat 3 g; 27% Calories from Fat; Chol 11 mg; Sod 22 mg.

Betty Anne Kyle, Lubbock

PARTY PUNCH

2 quarts cranapple juice	1 quart Sprite

Fill punch bowl half full with crushed ice. Add cranapple juice and Sprite; mix well. Garnish with orange and lemon slices. Yield: 25 servings.

Approx Per Serving: Cal 70; Prot <1 g; Carbo 18 g; Fiber <1 g;
    T Fat <1 g; 3% Calories from Fat; Chol 0 mg; Sod 6 mg.

This is quick and fits in with any party. Most folks really like it.

Jane Prince Jones, Lubbock

PERCOLATOR PUNCH

2½ cups pineapple juice
1¾ cups water
2 cups cranberry juice cocktail
1 tablespoon whole cloves

½ teaspoon whole allspice
3 cinnamon sticks, broken into pieces
½ teaspoon salt
½ cup packed brown sugar

Combine pineapple juice, water and cranberry juice cocktail in 8-cup percolator. Place cloves, allspice, cinnamon sticks, salt and brown sugar in percolator basket. Percolate for 10 minutes or until spices permeate punch. Yield: 16 servings.

Approx Per Serving: Cal 72; Prot <1 g; Carbo 18 g; Fiber <1 g;
    T Fat <1 g; 1% Calories from Fat; Chol 0 mg; Sod 72 mg.

Carol Huggins and Dahlia Hight, Lockney

RED HOT DRINK

1 46-ounce can pineapple juice
1 32-ounce can apple juice

1 to 2 tablespoons lemon juice
1 8-ounce package red hot candies

Combine juices in percolator. Place candies in percolator basket. Percolate as for coffee. Yield: 25 servings.

Approx Per Serving: Cal 82; Prot <1 g; Carbo 20 g; Fiber <1 g;
    T Fat <1 g; 1% Calories from Fat; Chol 0 mg; Sod 3 mg.

Our family has this every Christmas Eve.

Jennifer Pellham, Olton

STRAWBERRY PUNCH

3 envelopes strawberry drink mix
3 quarts water
3 cups sugar

1 46-ounce can pineapple juice
2 quarts ginger ale

Combine drink mix, water, sugar, pineapple juice and ginger ale in large container; mix well. Yield: 50 servings.

Approx Per Serving: Cal 74; Prot <1 g; Carbo 19 g; Fiber <1 g;
    T Fat <1 g; 0% Calories from Fat; Chol 0 mg; Sod 3 mg.

Latina Smith, Morton

LEMON SPICED TEA MIX

1¹/₃ cups Tang
¹/₃ cup instant lemon tea
1 teaspoon cinnamon

¹/₂ cup sugar
¹/₂ teaspoon ground cloves

Combine Tang, instant tea, cinnamon, sugar and cloves in bowl; mix well. Store in airtight container. Add boiling water to 1 tablespoon mix to make 1 cup tea. Yield: 35 servings.

Approx Per Serving: Cal 74; Prot <1 g; Carbo 19 g; Fiber 0 g;
    T Fat <1 g; 0% Calories from Fat; Chol 0 mg; Sod 8 mg.

Pat Moses, Slaton

SPICED TEA MIX

2 cups Tang
1 cup instant tea
2 cups sugar
1 teaspoon ground cloves

1 teaspoon cinnamon
1 tablespoon lemon-flavored drink
    mix

Combine Tang, instant tea, sugar, cloves, cinnamon and drink mix in bowl; mix well with slotted spoon. Store in airtight container. Add 1 cup hot water to 2 tablespoons mix to make 1 cup tea. Yield: 40 servings.

Approx Per Serving: Cal 118; Prot <1 g; Carbo 30 g; Fiber 0 g;
    T Fat <1 g; 0% Calories from Fat; Chol 0 mg; Sod 11 mg.

Beth A. Moore, Lubbock

Soups

Briscoe County

The walls of the Caprock
are bordered by the Prairie Dog Fork of the Red River.
The crevices and cliffs echo with bird call
at early light and encroaching night.
Andrew Briscoe, soldier of the Texas Republic,
come home.

R.S.

CREOLE BEEF STEW

1 clove of garlic, minced
1 teaspoon salt
1 teaspoon paprika
1 teaspoon thyme
1/8 teaspoon red pepper
1 pound beef stew meat, cut into
   1/2-inch cubes

3 to 4 tablespoons olive oil
2 tablespoons flour
1 onion, finely chopped
1 green bell pepper, finely chopped
1/2 cup chopped celery
1   16-ounce can tomatoes, chopped
2 cups hot cooked rice

Mash garlic and salt together in bowl to form paste. Stir in paprika, thyme and red pepper. Sprinkle over beef cubes. Brown beef in 2 tablespoons hot oil in heavy skillet; remove and set aside. Add enough remaining oil to pan drippings to measure 2 tablespoons. Stir in flour until blended. Cook for 2 to 3 minutes or until lightly browned. Add onion, green pepper and celery. Cook for 2 to 3 minutes, stirring constantly. Add tomatoes and beef. Cook, covered, over low heat for 1 1/2 hours or until beef is tender, stirring occasionally. Serve over rice.
Yield: 6 servings.

Approx Per Serving: Cal 292; Prot 17 g; Carbo 25 g; Fiber 2 g;
    T Fat 14 g; 42% Calories from Fat; Chol 43 mg; Sod 511 mg.

Barbara June Jones, Slaton

CATFISH STEW

4 pounds catfish
Salt and pepper to taste
8 ounces bacon, chopped
4 onions, chopped

8 potatoes, chopped
1   28-ounce can tomatoes
1   14-ounce bottle of catsup

Season fish with salt and pepper. Cook in water to cover in saucepan until fish flakes easily. Drain, reserving stock. Discard skin and bones; return fish meat to stock. Fry bacon in skillet until crisp. Drain, reserving pan drippings. Sauté onions in pan drippings until tender. Add bacon, onions, potatoes and tomatoes to fish stock. Simmer over low heat until potatoes are tender, adding additional water for desired consistency. Season with salt and pepper. Add catsup just before serving. Yield: 10 servings.

Approx Per Serving: Cal 286; Prot 8 g; Carbo 40 g; Fiber 4 g;
    T Fat 13 g; 37% Calories from Fat; Chol 60 mg; Sod 745 mg.

George Moore, Crosbyton

CHICKEN GUMBO

2 3-pound chickens
2 14-ounce cans chicken broth
2 16-ounce packages gumbo
   vegetables

2 16-ounce cans tomatoes
1/8 teaspoon red pepper
1 1/2 teaspoons salt

Rinse chickens and cut into pieces. Place in 5-quart saucepan. Add chicken broth. Bring to a boil; reduce heat. Simmer for 35 to 40 minutes. Remove chicken from broth. Shred chicken, discarding skin and bones; set aside. Cook broth until reduced by half. Add vegetables, tomatoes, red pepper and salt. Bring to a boil; reduce heat. Simmer for 25 minutes, stirring occasionally. Add chicken. Cook until heated through. Serve over rice, noodles or mashed potatoes. Yield: 12 servings.

Approx Per Serving: Cal 285; Prot 37 g; Carbo 13 g; Fiber 4 g;
    T Fat 9 g; 29% Calories from Fat; Chol 102 mg; Sod 724 mg.

This is an adaptation of Brunswick Stew from North Carolina.

Ruth Efird, Denver City

CREOLE GUMBO

3 slices bacon
3 pounds fresh okra, chopped
1 pound beef stew meat
8 ounces ham, chopped
1 green bell pepper, chopped

2 onions, chopped
1 28-ounce can whole tomatoes
3 quarts water
1 1/2 pounds shrimp, peeled

Fry bacon in cast-iron skillet until crisp. Drain, reserving pan drippings. Sauté okra in reserved pan drippings until browned; drain. Cook beef stew meat, ham, green pepper and onions in large stockpot until beef is browned. Add tomatoes, bacon, okra and water. Bring to a boil; reduce heat. Simmer for 2 hours, stirring occasionally. Add shrimp. Cook for 20 minutes longer. Serve with hot cooked rice. Yield: 12 servings.

Approx Per Serving: Cal 193; Prot 25 g; Carbo 13 g; Fiber 4 g;
    T Fat 5 g; 22% Calories from Fat; Chol 121 mg; Sod 503 mg.

Anne S. Glover, Lubbock

ULTIMATE GUMBO MCDONALD

2 teaspoons minced garlic	1 cup finely chopped green onions
1 onion, finely chopped	2 teaspoons cayenne pepper
1 green bell pepper, finely chopped	1 teaspoon black pepper
¼ cup unsalted butter	1 teaspoon white pepper
6 cups water	1 teaspoon salt
2 chicken bouillon cubes	2 teaspoons oregano
1 16-ounce package frozen sliced	1 tablespoon thyme
okra	3 tablespoons filé powder
4 large tomatoes, chopped	1 pound crab meat
1 cup chopped celery	3 pounds boiled shrimp

Sauté garlic, onion and green pepper in butter in skillet until tender. Bring water to a boil in large stockpot; reduce heat. Dissolve bouillon cubes in simmering water. Add sautéed mixture, okra, tomatoes, celery, green onions, peppers, salt, oregano, thyme and filé powder; mix well. Simmer, covered, for 1 hour. Add crab meat and shrimp. Simmer for 30 minutes longer. May add tomato paste to thicken sauce. Serve over hot cooked rice. Yield: 12 servings.

Approx Per Serving: Cal 219; Prot 33 g; Carbo 8 g; Fiber 1 g;
T Fat 6 g; 25% Calories from Fat; Chol 269 mg; Sod 774 mg.

Susan McDonald, Ransom Canyon

QUICK GOULASH

1 pound ground beef	1 9-ounce can tomatoes
1 onion, chopped	1 envelope chicken soup mix
1 clove of garlic, minced	3 to 4 cups water
1 tablespoon (heaping) flour	4 ounces Velveeta cheese, shredded

Brown ground beef, onion and garlic in skillet, stirring until ground beef is crumbly. Stir in flour. Add tomatoes, soup and water; mix well. Cook over medium heat for 10 to 15 minutes, stirring occasionally. Add cheese. Simmer until cheese is melted. Serve over corn bread or corn chips. Yield: 4 servings.

Approx Per Serving: Cal 390; Prot 29 g; Carbo 10 g; Fiber 2 g;
T Fat 26 g; 60% Calories from Fat; Chol 101 mg; Sod 795 mg.

Sheriff D.L. "Sonny" Keesee, Lubbock

SOPA DE CHICKEN

3 chicken breasts
8 ounces elbow macaroni
1/4 cup oil
1 small green bell pepper, chopped
1/2 small onion, chopped

1 16-ounce can whole tomatoes,
    chopped
1 teaspoon minced garlic
1/4 teaspoon cumin
Salt and pepper to taste

Rinse chicken. Cook in water to cover in saucepan for 40 minutes or until tender. Drain, reserving broth; cool. Chop chicken, discarding skin and bones. Cook macaroni in hot oil in skillet until light brown. Combine with reserved broth, chicken, green pepper, onion, tomatoes, garlic, cumin, salt and pepper in saucepan. Cook for 20 to 30 minutes or until macaroni is tender. Yield: 6 servings.

Approx Per Serving: Cal 312; Prot 19 g; Carbo 33 g; Fiber 3 g;
    T Fat 11 g; 33% Calories from Fat; Chol 37 mg; Sod 156 mg.

*This is an easy recipe long used by Spanish people. You can
use a whole chicken cut into pieces.*

Margie P. Garcia, Friona

CHILI-CHICKEN STEW

6 chicken breast filets
1 onion, chopped
1 green bell pepper, chopped
2 cloves of garlic, minced
1 tablespoon oil
2 14-ounce cans stewed tomatoes
1 15-ounce can pinto beans, drained
2/3 cup picante sauce

1 teaspoon chili powder
1/2 teaspoon salt
1 teaspoon ground cumin
3/4 cup shredded Cheddar cheese
6 tablespoons sour cream
6 tablespoons chopped avocado
6 tablespoons sliced green onions

Rinse chicken and pat dry; cut into 1-inch pieces. Brown chicken, onion, green pepper and garlic in hot oil in large saucepan. Add tomatoes, pinto beans, picante sauce, chili powder, salt and cumin; mix well. Simmer, covered, for 20 minutes, stirring occasionally. Remove to individual serving plates. Top each portion with cheese, sour cream, avocado and green onions. Yield: 6 servings.

Approx Per Serving: Cal 384; Prot 36 g; Carbo 28 g; Fiber 2 g;
    T Fat 15 g; 34% Calories from Fat; Chol 95 mg; Sod 1200 mg.

*This makes a wonderful stew the kids will love. May use leftover turkey
from Thanksgiving, which also cuts cooking time.*

Renee Wilson, Dimmitt

CHILI

3 pounds ground beef
3 onions, chopped
3 cloves of garlic, chopped
1 teaspoon oregano
1 teaspoon ground cumin
¼ cup chili powder

2 teaspoons cayenne pepper
1 tablespoon salt
2 tablespoons paprika
1 8-ounce can tomato sauce
6 cups water

Brown ground beef in skillet, stirring until crumbly. Rinse and drain. Combine with onions, garlic, oregano, cumin, chili powder, cayenne pepper, salt, paprika, tomato sauce and water in large saucepan. Simmer for 3 hours, stirring frequently. Yield: 8 servings.

Approx Per Serving: Cal 376; Prot 33 g; Carbo 7 g; Fiber 1 g;
T Fat 24 g; 58% Calories from Fat; Chol 111 mg; Sod 1070 mg.

Wanda Murdock, Dimmitt

VEGETABLE CHILI

2 green bell peppers, chopped
1 onion, chopped
2 tablespoons oil
1 zucchini, chopped
1 yellow squash, chopped
2 tablespoons chili powder
1 tablespoon sugar

¼ teaspoon salt
2 14-ounce cans stewed tomatoes
2 15-ounce cans pinto beans
2 15-ounce cans black beans
1 4-ounce can chopped green chilies
2 cups fresh or frozen corn

Sauté green peppers and onion in oil in 5-quart saucepan. Add zucchini, squash, chili powder, sugar and salt; mix well. Cook for 1 minute, stirring frequently. Add undrained tomatoes, undrained pinto beans, undrained black beans, undrained green chilies and corn; mix well. Bring to a boil; reduce heat. Simmer, covered, over medium-low heat for 20 minutes, stirring occasionally. Yield: 10 servings.

Approx Per Serving: Cal 228; Prot 10 g; Carbo 42 g; Fiber 2 g;
T Fat 4 g; 14% Calories from Fat; Chol 0 mg; Sod 1102 mg.

Ann Owens, Littlefield

MARTHA WHITTINGTON'S CORN CHOWDER

1 onion, chopped
2 teaspoons butter
1 16-ounce can tomato wedges,
   drained

2 17-ounce cans cream-style corn
4 cups milk
Salt and pepper to taste

Sauté onion in butter in skillet until tender. Combine with tomato wedges, corn, milk, salt and pepper in saucepan. Simmer until heated through, stirring frequently. Yield: 8 servings.

Approx Per Serving: Cal 189; Prot 7 g; Carbo 31 g; Fiber 4 g;
      T Fat 6 g; 25% Calories from Fat; Chol 19 mg; Sod 495 mg.

Betty Anne Kyle, Lubbock

INDIAN CORN STEW

1 pound ground beef
1 onion, chopped
1 tablespoon minced garlic
1 envelope chili seasoning mix

1 15-ounce can red beans
1 14-ounce can stewed tomatoes
1 12-ounce can corn, drained
1 cup tomato juice

Brown ground beef with onion and garlic in skillet, stirring until ground beef is crumbly; drain. Stir in chili seasoning mix. Simmer for 2 to 3 minutes, stirring occasionally. Add beans, tomatoes, corn and tomato juice; mix well. Bring to a boil; reduce heat. Simmer, covered, for 30 minutes. Serve with corn bread or corn chips. May also cook in slow cooker on Low all day. Yield: 6 servings.

Approx Per Serving: Cal 299; Prot 20 g; Carbo 32 g; Fiber 7 g;
      T Fat 12 g; 33% Calories from Fat; Chol 49 mg; Sod 811 mg.

Vickie Miller, Idalou

ONION-WINE SOUP

¹/₄ cup butter
5 onions, chopped
5 cups beef broth
¹/₂ cup chopped celery leaves
1 potato, sliced
1 cup dry white wine

1 tablespoon vinegar
2 teaspoons sugar
1 cup light cream
1 tablespoon minced parsley
Salt and pepper to taste

Melt butter in large saucepan. Stir in chopped onions. Add beef broth, celery leaves and potato. Bring to a boil; reduce heat. Simmer, covered, for 30 minutes. Purée mixture in blender. Return to saucepan. Add wine, vinegar and sugar, stirring well. Bring to a boil; reduce heat. Simmer for 5 minutes. Stir in cream, parsley, salt and pepper. Simmer gently until heated through, stirring frequently. Yield: 8 servings.

Approx Per Serving: Cal 221; Prot 4 g; Carbo 13 g; Fiber 2 g;
    T Fat 16 g; 67% Calories from Fat; Chol 49 mg; Sod 552 mg.

Former First Lady Nancy Reagan

TACO SOUP

2 pounds ground beef
1 small onion, chopped
1 envelope taco seasoning mix
1 envelope Italian salad dressing mix
1 16-ounce can pinto beans

1 16-ounce can kidney beans
2 16-ounce cans tomatoes
1 15-ounce can hominy
1 4-ounce can chopped green chilies,
    drained

Brown ground beef and onion in skillet until ground beef is crumbly; drain. Add taco seasoning mix and salad dressing mix; mix well. Pour into slow cooker. Add pinto beans, kidney beans, tomatoes, hominy and green chilies; mix well. Cook on High for 1 hour, stirring occasionally. Yield: 8 servings.

Approx Per Serving: Cal 401; Prot 29 g; Carbo 34 g; Fiber 6 g;
    T Fat 17 g; 38% Calories from Fat; Chol 74 mg; Sod 1493 mg.

Paula Corley, Springlake

Tortilla Soup

1   4-ounce can chopped green chilies,
   drained
3 onions, chopped
1 tablespoon minced garlic
1 cup oil
2   46-ounce cans tomato juice
1   16-ounce can ground tomatoes
2 tomato cans water

¼ cup beef bouillon
¼ cup chicken bouillon
2 tablespoons chili powder
5 ounces A-1 sauce
5 ounces Worcestershire sauce
3 tablespoons cumin
6 cups shredded Monterey Jack cheese
24 corn tortillas, cut into strips

Sauté green chilies, onions and garlic in oil in large stockpot. Add tomato juice, tomatoes, water, beef bouillon, chicken bouillon, chili powder, A-1 sauce, Worcestershire sauce and cumin; mix well. Simmer over low heat for 1 hour. Add cheese and sliced tortillas. Let stand for several minutes. Serve with crushed fried corn tortillas. Yield: 16 servings.

Approx Per Serving: Cal 443; Prot 16 g; Carbo 35 g; Fiber 6 g;
   T Fat 28 g; 56% Calories from Fat; Chol 39 mg; Sod 1036 mg.

I got this original recipe several years ago from "Cousin's Restaurant"
in Ruidoso, New Mexico. It is most delicious!

Hazel Donovan, Matador

Old-Fashioned Turkey and Dressing Soup

10 to 12 cups water
6 chicken bouillon cubes
2 onions, chopped
4 potatoes, peeled, cubed
2 cups sliced carrots
1 turnip, peeled, cubed
6 stalks celery, sliced

¼ head cabbage, sliced
¼ teaspoon pepper
Salt to taste
1 bay leaf
1 tablespoon chopped parsley
3 cups chopped cooked turkey
4 cups corn bread dressing

Bring water to a boil in large kettle. Add bouillon cubes, stirring until dissolved. Add onions, potatoes, carrots, turnip, celery, cabbage, pepper, salt, bay leaf and parsley. Simmer until vegetables are tender, stirring occasionally. Add turkey and dressing. Simmer until heated through. Remove bay leaf before serving.
Yield: 12 servings.

Approx Per Serving: Cal 198; Prot 14 g; Carbo 29 g; Fiber 3 g;
   T Fat 3 g; 12% Calories from Fat; Chol 27 mg; Sod 960 mg.

This recipe was originally published in the
***Lubbock Avalanche Journal** several years ago.*

Betty Scott, Slaton

Waylon's Winter-Vegetable Soup

2 pounds soupbones
3½ cups tomato juice
1 large red onion, chopped
¼ teaspoon chili powder
6 cups water
2 Turkish bay leaves
2 teaspoons Worcestershire sauce
2 teaspoons salt

1 16-ounce can tomato wedges
2 cups chopped potatoes
1 cup sliced celery
1 cup sliced carrots
1 10-ounce package frozen baby
  lima beans
1 10-ounce package frozen corn
1 cup uncooked macaroni

At 9:00 a.m. place soupbones, tomato juice, onion, chili powder, water, bay leaves, Worcestershire sauce and salt in large kettle. Cook over medium-low heat. You want it to boil very slowly, not rapidly. Boil until noon. If you need to leave the house you can—turn the soup down to simmer. However, you won't get the rich color to your stock, and your family will notice the difference. At 12:00 noon, take the soupbones out. Add tomato wedges, potatoes, celery and carrots. We'll simmer this for 1½ hours. After peppering generously, check stock to see that it's not too low. If it is, add more tomato juice and a 2-finger pinch of sugar. Add baby limas and corn. Continue simmering for 1½ hours. Remove from heat 30 minutes before serving and add macaroni. Let stand. Remove bay leaf. We like our macaroni *al dente* and our soup rich and tasty! A foolproof way would be to cook the macaroni separately, then add a few minutes before serving. Also, don't believe you can make good soup in 2½ hours. It's an all-day affair.
Yield: 10 servings.

Approx Per Serving: Cal 132; Prot 5 g; Carbo 29 g; Fiber 6 g;
    T Fat <1 g; 3% Calories from Fat; Chol 0 mg; Sod 843 mg.

Waylon Jennings, Nashville, Tennessee

Zucchini Soup

1 pound unpeeled zucchini, chopped
2 tablespoons chopped shallots
1 clove of garlic, minced
2 tablespoons butter

1¾ cups chicken broth
1 teaspoon curry powder
½ teaspoon salt
½ cup half and half

Sauté zucchini, shallots and garlic in butter in skillet for 10 to 20 minutes or until tender but not brown. Combine with chicken broth, curry powder and salt in blender container. Process until blended. Pour into saucepan; add half and half. Heat gently until heated through. Serve hot garnished with croutons, or serve cold garnished with chives. Yield: 4 servings.

Approx Per Serving: Cal 128; Prot 5 g; Carbo 6 g; Fiber 1 g;
    T Fat 10 g; 68% Calories from Fat; Chol 27 mg; Sod 670 mg.

First Lady Barbara Bush

Salads

Terry County

Until you've heard the sound of a pumpjack at midmorning
echoing across the flats of Terry County
lifting the spoils from the Earth's belly,
you've not known Texas.
You've not felt the intense tenancy of the people.

R.S.

Ambrosia Salad

8 ounces cream cheese, softened
3/4 cup sugar
2 bananas, sliced
2 18-ounce cans pineapple chunks, drained

1 10-ounce package frozen strawberries, drained
1/2 cup chopped pecans
9 ounces whipped topping

Combine cream cheese and sugar in mixer bowl; mix until fluffy. Add bananas, pineapple, strawberries and pecans; mix gently. Fold in whipped topping. Chill until serving time. Yield: 15 servings.

Approx Per Serving: Cal 224; Prot 2 g; Carbo 28 g; Fiber 2 g;
T Fat 12 g; 48% Calories from Fat; Chol 17 mg; Sod 51 mg.

Karla Stroud, Lubbock

Cherry Salad

1 6-ounce package cherry gelatin
2 1/2 cups boiling water

1 8-ounce can crushed pineapple
1 21-ounce can cherry pie filling

Dissolve gelatin in boiling water in bowl. Stir in undrained pineapple and cherry pie filling. Spoon into 9x13-inch dish. Chill until firm. Serve with whipped cream or mixture of sour cream, sugar and lemon juice. Yield: 15 servings.

Approx Per Serving: Cal 92; Prot 1 g; Carbo 23 g; Fiber 1 g;
T Fat <1 g; 0% Calories from Fat; Chol 0 mg; Sod 48 mg.

Dahlia Hight, Lockney

Congealed Cherry Salad

1 6-ounce package cherry gelatin
2 cups boiling water
1 16-ounce can whole cranberry sauce

1 20-ounce can crushed pineapple
1/2 cup Port
1/2 cup chopped pecans

Dissolve gelatin in boiling water in bowl. Stir in cranberry sauce. Let cool slightly. Add pineapple, wine and pecans; mix gently. Spoon into mold or dish. Chill until firm. Unmold or cut into squares to serve. Yield: 15 servings.

Approx Per Serving: Cal 156; Prot 2 g; Carbo 31 g; Fiber 1 g;
T Fat 3 g; 16% Calories from Fat; Chol 0 mg; Sod 46 mg.

Ophelia Florez, Friona

CREAM CHEESE CHRISTMAS SALAD

1   16-ounce can crushed pineapple,
    drained
1   6-ounce package lime gelatin
8 ounces cream cheese, softened

1   2-ounce jar chopped pimento,
    drained
1 cup chopped pecans
12 ounces whipped topping

Heat pineapple in saucepan until bubbly. Add gelatin, stirring to dissolve completely. Cool to room temperature. Combine cream cheese and pimento in bowl; mix well. Add gelatin mixture, pecans and whipped topping. Spoon into salad mold. Chill for 1 hour or until set. Unmold onto serving plate. Yield: 12 servings.

Approx Per Serving: Cal 296; Prot 4 g; Carbo 27 g; Fiber 1 g;
    T Fat 21 g; 60% Calories from Fat; Chol 21 mg; Sod 109 mg.

*We always serve this recipe of my mom's at Christmas
because of its festive green and red colors.*

Thresa Woods, Slaton

CINNAMON SALAD

1/2 cup red hot cinnamon candies
2 cups water
1   3-ounce package lemon gelatin
2 tablespoons lemon juice
1 1/4 cups chopped unpeeled apples

1/4 cup chopped walnuts
13 ounces cream cheese, softened
1/4 cup cream
1/8 teaspoon salt

Combine cinnamon candies with water in saucepan. Cook for 5 minutes or until candies dissolve, stirring frequently. Stir in gelatin until dissolved. Cool to room temperature. Add lemon juice. Chill until partially set. Fold in apples and walnuts. Spoon half the mixture into 8x8-inch dish. Chill until set. Combine cream cheese, cream and salt in bowl; mix well. Spoon evenly over congealed layer. Spread remaining gelatin mixture carefully over top. Chill until set. Cut into squares and serve on salad greens. Yield: 8 servings.

Approx Per Serving: Cal 325; Prot 5 g; Carbo 30 g; Fiber 1 g;
    T Fat 21 g; 57% Calories from Fat; Chol 61 mg; Sod 209 mg.

This holiday salad has been a tradition in my family for forty-five years.

Helen Bergen, El Paso

CRANBERRY FLUFF SALAD

12 ounces cranberries, ground	3 cups marshmallows
2 cups sugar	1 cup chopped pecans
1 15-ounce can crushed pineapple	1 cup whipping cream, whipped

Chill cranberries with sugar in bowl overnight. Add pineapple, marshmallows and pecans; mix well. Fold in whipped cream. Chill until serving time. Yield: 12 servings.

Approx Per Serving: Cal 349; Prot 2 g; Carbo 58 g; Fiber 2 g;
    T Fat 14 g; 35% Calories from Fat; Chol 27 mg; Sod 22 mg.

Kathy Bock, Earth

CRANBERRY CHRISTMAS SALAD

1½ cups ground fresh cranberries	2 cups boiling water
½ cup sugar	2 cups cold water
¼ teaspoon cinnamon	1 tablespoon lemon juice
⅛ teaspoon ground cloves	Sections of 1 orange, chopped
1 6-ounce package orange gelatin	½ cup chopped pecans

Combine cranberries, sugar, cinnamon and cloves in bowl; let stand for several minutes. Dissolve gelatin in boiling water in bowl. Stir in cold water and lemon juice. Chill until thickened. Fold in cranberry mixture, orange and pecans. Spoon into 6-cup mold. Chill until set. Unmold onto serving plate. Yield: 10 servings.

Approx Per Serving: Cal 164; Prot 2 g; Carbo 32 g; Fiber 2 g;
    T Fat 4 g; 21% Calories from Fat; Chol 0 mg; Sod 55 mg.

Linda Huffaker, Tahoka

CRANBERRY SALAD

2 cups cranberries	1 cup chopped celery
1 cup sugar	1 cup chopped apple
1 cup water	½ cup drained pineapple
1 6-ounce package cherry gelatin	1 cup chopped pecans
5 large marshmallows	

Cook cranberries and sugar in water in saucepan until cranberries pop. Stir in gelatin and marshmallows until dissolved. Fold in remaining ingredients. Spoon into salad mold. Chill until set. Unmold onto serving plate. Yield: 8 servings.

Approx Per Serving: Cal 319; Prot 4 g; Carbo 58 g; Fiber 3 g;
    T Fat 10 g; 27% Calories from Fat; Chol 0 mg; Sod 86 mg.

Myrtle Clayton, Springlake

LEMON GELATIN SALAD

1 envelope unflavored gelatin
1/4 cup water
1 3-ounce package lemon gelatin
1³/4 cups boiling water
1 cup pineapple juice
1/2 cup sugar
2 tablespoons flour

1 egg
1 8-ounce can crushed pineapple
2 bananas, sliced
1 cup miniature marshmallows
1 cup whipped topping
1/2 cup shredded Cheddar cheese

Soften unflavored gelatin in 1/4 cup water. Dissolve lemon gelatin in boiling water in bowl. Stir in unflavored gelatin until dissolved. Pour into shallow dish. Chill until set. Combine pineapple juice, sugar, flour and egg in saucepan; mix well. Cook until thickened, stirring constantly. Cool to room temperature. Mix pineapple, bananas and marshmallows in bowl. Cut congealed gelatin into ³/4-inch cubes. Combine with cooled custard and marshmallow mixture in bowl; mix gently. Top with whipped topping and cheese. Chill until serving time. Yield: 12 servings.

Approx Per Serving: Cal 170; Prot 3 g; Carbo 32 g; Fiber 1 g;
     T Fat 4 g; 19% Calories from Fat; Chol 23 mg; Sod 65 mg.

*This was a favorite recipe of my husband's mother and
always brings back sweet memories of her.*

Jenna V. Kellar, Earth

ORANGE GELATIN

1 3-ounce package vanilla pudding
   and pie filling mix
1 3-ounce package vanilla tapioca
   pudding mix

1 3-ounce package orange gelatin
3 cups water
1 11-ounce can mandarin oranges

Combine pudding mixes, gelatin and water in saucepan. Cook until thickened, stirring constantly. Reserve several mandarin orange sections for garnish. Fold remaining oranges into pudding mixture. Spoon into serving dishes. Garnish with reserved orange sections. Yield: 10 servings.

Approx Per Serving: Cal 107; Prot 1 g; Carbo 27 g; Fiber 1 g;
     T Fat <1 g; 0% Calories from Fat; Chol 0 mg; Sod 116 mg.

This easy favorite was originated by a Crosby County 4-H member.

Colleen Chadwick, Plainview

PINK ARCTIC SALAD

8 ounces cream cheese, softened
2 tablespoons sugar
2 tablespoons mayonnaise
1 16-ounce can cranberry sauce
1 12-ounce can crushed pineapple

½ cup chopped pecans
2 tablespoons thawed frozen orange
  juice concentrate
½ cup whipping cream, whipped

Blend cream cheese, sugar and mayonnaise in bowl. Add cranberry sauce, drained pineapple, pecans and orange juice concentrate; mix well. Fold in whipped cream. Spoon into freezer container. Freeze until firm. Yield: 10 servings.

Approx Per Serving: Cal 281; Prot 3 g; Carbo 28 g; Fiber 2 g;
    T Fat 19 g; 58% Calories from Fat; Chol 43 mg; Sod 101 mg.

Betty Anne Kyle, Lubbock

CHRISTMAS SALAD

2 3-ounce packages strawberry
   gelatin
5 cups boiling water

⅔ cup sour cream
2 3-ounce packages lime gelatin

Dissolve strawberry gelatin in 2½ cups boiling water in bowl. Stir in ⅓ cup sour cream. Spoon into 6-cup ring mold. Chill for 15 minutes or until thickened. Dissolve lime gelatin in 2½ cups boiling water in bowl. Stir in ⅓ cup sour cream. Spoon carefully over strawberry layer. Chill for 2 hours or longer. Unmold onto serving plate. May substitute vanilla yogurt for sour cream. Yield: 12 servings.

Approx Per Serving: Cal 132; Prot 3 g; Carbo 26 g; Fiber 0 g;
    T Fat 3 g; 17% Calories from Fat; Chol 6 mg; Sod 97 mg.

Charity Martinez, Earth

DUMP-IT SALAD

1 16-ounce can crushed pineapple
2 21-ounce cans strawberry pie
   filling
1 cup chopped pecans

2 bananas, mashed
1 14-ounce can sweetened
   condensed milk
24 ounces whipped topping

Combine drained pineapple and remaining ingredients in bowl; mix gently. Spoon into serving dish. Chill for 1 hour or longer. Yield: 16 servings.

Approx Per Serving: Cal 363; Prot 4 g; Carbo 50 g; Fiber 2 g;
    T Fat 18 g; 43% Calories from Fat; Chol 8 mg; Sod 65 mg.

Darla Mason, Slaton

CABBAGE CHICKEN SALAD

1 4-ounce can chicken
4 green onions, chopped
2 tablespoons sliced almonds
2 teaspoons sesame seed
1/2 cup corn oil
2 teaspoons vinegar

2 teaspoons sugar
1 teaspoon each MSG and salt
1/2 teaspoon pepper
1/2 head cabbage, shredded
1 3-ounce package chicken-flavored
   ramen noodles

Combine first 4 ingredients in bowl. Add oil, vinegar, sugar, MSG, salt and pepper; mix well. Add cabbage, broken noodles and seasoning packet from noodles; mix gently. Chill, covered, overnight. Yield: 10 servings.

Approx Per Serving: Cal 165; Prot 4 g; Carbo 8 g; Fiber 1 g;
    T Fat 14 g; 72% Calories from Fat; Chol 0 mg; Sod 838 mg.

Jane Davis, Post

CHICKEN AND GRAPE SALAD

4 cups chopped cooked chicken
1 cup chopped celery
1 cup seedless grape halves
1 3-ounce package slivered almonds

1 teaspoon salt
1/4 teaspoon pepper
3/4 cup mayonnaise
1/4 cup sour cream

Mix chicken, celery, grapes, toasted almonds and remaining ingredients in order listed in bowl. Serve in lettuce cups. Yield: 4 servings.

Approx Per Serving: Cal 751; Prot 46 g; Carbo 14 g; Fiber 3 g;
    T Fat 58 g; 68% Calories from Fat; Chol 156 mg; Sod 925 mg.

Diana Phillips, Abernathy

CHICKEN SALAD

4 chicken breasts
1 stalk celery
Salt to taste
3/4 cup chopped celery

1 1/2 cups mayonnaise
1/4 teaspoon lemon juice
2 tablespoons creamy buttermilk and
   chives salad dressing

Rinse chicken. Cook with 1 stalk celery and salt in water to cover in saucepan until tender. Drain and chop chicken; chill. Combine with 3/4 cup celery in bowl. Stir in mixture of remaining ingredients; chill. Serve on lettuce leaves. Yield: 4 servings.

Approx Per Serving: Cal 777; Prot 28 g; Carbo 4 g; Fiber 1 g;
    T Fat 73 g; 84% Calories from Fat; Chol 123 mg; Sod 621 mg.

Sue Forbes, O'Donnell

Wildly Delicious Turkey Salad

1 6-ounce package long grain and
  wild rice mix, cooked, chilled
2 cups chopped cooked turkey
1 cup packed sliced spinach leaves
2 green onions with tops, sliced
1/3 cup dry white wine

1/4 cup oil
2 tablespoons sugar
3/4 teaspoon salt
1/4 teaspoon pepper
10 cherry tomatoes, cut into halves
1 11-ounce can mandarin oranges

Combine rice, turkey, spinach and green onions in bowl; mix well. Blend wine, oil, sugar, salt and pepper in bowl. Add to salad; mix well. Add tomatoes; mix lightly. Top with sliced mandarin oranges. Yield: 6 servings.

Approx Per Serving: Cal 327; Prot 18 g; Carbo 37 g; Fiber 2 g;
    T Fat 12 g; 33% Calories from Fat; Chol 36 mg; Sod 765 mg.

Doris Richards, Friona

Tuna and Macaroni Salad

5 cups cooked macaroni
1 cup grated carrots
1/2 cup chopped green bell pepper
1/2 cup chopped onion

Salt and pepper to taste
1 11-ounce can tuna, drained
1/2 cup plain yogurt
1/2 cup mayonnaise-type salad dressing

Mix first 4 ingredients in bowl. Add salt, pepper and tuna; toss lightly. Add mixture of yogurt and salad dressing; mix gently. Chill until serving time. Yield: 6 servings.

Approx Per Serving: Cal 300; Prot 21 g; Carbo 36 g; Fiber 2 g;
    T Fat 8 g; 24% Calories from Fat; Chol 37 mg; Sod 341 mg.

Doris Richards, Friona

Asparagus Salad

8 ounces cream cheese, chopped
1 10-ounce can cream of asparagus
  soup, heated
1 3-ounce package lime gelatin
1/2 cup mayonnaise

1/2 cup water
1/2 cup chopped green bell pepper
3/4 cup chopped celery
1 tablespoon grated onion

Stir cream cheese into hot soup until melted. Stir in gelatin until dissolved. Add mayonnaise and water; mix well. Fold in vegetables. Spoon into 2-quart mold. Chill overnight. Unmold onto serving plate. Yield: 8 servings.

Approx Per Serving: Cal 265; Prot 4 g; Carbo 14 g; Fiber 1 g;
    T Fat 22 g; 73% Calories from Fat; Chol 41 mg; Sod 206 mg.

Mary Lou Caceres, El Paso

Fresh Broccoli Salad

1 small purple onion, thinly sliced	1 cup mayonnaise
Flowerets of 1 bunch broccoli	2 tablespoons sugar
12 ounces bacon, crisp-fried, crumbled	2 tablespoons vinegar

Pour boiling water over onion in bowl. Let stand for 30 to 60 seconds; drain. Add broccoli and bacon; mix well. Add mixture of mayonnaise, sugar and vinegar; mix well. Chill until serving time. Yield: 6 servings.

Approx Per Serving: Cal 400; Prot 8 g; Carbo 10 g; Fiber 2 g;
    T Fat 38 g; 83% Calories from Fat; Chol 36 mg; Sod 496 mg.

Diana Phillips, Abernathy

Chili Salad

1 medium head lettuce, torn	1/4 cup chopped black olives
3 cups corn chips	1/2 cup shredded Cheddar cheese
1 large tomato, chopped	1 15-ounce can ranch-style beans

Combine lettuce, corn chips, tomato, olives and cheese in salad bowl; toss to mix. Heat beans in saucepan until bubbly; drain. Add to salad; toss lightly. May add chili powder and French salad dressing if desired. Yield: 6 servings.

Approx Per Serving: Cal 286; Prot 8 g; Carbo 30 g; Fiber 2 g;
    T Fat 16 g; 48% Calories from Fat; Chol 10 mg; Sod 574 mg.

Joan Blackmon, Lubbock

Corn Bread Salad

1 8-ounce package corn bread mix	6 slices bacon, crisp-fried, crumbled
3 medium tomatoes, chopped	1 1/2 cups mayonnaise-type salad
1/2 cup each chopped green bell	dressing
pepper, onion and sweet pickles	1/2 cup sweet pickle juice

Prepare and bake corn bread using package directions. Cool and crumble corn bread. Combine tomatoes, green pepper, onion, pickles and bacon in bowl; mix well. Blend salad dressing and pickle juice in small bowl. Alternate layers of corn bread, vegetable mixture and salad dressing mixture in serving bowl until all ingredients are used. Yield: 6 servings.

Approx Per Serving: Cal 498; Prot 7 g; Carbo 55 g; Fiber 1 g;
    T Fat 30 g; 52% Calories from Fat; Chol 47 mg; Sod 3628 mg.

Rhonda Bentley, Friona

Shoe Peg Salad

1 16-ounce can white Shoe Peg corn
1 16-ounce can green peas
1 2-ounce jar chopped pimento
1 16-ounce can cut green beans
1/3 cup vinegar
1/3 cup oil
1/3 cup sugar
Salt to taste
1/2 cup chopped red onion
1/4 cup chopped green onions
4 stalks celery, chopped
1/2 cup chopped green bell pepper

Drain first 4 vegetables. Bring vinegar, oil, sugar and salt to a boil in saucepan, stirring to dissolve sugar. Cool to room temperature. Combine vegetables in bowl. Add cooled dressing; mix well. Chill for 8 hours to 4 days. Yield: 10 servings.

Approx Per Serving: Cal 175; Prot 4 g; Carbo 25 g; Fiber 4 g;
   T Fat 8 g; 38% Calories from Fat; Chol 0 mg; Sod 333 mg.

Hazel Alexander, Levelland

Sauerkraut Salad

1 16-ounce can sauerkraut
1/2 cup chopped onion
1/2 cup chopped green bell pepper
1 2-ounce jar chopped pimento
1 (scant) cup sugar
1 teaspoon salt

Combine sauerkraut, onion, green pepper, pimento, sugar and salt in bowl; mix well. Chill for 3 hours or longer. Yield: 6 servings.

Approx Per Serving: Cal 151; Prot 1 g; Carbo 38 g; Fiber 2 g;
   T Fat <1 g; 1% Calories from Fat; Chol 0 mg; Sod 857 mg.

Myrtle Clayton, Springlake

Seven-Layer Salad

1 head lettuce, chopped
1/2 cup each chopped celery, green
   onions and green bell pepper
1 10-ounce package frozen green
   peas, thawed
1 cup mayonnaise
2 tablespoons sugar
6 slices bacon, crisp-fried, crumbled
1 cup shredded Cheddar cheese

Layer lettuce, celery, green onions, green pepper and peas in order listed in large glass bowl. Blend mayonnaise and sugar in small bowl. Spread over layers. Top with bacon and cheese. Chill, covered with foil, overnight. Yield: 8 servings.

Approx Per Serving: Cal 328; Prot 8 g; Carbo 11 g; Fiber 3 g;
   T Fat 29 g; 78% Calories from Fat; Chol 35 mg; Sod 369 mg.

Dawn Wolf, Abernathy

TWENTY-FOUR HOUR SALAD

1 head lettuce, torn
1 green bell pepper, sliced into rings
1 onion, sliced into rings
1 7-ounce can water chestnuts, drained
1 carrot, shredded

1 10-ounce package frozen peas, thawed
2 cups mayonnaise
1/4 teaspoon sugar
1 cup shredded Monterey Jack cheese
1 cup shredded Cheddar cheese

Layer lettuce, green pepper, onion, water chestnuts, carrot and peas in large salad bowl. Spread with mixture of mayonnaise and sugar. Top with cheeses. Garnish with bacon bits. Chill, tightly covered, for 24 hours. Yield: 10 servings.

Approx Per Serving: Cal 448; Prot 8 g; Carbo 11 g; Fiber 3 g;
    T Fat 42 g; 83% Calories from Fat; Chol 48 mg; Sod 419 mg.

Bettye Hausmann, Earth

TANGY VEGETABLE SALAD

3/4 cup apple cider vinegar
1/2 cup corn oil
1 cup sugar
1 1/2 teaspoons salt
1 teaspoon white pepper
8 green onions with tops, finely chopped

1 cup finely chopped celery
1 15-ounce can Shoe Peg corn, drained
1 7-ounce can green peas, drained
1 2-ounce jar chopped pimento, drained

Combine vinegar, oil, sugar, salt and white pepper in saucepan. Bring to a boil, stirring to mix well. Cool to room temperature. Combine green onions, celery, corn, peas and pimento in bowl. Add marinade; mix well. Marinate in refrigerator for 2 hours to several days. Drain to serve. Yield: 8 servings.

Approx Per Serving: Cal 287; Prot 3 g; Carbo 41 g; Fiber 3 g;
    T Fat 14 g; 42% Calories from Fat; Chol 0 mg; Sod 592 mg.
    Nutritional information includes entire amount of marinade.

Janet Gentry, Lubbock

Congealed Tomato Salad

1¹/₂ envelopes unflavored gelatin
¹/₂ cup cold water
1   10-ounce can tomato soup
6 ounces cream cheese, softened

1 cup mayonnaise
¹/₂ cup each chopped celery, onion,
   carrot and green bell pepper

Soften gelatin in cold water. Bring soup to a boil in saucepan. Stir in gelatin until dissolved. Blend cream cheese and mayonnaise in bowl. Add soup mixture. Stir in chopped celery, onion, carrot and green pepper. Spoon into salad mold. Chill until set. Unmold onto serving plate. May add olives if desired. Yield: 8 servings.

Approx Per Serving: Cal 308; Prot 4 g; Carbo 8 g; Fiber 1 g;
   T Fat 30 g; 85% Calories from Fat; Chol 40 mg; Sod 475 mg.

Rita Tyson, Morton

French-Russian Dressing

¹/₂ cup oil
2 tablespoons white vinegar
¹/₄ cup catsup

2 tablespoons finely minced red onion
Salt to taste
1 teaspoon cayenne pepper

Combine oil, vinegar, catsup, onion, salt and cayenne pepper in jar; seal tightly. Shake to mix well. Serve on salad or salad greens. Store in refrigerator. Yield: 16 (1-tablespoon) servings.

Approx Per Serving: Cal 66; Prot <1 g; Carbo 1 g; Fiber <1 g;
   T Fat 7 g; 91% Calories from Fat; Chol 0 mg; Sod 45 mg.

Betty Dennis, Gail

French Salad Dressing

¹/₂ cup sugar
¹/₂ teaspoon dry mustard
¹/₂ teaspoon white pepper
¹/₂ teaspoon salt
1 large onion, grated

2 cloves of garlic, minced
1 cup oil
¹/₂ cup catsup
¹/₃ cup lemon juice

Combine sugar, dry mustard, white pepper, salt, onion, garlic, oil, catsup and lemon juice in order listed in mixer bowl, mixing well after each addition. Store in airtight container in refrigerator. Yield: 50 (1-tablespoon) servings.

Approx Per Serving: Cal 51; Prot <1 g; Carbo 3 g; Fiber <1 g;
   T Fat 4 g; 76% Calories from Fat; Chol 0 mg; Sod 50 mg.

Hazel Donovan, Matador

Vegetables & Side Dishes

Castro County

Playas sparkle in the late afternoon,
prairie jewels around the necks of Nazareth and Tam Annie,
the light of the stars push down,
the wind wanders lazily across Castro County,
our constant companion.

R.S.

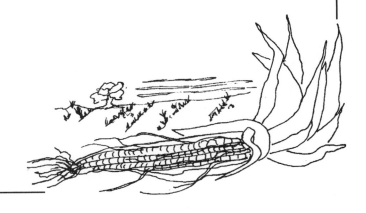

BAKED BEANS ROYALE

1/2 cup minced onion
2 tablespoons margarine
1/2 cup chopped celery
1 10-ounce can Ro-Tel tomatoes and
 green chilies

3 28-ounce cans pork and beans
1/2 cup dark molasses
Salt and pepper to taste
3 slices bacon, cut into halves

Sauté onion in margarine in skillet. Combine celery, tomatoes and green chilies and pork and beans in bowl; mix well. Add onion, molasses, salt and pepper; mix well. Pour into large greased baking dish. Arrange bacon slices over top. Bake, covered, at 325 degrees for 1 to 1 1/2 hours or until done to taste. Yield: 15 servings.

Approx Per Serving: Cal 226; Prot 9 g; Carbo 40 g; Fiber 9 g;
 T Fat 4 g; 17% Calories from Fat; Chol 12 mg; Sod 660 mg.

This recipe could also be prepared in slow cooker.
Cook on Low for 4 to 5 hours.

Mrs. T. Kinder Farris, Floydada

BEAN TOSS

1 16-ounce can pork and beans,
 drained
1 cup finely chopped celery
1/3 cup chopped sweet pickle
1/4 cup finely chopped onion
1 cup shredded sharp Cheddar cheese

1/2 teaspoon salt
1/2 teaspoon chili powder
1/2 teaspoon Worcestershire sauce
Several drops of hot pepper sauce
1/2 cup mayonnaise
1 cup coarsely crushed corn chips

Combine beans, celery, pickle, onion and cheese in bowl; mix well. Add salt, chili powder, Worcestershire sauce, hot pepper sauce and mayonnaise; mix well. Spoon into greased 1-quart shallow baking dish. Sprinkle with corn chips. Bake at 450 degrees for 10 to 15 minutes. May garnish with green bell pepper rings. Yield: 6 servings.

Approx Per Serving: Cal 366; Prot 10 g; Carbo 28 g; Fiber 5 g;
 T Fat 25 g; 60% Calories from Fat; Chol 36 mg; Sod 844 mg.

This recipe was given to me 22 years ago while I was living in Germany.
It is good with many types of food.

Helen Bergen, El Paso

Pinto Beans Muy Caliente

1 pound pinto beans
1½ teaspoons crushed red pepper
1 teaspoon salt
1 large clove of garlic, minced
2 cups chopped onions
4 slices bacon, chopped

2 10-ounce cans Rotel tomatoes
¼ cup chopped parsley
½ teaspoon ground cumin
½ teaspoon ground marjoram
5 teaspoons chili powder
1 teaspoon salt

Soak beans overnight in water to cover in saucepan. Drain beans. Add fresh water to cover, red pepper, 1 teaspoon salt and garlic. Bring to a boil. Reduce heat. Simmer for 1½ hours or until beans are tender, stirring occasionally. Sauté onions with bacon in skillet until onions are tender. Add tomatoes, parsley, cumin, marjoram, chili powder and 1 teaspoon salt to onion mixture; mix well. Simmer for 45 minutes. Add to beans. Simmer for 20 minutes longer. Yield: 8 servings.

Approx Per Serving: Cal 239; Prot 16 g; Carbo 41 g; Fiber 14 g;
 T Fat 3 g; 9% Calories from Fat; Chol 3 mg; Sod 899 mg.

Lee Ruth Krieg, Lubbock

Cajun Black-Eyed Peas

1 pound dried black-eyed peas
1 onion, chopped
¼ cup chopped garlic
1 cup white Sauterne wine

4 green cayenne peppers
4 ounces salt pork, chopped
½ cup olive oil

Rinse black-eyed peas. Place in large bowl; cover with water. Add onion, garlic, wine and whole peppers. Soak, covered with towel, overnight. Sauté salt pork in olive oil in large skillet until light brown. Add black-eyed peas mixture. Bring to a boil. Reduce heat. Simmer for 1 hour or until peas are tender, adding water as needed. Serve over hot cooked white rice or with corn bread. May substitute fresh black-eyed peas for dried but will need to cook longer. May substitute ham hocks or ham steak for salt pork and 3 jalapeño peppers for cayenne peppers.
Yield: 6 servings.

Approx Per Serving: Cal 507; Prot 21 g; Carbo 54 g; Fiber 22 g;
 T Fat 22 g; 40% Calories from Fat; Chol 5 mg; Sod 108 mg.

This has become a favorite at my family's holiday meals.
It has a new and unusual flavor.

Debbie Steffens, Slaton

BROCCOLI AND SPINACH CASSEROLE

2 10-ounce packages frozen chopped broccoli	1 cup yogurt
2 10-ounce packages frozen chopped spinach	1 cup sour cream
	1 envelope dry onion soup mix
	½ cup shredded Cheddar cheese

Combine broccoli, spinach and boiling water to cover in saucepan. Cook until vegetables are thawed; drain well. Combine yogurt, sour cream and soup mix in bowl. Add drained vegetables; mix well. Spray 9x13-inch baking dish with non-stick cooking spray. Pour vegetable mixture into baking dish; sprinkle with cheese. Bake at 325 degrees for 30 minutes or until hot and bubbly. Yield: 12 servings.

Approx Per Serving: Cal 100; Prot 5 g; Carbo 7 g; Fiber 3 g;
    T Fat 6 g; 53% Calories from Fat; Chol 16 mg; Sod 152 mg.

Yolonda Kelly, Lubbock

COOKED PURPLE CABBAGE

1 head purple cabbage, finely shredded	¼ cup raisins
⅓ cup oil	Lemon juice to taste
1 tablespoon grated onion	1 apple, finely chopped
	½ cup grape jam

Combine all ingredients in large saucepan. Cook on low heat for 20 to 25 minutes or until cabbage is tender, mixing gently with fork occasionally. Yield: 6 servings.

Approx Per Serving: Cal 223; Prot 1 g; Carbo 30 g; Fiber 2 g;
    T Fat 12 g; 47% Calories from Fat; Chol 0 mg; Sod 12 mg.

Helen Otken, Lubbock

CORN CASSEROLE

1 7-ounce package corn bread mix	1 17-ounce can cream-style corn
1 cup sour cream	½ cup melted margarine
1 17-ounce can whole kernel corn	1 cup shredded Cheddar cheese

Combine first 5 ingredients in bowl; mix well. Pour into greased 9x13-inch baking dish. Bake at 350 degrees for 30 minutes. Sprinkle with cheese. Bake for 20 to 30 minutes longer or until firm. Yield: 12 servings.

Approx Per Serving: Cal 233; Prot 5 g; Carbo 20 g; Fiber 1 g;
    T Fat 16 g; 58% Calories from Fat; Chol 18 mg; Sod 457 mg.

Magoline James, Olton

BEEFY CORN CASSEROLE

2 tablespoons chopped onion
1/2 cup shredded dried beef
3 tablespoons butter
3 eggs, beaten
1/4 cup milk

2 teaspoons salt
1/2 cup shredded Cheddar cheese
1 12-ounce can whole kernel corn,
   drained

Sauté onion and dried beef in butter in skillet until onion is tender. Combine with eggs, milk, salt, cheese and corn in bowl; mix well. Pour into greased casserole. Bake at 350 degrees for 30 minutes. Yield: 6 servings.

Approx Per Serving: Cal 197; Prot 10 g; Carbo 12 g; Fiber 1 g;
    T Fat 13 g; 57% Calories from Fat; Chol 149 mg; Sod 1315 mg.

Dahlia Hight, Lockney

CORN AND RICE CASSEROLE

2 16-ounce cans cream-style corn
1/2 cup chopped green bell pepper
1/2 cup chopped onion
1 cup uncooked minute rice
2 tablespoons sugar

1 2-ounce jar chopped pimento
1 4-ounce can chopped green chilies
Salt and pepper to taste
1 cup shredded Cheddar cheese

Combine corn, green pepper, onion, rice, sugar, pimento, green chilies, salt and pepper in bowl; mix well. Pour into greased 1½-quart casserole. Bake, uncovered, at 350 degrees for 25 minutes. Sprinkle with cheese. Bake for 10 minutes longer. Yield: 12 servings.

Approx Per Serving: Cal 137; Prot 4 g; Carbo 24 g; Fiber 2 g;
    T Fat 4 g; 22% Calories from Fat; Chol 10 mg; Sod 342 mg.

Maurine Chisholm, Littlefield

Onion Patties

³/₄ cup flour	¹/₂ teaspoon salt
2 teaspoons baking powder	1 tablespoon cornmeal
1 tablespoon sugar	2¹/₂ cups finely chopped onions
¹/₂ cup dry milk powder	Oil for deep frying

Combine flour, baking powder, sugar, dry milk powder, salt and cornmeal in bowl; mix well. Add enough cold water for a thick batter. Add onions; mix well. Drop by teaspoonfuls into deep hot oil in deep-fryer. Cook until golden brown. Drain on paper towels. Yield: 12 servings.

Approx Per Serving: Cal 57; Prot 2 g; Carbo 12 g; Fiber 1 g;
    T Fat <1 g; 3% Calories from Fat; Chol 1 mg; Sod 160 mg.
    Nutritional information does not include oil for deep frying.

Try these. They are so much easier than onion rings.

Leta Kelley, Earth

Gourmet Potatoes

6 medium potatoes	1 teaspoon salt
2 cups shredded Cheddar cheese	¹/₄ teaspoon pepper
¹/₄ cup margarine	2 tablespoons margarine
1¹/₂ cups sour cream	Paprika to taste
¹/₃ cup chopped green onions	

Cook potatoes in water to cover in saucepan until tender. Cool; peel and grate. Melt cheese and ¹/₄ cup margarine together in saucepan. Remove from heat. Add sour cream, green onions, salt and pepper; mix well. Pour over grated potatoes, stirring just until mixed. Spoon into greased 9x13-inch baking dish. Dot with 2 tablespoons margarine; sprinkle with paprika. Bake, uncovered, at 350 degrees for 30 minutes. Yield: 6 servings.

Approx Per Serving: Cal 497; Prot 14 g; Carbo 31 g; Fiber 2 g;
    T Fat 36 g; 64% Calories from Fat; Chol 65 mg; Sod 760 mg.

Susan Coleman, Dimmitt

Sour Cream Potatoes

2 cups water
1 teaspoon salt
1/4 cup butter
3/4 cup milk
2 cups potato flakes

2 cups shredded Cheddar cheese
5 or 6 slices crisp-fried bacon,
  crumbled
1 cup sour cream
1 tablespoon dried chives

Combine water, salt, butter and milk in saucepan. Bring to a boil, stirring occasionally. Remove from heat. Stir in potato flakes. Reserve 1/2 cup cheese. Add remaining cheese, bacon, sour cream and chives; mix well. Spoon into greased casserole; sprinkle with reserved cheese. Bake at 350 degrees for 20 to 25 minutes or until light brown. Yield: 8 servings.

Approx Per Serving: Cal 448; Prot 14 g; Carbo 44 g; Fiber 3 g;
    T Fat 25 g; 49% Calories from Fat; Chol 65 mg; Sod 660 mg.

Our family likes these because they're like stuffed baked potatoes.

Jennifer Pellham, Olton

Spinach Casserole

1   10-ounce package frozen chopped
    spinach
1 tablespoon grated onion
2 eggs, beaten
1/2 cup sour cream

1 tablespoon flour
2 tablespoons melted butter
1 cup grated Parmesan cheese
Salt and pepper to taste

Cook spinach with onion in a small amount of water in saucepan using package directions; drain. Combine eggs, sour cream, flour, butter, Parmesan cheese, salt and pepper in bowl; mix well. Stir in spinach. Spoon into greased casserole. Bake at 350 degrees for 25 to 30 minutes or until hot and bubbly. Yield: 4 servings.

Approx Per Serving: Cal 272; Prot 15 g; Carbo 8 g; Fiber 2 g;
    T Fat 21 g; 67% Calories from Fat; Chol 150 mg; Sod 536 mg.

Linda Moorhouse, Guthrie

CHEESY SPINACH CASSEROLE

2   10-ounce packages frozen chopped
   spinach
4 ounces Cheddar cheese, shredded
4 ounces Monterey Jack cheese,
   shredded

6 ounces cottage cheese
3 eggs, beaten
Salt to taste
2 tablespoons flour
2 tablespoons melted butter

Cook spinach in nonstick skillet using package directions; drain. Add cheeses, eggs, salt, flour and butter; mix well. Spoon into 8x8-inch baking dish. Bake at 350 degrees for 1 hour. Yield: 8 servings.

Approx Per Serving: Cal 214; Prot 14 g; Carbo 6 g; Fiber 2 g;
   T Fat 15 g; 62% Calories from Fat; Chol 119 mg; Sod 361 mg.

Martha Beach, Lubbock

FRESH PEACH AND SQUASH CASSEROLE

2¹/₂ cups sliced peeled yellow or
   zucchini squash
1 cup sliced fresh peaches

2 tablespoons brown sugar
Salt to taste
2¹/₂ tablespoons butter

Alternate layers of squash and peaches in greased 2-quart casserole. Sprinkle with brown sugar and salt. Dot with butter. Bake, covered, at 350 degrees for 45 to 60 minutes or until squash is tender. Yield: 4 servings.

Approx Per Serving: Cal 124; Prot 1 g; Carbo 15 g; Fiber 2 g;
   T Fat 7 g; 51% Calories from Fat; Chol 19 mg; Sod 66 mg.

Carrie Tatum, Friona

SQUASH CASSEROLE

3 cups squash
1   10-ounce can cream of chicken
   soup
3 tablespoons chopped pimento

3 tablespoons melted butter
Salt and pepper to taste
¹/₂ cup bread crumbs

Cook squash in a small amount of water in saucepan for 5 minutes; drain. Combine soup, pimento and butter in bowl; mix well. Add squash, salt and pepper; mix well. Pour into greased casserole; sprinkle with bread crumbs. Bake at 375 degrees for 15 minutes. Yield: 6 servings.

Approx Per Serving: Cal 142; Prot 3 g; Carbo 13 g; Fiber 2 g;
   T Fat 9 g; 56% Calories from Fat; Chol 20 mg; Sod 483 mg.

Dahlia Hight, Lockney

SQUASH-CHILI CASSEROLE

Salt to taste
3 cups grated yellow squash
3/4 cup sliced green onions
1 1/2 tablespoons melted margarine
1 tablespoon flour
1 4-ounce can chopped green chilies

1 cup shredded Cheddar cheese
3 eggs, beaten
1 cup whipping cream
1/2 teaspoon salt
1/4 teaspoon pepper
1/2 cup shredded Cheddar cheese

Sprinkle salt on squash in bowl. Let stand for 30 minutes; drain well. Pat dry. Sauté green onions in margarine in skillet until tender. Add squash. Cook for several minutes, stirring gently. Stir in flour. Cook for 1 minute, stirring frequently. Spoon into greased 9x13-inch baking dish. Sprinkle with green chilies and 1 cup cheese. Combine eggs, whipping cream, 1/2 teaspoon salt and pepper in bowl; beat well. Pour over squash. Bake at 400 degrees for 15 minutes. Reduce over temperature to 350 degrees. Bake for 20 minutes longer. Sprinkle with remaining 1/2 cup cheese. Bake for 5 minutes longer. Let stand for 5 minutes before serving. Yield: 10 servings.

Approx Per Serving: Cal 228; Prot 8 g; Carbo 6 g; Fiber 1 g;
    T Fat 20 g; 76% Calories from Fat; Chol 119 mg; Sod 359 mg.

Rita Tyson, Morton

SWEET POTATO CASSEROLE

3 cups mashed cooked sweet potatoes
1 cup sugar
2 eggs, beaten
1/2 cup milk
1/4 cup melted margarine
1/2 teaspoon salt

1 teaspoon vanilla extract
1 cup packed brown sugar
1/2 cup self-rising flour
1/4 cup margarine
1 cup chopped pecans

Combine sweet potatoes, sugar, eggs, milk, 1/4 cup melted margarine, salt and vanilla in bowl; mix well. Spoon into greased casserole. Combine brown sugar and flour in bowl; mix well. Cut in 1/4 cup margarine until crumbly. Stir in pecans. Sprinkle over sweet potato mixture. Bake at 350 degrees for 30 minutes. Yield: 8 servings.

Approx Per Serving: Cal 613; Prot 6 g; Carbo 98 g; Fiber 2 g;
    T Fat 24 g; 34% Calories from Fat; Chol 55 mg; Sod 407 mg.

Hazel Donovan, Matador

Zucchini Quiche

4 cups thinly sliced zucchini
1 cup coarsely chopped onion
1/2 cup margarine
2 tablespoons parsley flakes
1/2 teaspoon salt
1/2 teaspoon garlic powder
1/2 teaspoon pepper

1/4 teaspoon basil
1/4 teaspoon oregano
2 eggs, beaten
8 ounces mozzarella cheese, shredded
1 8-count can crescent rolls
2 teaspoons Dijon mustard

Sauté zucchini and onion in margarine in skillet until tender. Remove from heat. Add parsley flakes, salt, garlic powder, pepper, basil and oregano; mix well. Combine eggs and cheese in bowl; beat well. Add vegetable mixture; mix well. Unroll crescent roll dough; separate into triangles. Press on bottom and up sides of 11-inch quiche dish; seal edges together. Spread mustard over dough. Spoon vegetable mixture into prepared dish. Bake at 375 degrees for 18 to 20 minutes or until knife inserted near center comes out clean. Let stand for several minutes before serving. Yield: 6 servings.

Approx Per Serving: Cal 426; Prot 13 g; Carbo 21 g; Fiber 1 g;
    T Fat 32 g; 69% Calories from Fat; Chol 100 mg; Sod 874 mg.

Mildred McAllister, Ft. Worth

Mixed Vegetable Casserole

1 cup sliced celery
1 10-ounce can cream of celery soup
1 15-ounce can cut asparagus, drained
1 15-ounce can tiny party peas, drained

1 15-ounce can French-style green beans, drained
1 8-ounce can sliced water chestnuts, drained
1/2 cup fine bread crumbs
1/2 cup grated Parmesan cheese

Cook celery in a small amount of water in saucepan until tender. Drain, reserving cooking liquid. Combine soup and enough reserved liquid to make of desired consistency; mix well. Alternate layers of soup and drained vegetables in greased casserole. Sprinkle with bread crumbs and cheese. Bake at 325 degrees for 30 to 40 minutes or until hot and bubbly. Yield: 10 servings.

Approx Per Serving: Cal 115; Prot 6 g; Carbo 17 g; Fiber 4 g;
    T Fat 3 g; 23% Calories from Fat; Chol 7 mg; Sod 639 mg.

Betty Anne Kyle, Lubbock

VEGETABLES CHOW MEIN

1/2 medium head cabbage, shredded
2 small carrots, cut julienne-style
1 green bell pepper, cut julienne-style
1 onion, shredded
1 clove of garlic, minced

1/2 medium head cauliflower, thinly
  sliced
2/3 cup thinly sliced celery
1 tablespoon oil
Salt and pepper to taste

Stir-fry cabbage, carrots, green pepper, onion, garlic, cauliflower and celery in hot oil in skillet for 4 to 5 minutes or until vegetables are tender-crisp. Add salt and pepper; mix well. Serve over hot cooked rice. Yield: 6 servings.

Approx Per Serving: Cal 56; Prot 2 g; Carbo 8 g; Fiber 3 g;
    T Fat 3 g; 37% Calories from Fat; Chol 0 mg; Sod 28 mg.

Doreen Vernon, Lubbock

CHILIES RELLENOS CASSEROLE

1/2 pound sharp Cheddar cheese
1 4-ounce can chopped green chilies
2 eggs, beaten

2 cups milk
1/2 cup flour
1 teaspoon salt

Cut cheese into 3-inch strips. Layer with green chilies in greased 2-quart casserole. Blend remaining ingredients in blender container. Pour over layers. Bake at 350 degrees for 35 to 40 minutes or until hot and bubbly. Yield: 6 servings.

Approx Per Serving: Cal 271; Prot 15 g; Carbo 14 g; Fiber <1 g;
    T Fat 17 g; 57% Calories from Fat; Chol 122 mg; Sod 781 mg.

Barbara Amerson, Abernathy

FRITO FEAST

12 ounces corn chips, crushed
2 17-ounce cans chili

2 17-ounce cans cream-style corn
1 cup shredded Cheddar cheese

Layer half the corn chips, chili, corn, cheese and remaining corn chips in greased 9x13-inch microwave-safe dish. Microwave on Medium-High for 7 minutes or until heated through, stirring several times. Great as a main dish! Yield: 12 servings.

Approx Per Serving: Cal 394; Prot 11 g; Carbo 35 g; Fiber 3 g;
    T Fat 24 g; 54% Calories from Fat; Chol 10 mg; Sod 1041 mg.

Patsy Allen, Friona

President Reagan's Favorite Macaroni and Cheese

8 ounces uncooked macaroni
1 teaspoon butter
1 egg, beaten
1 teaspoon salt
1 teaspoon dry mustard

1 tablespoon hot water
1 cup milk
3 cups shredded sharp Cheddar
   cheese

Cook macaroni using package directions; drain. Stir butter and egg into hot macaroni. Mix salt, mustard and hot water in bowl. Add milk; mix well. Add 2 cups cheese to milk mixture; mix well. Add macaroni mixture; mix well. Pour into buttered casserole. Sprinkle with remaining cheese. Bake at 350 degrees for 45 minutes or until set and top is crusty. Yield: 4 servings.

Approx Per Serving: Cal 615; Prot 32 g; Carbo 47 g; Fiber 2 g;
   T Fat 33 g; 48% Calories from Fat; Chol 153 mg; Sod 1107 mg.

Former First Lady Nancy Reagan

Davis Family Special

16 ounces uncooked macaroni
1 onion, chopped
1 green bell pepper, chopped
1/2 cup margarine

1 16-ounce can stewed tomatoes
Garlic powder to taste
16 ounces Cheddar cheese, shredded

Cook macaroni using package directions; drain. Sauté onion and green pepper in margarine in skillet until tender. Add tomatoes and garlic powder. Simmer for 30 minutes, stirring occasionally. Add to macaroni; mix well. Spray 10x14-inch baking dish with nonstick cooking spray. Pour macaroni mixture into prepared baking dish. Top with cheese. Bake at 350 degrees for 30 minutes or until hot and bubbly. Yield: 12 servings.

Approx Per Serving: Cal 377; Prot 15 g; Carbo 33 g; Fiber 2 g;
   T Fat 21 g; 49% Calories from Fat; Chol 40 mg; Sod 446 mg.

Patsy Vessels, Slaton

FETTUCINI

1 pound medium mushrooms, sliced	4 ounces Parmesan cheese, grated
1/4 cup butter	1/2 cup whipping cream
16 ounces fettucini, cooked	1/4 teaspoon freshly ground pepper

Sauté mushrooms in butter in skillet over medium heat for 5 minutes. Remove from heat. Combine with fettucini and remaining ingredients in saucepan. Cook until heated through, stirring gently occasionally. Yield: 8 servings.

Approx Per Serving: Cal 390; Prot 15 g; Carbo 46 g; Fiber 4 g;
T Fat 16 g; 38% Calories from Fat; Chol 47 mg; Sod 321 mg.

Mrs. R. W. Blake, Lubbock

MACARONI CASSEROLE

16 ounces small elbow macaroni, cooked	1/4 cup chopped onion
4 cups grated sharp Cheddar cheese	1/4 cup chopped green bell pepper
1 10-ounce can cream of mushroom soup	3 tablespoons butter
1 4-ounce can mushrooms	1 4-ounce package Roquefort cheese
1 cup mayonnaise	1 1/2 cups cracker crumbs

Mix first 7 ingredients in bowl. Spoon into greased 1 1/2-quart casserole. Melt butter and Roquefort cheese in saucepan over low heat, stirring constantly. Stir in crumbs. Sprinkle over macaroni mixture. Bake at 350 degrees for 30 minutes. Yield: 8 servings.

Approx Per Serving: Cal 833; Prot 26 g; Carbo 60 g; Fiber 3 g;
T Fat 54 g; 59% Calories from Fat; Chol 106 mg; Sod 1352 mg.

Brenda Farr, Lubbock

MACARONI PIE

4 ounces elbow macaroni, cooked	2 cups milk
4 ounces spaghetti, cooked	4 eggs, beaten
1 1/2 cups shredded sharp Cheddar cheese	1/4 cup butter
	1/2 teaspoon salt

Alternate layers of macaroni, spaghetti and cheese in greased 2-quart casserole, ending with cheese. Combine milk, eggs and butter in saucepan. Cook for 2 minutes or until thickened, stirring constantly. Stir in salt. Pour over layers. Bake, covered, at 375 degrees for 30 minutes or until bubbly. Yield: 8 servings.

Approx Per Serving: Cal 318; Prot 14 g; Carbo 25 g; Fiber 1 g;
T Fat 18 g; 51% Calories from Fat; Chol 153 mg; Sod 374 mg.

Doreen Vernon, Lubbock

Lemon Rice

2¹/₂ cups canned chicken broth
¹/₄ teaspoon salt
¹/₂ teaspoon minced garlic
1 cup long-grain rice

1 tablespoon finely grated lemon rind
¹/₂ teaspoon tarragon
¹/₈ teaspoon white pepper
1 teaspoon butter

Combine chicken broth, salt and garlic in heavy saucepan. Bring to a boil, stirring occasionally. Stir in rice. Simmer, covered, for 15 minutes or until all the liquid is absorbed. Remove from heat. Stir in remaining ingredients. Yield: 4 servings.

Approx Per Serving: Cal 202; Prot 6 g; Carbo 38 g; Fiber 1 g;
    T Fat 2 g; 10% Calories from Fat; Chol 3 mg; Sod 628 mg.

Susan McDonald, Ransom Canyon

Festive Rice

²/₃ cup long-grain rice
1 teaspoon freshly grated lemon rind
¹/₄ teaspoon turmeric
1 tablespoon vegetable oil

1¹/₂ cups coconut milk
1 bay leaf
¹/₈ teaspoon salt
1 red bell pepper, cut into strips

Cook rice, lemon rind and turmeric together in hot oil in skillet for 2 minutes, stirring constantly. Add coconut milk, bay leaf and salt. Bring to a boil, stirring occasionally. Reduce heat. Simmer, covered, for 15 minutes or until rice is tender. Remove bay leaf. Press rice mixture into 2 oiled ¹/₂-cup cone-shaped molds. Invert onto serving plate. Garnish with red pepper strips. Serve immediately.
Yield: 4 servings.

Approx Per Serving: Cal 312; Prot 4 g; Carbo 28 g; Fiber 1 g;
    T Fat 22 g; 61% Calories from Fat; Chol 0 mg; Sod 79 mg.

Susan McDonald, Ransom Canyon

Special Rice

2   10-ounce cans beef consommé
1 cup rice

¹/₄ cup melted margarine
1 small onion, chopped

Combine all ingredients in bowl; mix well. Pour into greased baking dish. Bake at 350 degrees for 1 hour or until liquid is absorbed. Yield: 6 servings.

Approx Per Serving: Cal 209; Prot 7 g; Carbo 28 g; Fiber 1 g;
    T Fat 8 g; 34% Calories from Fat; Chol 0 mg; Sod 582 mg.

Paula Wilson, Friona

Meats

Crosby County

From Courthouse Mountain,

to the corners of the Blanco Canyon,

to the Silver Falls of the White River,

the ghosts of Indian hunters and Stephen Crosby

walk the rim of the Caprock.

R.S.

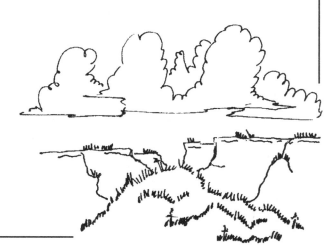

Barbecued Roast

1 3-pound beef roast
1 small onion, cut into chunks
1/2 teaspoon red pepper
4 teaspoons brown sugar
1 teaspoon dry mustard
2 tablespoons Worcestershire sauce
1/4 teaspoon pepper sauce
1/2 cup catsup
1/4 cup vinegar
1 cup water
4 teaspoons liquid smoke
1 teaspoon chili powder

Brown roast in large saucepan. Place onion chunks on roast. Combine red pepper, brown sugar, dry mustard, Worcestershire sauce, pepper sauce, catsup, vinegar, water, liquid smoke and chili powder in bowl; mix well. Pour over roast. Cook for 2 hours or to desired degree of doneness. Yield: 12 servings.

Approx Per Serving: Cal 173; Prot 22 g; Carbo 6 g; Fiber <1 g;
T Fat 7 g; 35% Calories from Fat; Chol 64 mg; Sod 181 mg.
Nutritional information does not include liquid smoke.

Hazel Alexander, Levelland

Beef Stroganoff

1 1/2 pounds round steak
1/2 cup finely chopped onion
2 tablespoons bacon drippings
2 beef bouillon cubes
2 1/2 cups boiling water
2 tablespoons flour
1 teaspoon salt
1/2 teaspoon pepper
1 cup sour cream
4 cups hot cooked rice

Trim fat from steak; cut into finger-length strips. Brown onion in bacon drippings in skillet. Add steak. Cook until browned. Dissolve bouillon cubes in boiling water. Add to skillet. Stir in flour, salt and pepper. Cook until thickened, stirring constantly. Spoon into baking dish. Bake at 300 degrees for 50 to 60 minutes or until heated through. Stir in sour cream. Spoon over hot cooked rice.
Yield: 8 servings.

Approx Per Serving: Cal 328; Prot 19 g; Carbo 28 g; Fiber 1 g;
T Fat 15 g; 41% Calories from Fat; Chol 82 mg; Sod 559 mg.

*This recipe was clipped from the **Oklahoma City Times** newspaper.*

Jane B. McCulley, Floydada

Cube Steaks Parmesan

1 egg
¹/₈ teaspoon pepper
1 tablespoon water
¹/₄ cup crushed saltine crackers
2 tablespoons grated Parmesan cheese

5 4-ounce cube steaks
2 tablespoons oil
1 8-ounce can pizza sauce
2 tablespoons grated Parmesan cheese

Mix egg, pepper and water in small bowl. Mix cracker crumbs and 2 tablespoons cheese in medium bowl. Dip steaks first into egg mixture, then into crumb mixture. Brown in hot oil in skillet; drain. Stir pizza sauce into skillet. Simmer, covered, over low heat for 20 minutes, adding a small amount of water if needed to keep sauce from sticking. Sprinkle with 2 tablespoons cheese. Yield: 5 servings.

Approx Per Serving: Cal 274; Prot 25 g; Carbo 6 g; Fiber <1 g;
T Fat 16 g; 53% Calories from Fat; Chol 111 mg; Sod 381 mg.

*This recipe came from **Better Homes and Gardens'** all-time
favorite beef recipes. Our family calls it pizza steak.*

Kathy Bock, Earth

Pepper Cuts

2 pounds round steak
2 tablespoons oil
1 cup chopped onion
2 green bell peppers, cut into ¹/₂-inch
  strips

Seasoned salt to taste
Pepper to taste
¹/₂ cup water

Cut steak cross grain into ¹/₄-inch strips. Brown in hot oil in skillet. Add onion and green peppers; mix well. Sprinkle with seasoned salt and pepper. Add a small amount of water. Simmer, covered, over low heat for 20 minutes, adding remaining water gradually to keep mixture from scorching. Yield: 4 servings.

Approx Per Serving: Cal 380; Prot 43 g; Carbo 5 g; Fiber 1 g;
T Fat 20 g; 48% Calories from Fat; Chol 128 mg; Sod 71 mg.

*This recipe is a good way to use less expensive cuts of meat. Serve
with rice and a salad or use in fajitas.*

Richard Young, Dimmitt

BARBECUPS

1 12-count can biscuits	1 tablespoon minced onion
1 pound ground beef	2 tablespoons brown sugar
1/2 cup barbecue sauce	3/4 cup shredded Cheddar cheese

Press biscuit dough into ungreased muffin cups into shape of cups. Brown ground beef in skillet; drain. Stir in barbecue sauce, onion and brown sugar. Spoon into dough cups. Sprinkle with cheese. Bake at 400 degrees for 10 to 12 minutes or until cheese is melted. Yield: 12 servings.

Approx Per Serving: Cal 186; Prot 10 g; Carbo 13 g; Fiber <1 g;
T Fat 10 g; 49% Calories from Fat; Chol 33 mg; Sod 400 mg.

Phyllis Redman, Morton

GROUND BEEF AND SAUERKRAUT

1 pound ground beef	1 16-ounce can sauerkraut
1/2 onion, chopped	1/4 teaspoon each thyme and oregano
1/2 green bell pepper, chopped	Cayenne pepper to taste

Brown ground beef in saucepan; drain. Add onion and green pepper. Cook until onion is transparent. Stir in sauerkraut, thyme, oregano and pepper. Yield: 4 servings.

Approx Per Serving: Cal 260; Prot 22 g; Carbo 7 g; Fiber 3 g;
T Fat 16 g; 56% Calories from Fat; Chol 74 mg; Sod 816 mg.

Joline Bolden, Levelland

DEEP-DISH TACO SQUARES

8 ounces ground beef	1/2 cup sour cream
1 cup baking mix	1/3 cup mayonnaise
1/4 cup cold water	1/2 cup shredded Cheddar cheese
2 tomatoes, thinly sliced	1 tablespoon chopped onion
1/2 cup chopped green bell pepper	

Brown ground beef in skillet; drain. Combine baking mix and water in bowl; mix until soft dough forms. Pat into 8x8-inch baking pan. Layer ground beef, tomatoes and green pepper over dough. Combine sour cream, mayonnaise, cheese and onion in bowl; mix well. Spoon over all. Bake at 375 degrees for 20 to 25 minutes or until edges of dough are light brown. Yield: 4 servings.

Approx Per Serving: Cal 516; Prot 18 g; Carbo 26 g; Fiber 1 g;
T Fat 38 g; 66% Calories from Fat; Chol 75 mg; Sod 641 mg.

Dahlia Hight, Lockney

COWBOY CASSEROLE

1¹/₂ pounds ground beef
4 tablespoons oil
2 stalks celery, cut into thin strips
1 slice green bell pepper
³/₄ cup chopped onion
1 cup uncooked rice
1 28-ounce can chopped tomatoes

2 teaspoons salt
2 teaspoons chili powder
¹/₂ teaspoon pepper
1 teaspoon Worcestershire sauce
Tabasco sauce to taste
1 cup chopped large black olives
8 ounces Monterey Jack cheese, sliced

Brown ground beef in 2 tablespoons oil in skillet; drain. Remove ground beef to 2-quart casserole. Add remaining 2 tablespoons oil, celery, green pepper, onion and rice to skillet. Cook until rice is browned. Add undrained tomatoes, salt, chili powder, pepper, Worcestershire sauce, Tabasco sauce and half the olives; mix well. Bring to a boil. Pour over ground beef. Bake, covered, at 325 degrees for 1 hour. Layer remaining olives and cheese over baked layers. Broil for 5 minutes or until cheese is bubbly. Yield: 8 servings.

Approx Per Serving: Cal 487; Prot 26 g; Carbo 26 g; Fiber 3 g;
    T Fat 33 g; 59% Calories from Fat; Chol 82 mg; Sod 1078 mg.

Zita LaMaster, Perryton

GREEN ENCHILADAS

1 pound lean ground beef
1 teaspoon salt
¹/₄ teaspoon garlic
8 ounces Longhorn cheese, shredded
1 cup chopped onion
1 10-ounce can cream of chicken
    soup

8 ounces Velveeta cheese, grated
1 4-ounce can green chilies
1 2-ounce jar chopped pimento
12 tortillas
¹/₂ cup corn oil

Combine ground beef, salt and garlic in skillet. Brown ground beef, stirring until crumbly; drain. Add longhorn cheese and onion; mix well. Combine chicken soup and Velveeta cheese in top of double boiler. Cook until cheese is melted, stirring frequently. Add green chilies and pimento; mix well. Soften tortillas in hot oil in skillet; drain well on both sides on paper towels. Fill each tortilla with ground beef mixture; fold to enclose filling. Place seam side down in greased 8x10-inch baking dish. Pour cheese sauce over all. Bake, covered with foil, at 350 degrees for 30 minutes. Yield: 8 servings.

Approx Per Serving: Cal 598; Prot 28 g; Carbo 26 g; Fiber 4 g;
    T Fat 44 g; 65% Calories from Fat; Chol 97 mg; Sod 1261 mg.

Sygale Hall, Morton

LASAGNA

3 medium onions, chopped
2 cloves of garlic, minced
1 tablespoon butter
1 pound ground beef
1 pound ground pork
2 15-ounce cans tomato sauce
1 6-ounce can tomato paste
1¹/₂ cups water

1 teaspoon salt
¹/₂ teaspoon pepper
¹/₂ teaspoon oregano
2 pounds ricotta cheese
2 eggs
8 lasagna noodles, cooked
3 cups shredded mozzarella cheese
¹/₂ cup grated Parmesan cheese

Sauté onions and garlic in butter in large skillet until tender. Add ground beef and ground pork. Cook until ground beef and ground pork are brown, stirring until crumbly; drain. Add tomato sauce, tomato paste, water, salt, pepper and oregano; mix well. Simmer, covered, for 25 minutes, stirring occasionally. Combine ricotta cheese and eggs in bowl; mix well. Layer half the lasagna noodles, ¹/₃ of the meat sauce, half the ricotta mixture and half the mozzarella cheese in greased baking dish. Repeat layers. Top with remaining meat sauce and Parmesan cheese. Bake at 350 degrees for 25 minutes or until hot and bubbly. Cool for 15 minutes before cutting into squares. Yield: 10 servings.

Approx Per Serving: Cal 611; Prot 45 g; Carbo 34 g; Fiber 3 g;
  T Fat 33 g; 49% Calories from Fat; Chol 184 mg; Sod 1095 mg.

Mrs. R. W. Blake, Lubbock

ONE-STEP LASAGNA

1¹/₂ cups water
2 15-ounce jars spaghetti sauce
16 ounces uncooked lasagna noodles
15 ounces ricotta cheese

8 ounces mozzarella cheese, thinly
  sliced
¹/₂ cup grated Parmesan cheese

Combine water and spaghetti sauce in bowl; mix well. Spoon 1¹/₂ cups sauce into 9x13-inch baking dish. Arrange ¹/₃ of the uncooked noodles over sauce, overlapping slightly. Layer half the ricotta cheese, half the mozzarella cheese and 2 tablespoons Parmesan cheese over noodles. Repeat layers. Layer remaining uncooked noodles, remaining sauce and remaining Parmesan cheese over all. Bake, lightly covered with foil, at 350 degrees for 1 hour or until noodles are tender. Let stand, covered, on rack for 10 minutes before cutting. Yield: 10 servings.

Approx Per Serving: Cal 419; Prot 19 g; Carbo 49 g; Fiber 1 g;
  T Fat 17 g; 35% Calories from Fat; Chol 42 mg; Sod 620 mg.

We won first place in outdoor cooking with this recipe. We cooked it for 30 minutes in a #14 Dutch oven with 20 briquettes under and 15 briquettes on top.

Kathy Hunt, Lubbock

MARY'S MEAT LOAF WITH CREOLE SAUCE

1 pound ground round beef
1 egg, beaten
1 tablespoon minced onion
1/4 teaspoon pepper
1/2 teaspoon seasoned salt
1 cup tomato juice
1/2 cup cracker crumbs
1/4 cup tomato juice
2 tablespoons water
1/2 cup chopped green bell pepper

1/2 cup chopped onion
3 tablespoons margarine
2 tablespoons flour
1/4 teaspoon pepper
1/8 teaspoon Tabasco sauce
2 tablespoons brown sugar
1 1/2 tablespoons vinegar
1/4 bay leaf
4 cups tomatoes
1 tablespoon Worcestershire sauce

Combine ground beef, egg, minced onion, 1/4 teaspoon pepper, seasoned salt, 1 cup tomato juice and cracker crumbs in bowl; mix well. Spoon into greased 8x8-inch baking pan. Mix 1/4 cup tomato juice and 2 tablespoons water in bowl. Pour over meat loaf. Bake at 350 degrees for 45 minutes or until cooked through. Sauté green pepper and remaining onion in margarine in skillet until tender. Stir in flour until well mixed. Add 1/4 teaspoon pepper, Tabasco sauce, brown sugar, vinegar, bay leaf, tomatoes and Worcestershire sauce; mix well. Simmer over low heat for 25 minutes, stirring occasionally. Discard bay leaf. May serve with meat loaf or add 3 or 4 tablespoons sauce over meat loaf while it is baking.
Yield: 4 servings.

Approx Per Serving: Cal 473; Prot 26 g; Carbo 32 g; Fiber 4 g;
    T Fat 28 g; 52% Calories from Fat; Chol 131 mg; Sod 813 mg.

Kay Lepard, Muleshoe

MICROWAVE MEAT LOAF

1 pound ground beef
1/2 cup chopped green bell pepper
1/4 cup chopped onion
1 egg
1 tablespoon Worcestershire sauce

1/3 cup oats
Salt and pepper to taste
1   6-ounce can tomato juice
1 cup catsup

Combine ground beef, green pepper, onion, egg, Worcestershire sauce, oats, salt, pepper, tomato juice and 3/4 cup catsup in bowl; mix well. Spoon into microwave-safe dish. Microwave on High for 8 to 10 minutes or until cooked through, stirring halfway through cooking time. Top with remaining catsup. Microwave for 1 minute longer. May also cook in individual dishes for 2 1/2 minutes.
Yield: 6 servings.

Approx Per Serving: Cal 243; Prot 17 g; Carbo 17 g; Fiber 2 g;
    T Fat 12 g; 44% Calories from Fat; Chol 85 mg; Sod 656 mg.

Doris Vandiver, Muleshoe

Apricot Meat Loaf

2 pounds ground beef
1 cup chopped uncooked dried
   apricots
1/2 cup crushed cornflakes

2 eggs
1 1/2 teaspoons salt
1/8 teaspoon pepper
1/2 cup packed brown sugar

Combine first 6 ingredients in bowl; mix lightly. Press into greased 5x9-inch loaf pan. Bake at 350 degrees for 1 hour. Sprinkle brown sugar on top. Bake for 5 to 10 minutes longer or until brown sugar is melted. Yield: 12 servings.

Approx Per Serving: Cal 272; Prot 16 g; Carbo 27 g; Fiber 2 g;
   T Fat 12 g; 38% Calories from Fat; Chol 85 mg; Sod 363 mg.

Joann Stewart, Lubbock

Mexican Casserole

2 pounds ground chuck
1 medium onion, chopped
1 envelope taco seasoning mix

1 15-ounce can refried beans
10 ounces Cheddar cheese, shredded
1 10-count can biscuits

Brown ground chuck with onion in skillet, stirring until ground chuck is crumbly; drain. Add taco seasoning mix; mix well. Heat beans in saucepan. Layer ground chuck mixture, beans and cheese in 8x8-inch baking dish. Top with biscuits. Bake using biscuit package directions. Yield: 4 servings.

Approx Per Serving: Cal 1075; Prot 71 g; Carbo 56 g; Fiber 11 g;
   T Fat 63 g; 53% Calories from Fat; Chol 225 mg; Sod 2516 mg

Johnnie Hill, Sundown

Cabbage Pie

1 pound ground beef
1/2 onion, chopped
1/2 head cabbage, finely chopped

1 8-count can crescent rolls
4 cheese slices

Brown ground beef with onion in skillet, stirring frequently; drain. Remove from heat. Stir in cabbage. Unroll roll dough. Separate into 2 rectangles. Press 1 rectangle onto greased 9x9-inch baking dish; top with ground beef mixture. Spread remaining dough rectangle over top. Bake at 400 degrees for 10 minutes or until brown. Arrange cheese slices on top. Bake until cheese is melted. Yield: 4 servings.

Approx Per Serving: Cal 551; Prot 31 g; Carbo 26 g; Fiber 1 g;
   T Fat 36 g; 59% Calories from Fat; Chol 101 mg; Sod 937 mg.

Debbie Steffens, Slaton

TOPSY TURVY PIE

1 pound ground chuck
1/2 cup chopped onion
1/4 cup chopped green bell pepper
Salt to taste

1 8-ounce can tomato sauce
2 cups baking mix
2/3 cup milk

Brown ground chuck with onion and green pepper in skillet, stirring until ground chuck is crumbly; drain. Add salt and tomato sauce; mix well. Spoon into greased 9-inch round baking dish. Combine baking mix and milk in bowl; mix well. Roll out dough on floured surface to fit baking dish. Place dough on top of ground beef mixture. Bake at 425 degrees for 15 to 20 minutes or until brown. Yield: 4 servings.

Approx Per Serving: Cal 552; Prot 28 g; Carbo 50 g; Fiber 1 g;
T Fat 27 g; 44% Calories from Fat; Chol 80 mg; Sod 1219 mg.

LaVerne Stolle, Slaton

CORN PONE PIE

1 pound lean ground beef
1 onion, chopped
Salt, black pepper and chili pepper
to taste
1 4-ounce can chopped green chilies

1 16-ounce can ranch-style beans
1 16-ounce can tomato pieces
16 ounces American cheese, shredded
1 6-ounce package corn bread mix

Brown ground beef in skillet, stirring until crumbly. Add onion. Cook until tender; drain. Combine ground beef mixture, salt, black pepper, chili pepper and green chilies in bowl; mix well. Add undrained beans and undrained tomato pieces; mix well. Spoon into 10-inch cast-iron skillet. Top with cheese. Prepare corn bread mix using package directions. Spoon batter over cheese. Bake at 350 degrees for 40 to 45 minutes or until brown. Yield: 6 servings.

Approx Per Serving: Cal 684; Prot 39 g; Carbo 42 g; Fiber 1 g;
T Fat 41 g; 54% Calories from Fat; Chol 141 mg; Sod 3847 mg.

Valerie Martin, Sundown

Grandma's Spaghetti

2 pounds ground beef
1 medium onion, chopped
1 medium green bell pepper, chopped
1 cup finely chopped celery
3 tablespoons chili powder

Salt to taste
1 cup (about) tomato juice
8 ounces uncooked elbow macaroni
1 cup shredded Cheddar cheese

Brown ground beef in large skillet, stirring until crumbly; drain. Add onion, green pepper, celery, chili powder and salt; mix well. Simmer over low heat for 10 minutes, stirring occasionally. Stir in enough tomato juice to make of desired consistency. Cook macaroni using package directions; drain. Add to ground beef mixture; mix well. Sprinkle with cheese. Turn off heat. Let stand, covered, for 15 minutes before serving. Yield: 6 servings.

Approx Per Serving: Cal 556; Prot 39 g; Carbo 36 g; Fiber 4 g;
    T Fat 29 g; 47% Calories from Fat; Chol 119 mg; Sod 408 mg.

*The children's grandmother started making her style
of "spaghetti" back in the early Fifties.*

Richard Young, Dimmitt

Spaghetti Bake

1½ pounds ground beef
1 cup chopped onion
1 tablespoon dried minced garlic
1   28-ounce can tomatoes, chopped
1   15-ounce can tomato sauce
1   4-ounce can mushroom pieces

1½ teaspoons oregano
1 teaspoon salt
1 teaspoon basil
8 ounces spaghetti, broken, cooked
1½ cups shredded mozzarella cheese
⅓ cup grated Parmesan cheese

Brown ground beef with onion and garlic in skillet, stirring until ground beef is crumbly; drain. Add undrained tomatoes, tomato sauce, mushrooms, oregano, salt and basil; mix well. Bring to a boil. Simmer over low heat for 20 minutes, stirring occasionally. Add spaghetti; mix well. Layer half the spaghetti mixture, mozzarella cheese, remaining spaghetti mixture and Parmesan cheese in greased 9x13-inch baking dish. Bake at 375 degrees for 30 minutes. Yield: 12 servings.

Approx Per Serving: Cal 267; Prot 18 g; Carbo 22 g; Fiber 2 g;
    T Fat 12 g; 41% Calories from Fat; Chol 50 mg; Sod 667 mg.

Betty Parish, Earth

HAM LOAF

1½ pounds ground cured ham
1 pound ground pork shoulder
2 eggs, beaten
⅔ cup milk
1 cup cracker crumbs

½ cup tomato juice
1 cup packed brown sugar
½ cup vinegar
2 teaspoons mustard

Combine ground ham and ground pork with eggs in bowl; mix well. Add milk and cracker crumbs; mix well. Shape into loaf; place in greased 9x13-inch baking dish. Pour tomato juice over loaf. Combine brown sugar, vinegar and mustard in saucepan; mix well. Bring to a boil; pour over ham loaf. Bake at 375 degrees for 1 hour and 15 minutes, basting with sauce every 15 minutes. Yield: 8 servings.

Approx Per Serving: Cal 437; Prot 38 g; Carbo 44 g; Fiber 1 g;
     T Fat 12 g; 25% Calories from Fat; Chol 148 mg; Sod 1339 mg.

Mary Edna Hendrix, Dimmitt

SCALLOPED POTATOES AND HAM

6 to 8 medium potatoes
1 pound canned ham, cubed
3 tablespoons melted butter
¾ cup bread crumbs
½ teaspoon paprika
⅛ teaspoon thyme

1 teaspoon dry mustard
1 teaspoon salt
⅛ teaspoon pepper
½ to 1 cup milk
2 teaspoons flour
8 slices American cheese

Peel and slice potatoes. Cook potatoes in a small amount of water in saucepan for 10 to 15 minutes or until tender; drain, reserving 1 cup liquid. Combine potatoes, ham, butter, bread crumbs, paprika, thyme, mustard, salt, pepper, mixture of milk and flour and reserved cooking liquid in bowl. Cut 4 slices cheese into small pieces. Add to potato mixture; mix well. Spray baking dish with nonstick cooking spray. Spoon into baking dish. Top with remaining cheese slices. Bake, covered, at 350 degrees for 30 minutes. Yield: 10 servings.

Approx Per Serving: Cal 325; Prot 20 g; Carbo 29 g; Fiber 2 g;
     T Fat 14 g; 40% Calories from Fat; Chol 60 mg; Sod 1239 mg.

Joann Rackler, Springlake

PORK CHOP CASSEROLE

6 pork chops
1 10-ounce can cream of mushroom
   soup
1/4 cup water

1 cup sour cream
2 tablespoons chopped parsley
2 potatoes, thinly sliced
Salt and pepper to taste

Brown pork chops in skillet. Combine soup, water, sour cream and parsley in bowl; mix well. Alternate layers of potatoes sprinkled with salt and pepper and sauce in greased 2-quart casserole. Top with pork chops. Bake, covered, at 375 degrees for 1¼ hours. Yield: 6 servings.

Approx Per Serving: Cal 408; Prot 35 g; Carbo 16 g; Fiber 1 g;
    T Fat 22 g; 49% Calories from Fat; Chol 115 mg; Sod 483 mg.

Pansy Byers, Dimmitt

PORK CHOPS AND RICE

1½ to 2 pounds pork chops
1 cup uncooked rice
1 10-ounce can cream of mushroom
   soup

1 soup can milk

Brown pork chops in nonstick skillet. Cook rice using package directions. Combine rice, soup and milk in bowl; mix well. Place pork chops in greased 8x11-inch baking dish; top with rice mixture. Bake at 325 degrees for 1 hour. Yield: 6 servings.

Approx Per Serving: Cal 405; Prot 34 g; Carbo 31 g; Fiber <1 g;
    T Fat 15 g; 34% Calories from Fat; Chol 99 mg; Sod 477 mg.

This was handed down from my grandmother in Pampa, Texas.
It refrigerates and reheats well.

Gwen Parish, Earth

Poultry & Seafood

Dickens County

The spirit of the cowboy rides Dickens County
through the Croton Breaks.
Riding atop the chocolate sand soil,
guarded by Soldier's Mound,
they come at night to Haystack Mountain,
with the creak of leather and the soothing song of the guitar.

R.S.

THE FAMOUS CAPROCK COUNCIL CHICKEN SPAGHETTI

1 10-ounce can cream of mushroom
   ·soup
1 10-ounce can cream of celery soup
1 10-ounce can Cheddar cheese soup
1 10-ounce can cream of chicken
   soup
1/3 cup chopped green bell pepper
1/4 cup chopped onion
1 2-ounce jar chopped pimento

1 2-ounce can mushrooms
2 ounces sharp Cheddar cheese,
   shredded
Salt and pepper to taste
3 pounds chicken, cooked, chopped
8 ounces spaghetti, cooked
1/2 cup grated Parmesan cheese
1 2-ounce package sliced almonds

Combine soups, green pepper, onion, pimento, mushrooms and Cheddar cheese in saucepan. Cook over low heat for 30 minutes, stirring frequently. Add salt, pepper and chicken. Cook until heated through. Stir in cooked spaghetti. Spoon into greased 9x13-inch baking dish. Sprinkle with half the Parmesan cheese, almonds and remaining Parmesan cheese. Bake at 350 degrees for 30 minutes or until hot and bubbly. Yield: 10 servings.

Approx Per Serving: Cal 404; Prot 30 g; Carbo 28 g; Fiber 2 g;
   T Fat 19 g; 42% Calories from Fat; Chol 82 mg; Sod 1097 mg.

Lee Ruth Krieg, Lubbock

CHICKEN ENCHILADAS

12 flour tortillas
2 cups chopped cooked chicken
1 4-ounce can chopped green chilies
12 ounces Monterey Jack cheese,
   shredded

2 tablespoons butter
1 tablespoon flour
1 1/4 cups chicken broth
1 cup sour cream

Wrap tortillas in foil. Heat in 350-degree oven for 10 minutes to soften. Combine chicken and half the green chilies in bowl; mix well. Place 2 tablespoons chicken mixture and 1 tablespoon cheese on each tortilla, rolling to enclose. Place seam side down in greased 9x13-inch baking dish. Melt butter in saucepan. Stir in flour until well mixed. Add chicken broth; mix well. Cook over medium heat until thick and bubbly, stirring constantly. Remove from heat. Stir in sour cream and remaining green chilies. Pour over enchiladas; top with remaining cheese. Bake at 350 degrees for 20 to 30 minutes or until bubbly. Yield: 12 servings.

Approx Per Serving: Cal 322; Prot 18 g; Carbo 22 g; Fiber 1 g;
   T Fat 19 g; 52% Calories from Fat; Chol 61 mg; Sod 480 mg.

Dawn Wolf, Abernathy

CHICKEN OLÉ

2 cups chopped cooked chicken	1/2 cup sour cream
4 cups cooked wide noodles	1 teaspoon salt
1/4 cup chopped onion	1/2 teaspoon pepper
1 4-ounce can chopped green chilies	1 cup shredded Cheddar cheese
1 10-ounce can cream of chicken	1/2 to 3/4 cup chicken broth
soup	1/2 cup shredded Cheddar cheese

Combine chicken, noodles, onion, green chilies, chicken soup, sour cream, salt, pepper and 1 cup Cheddar cheese in bowl; mix well. Add enough chicken broth to moisten. Spoon into greased 2-quart casserole. Sprinkle with remaining 1/2 cup cheese. Bake at 350 degrees for 45 minutes to 1 hour or until hot and bubbly. May substitute Parmesan cheese for 1/2 cup Cheddar cheese. Yield: 8 servings.

Approx Per Serving: Cal 326; Prot 21 g; Carbo 24 g; Fiber 2 g;
   T Fat 16 g; 44% Calories from Fat; Chol 88 mg; Sod 910 mg.

Ophelia Florez, Friona

CHICKEN CASSEROLE

12 ounces uncooked wide noodles	1 large green bell pepper, chopped
3 10-ounce cans chicken broth	1 10-ounce can cream of celery soup
12 ounces chopped cooked chicken	1 10-ounce can cream of mushroom
16 ounces shredded Velveeta cheese	soup
1 4-ounce jar chopped pimentos	Salt and pepper to taste

Combine noodles and chicken broth in saucepan. Cook over low heat until liquid is absorbed, stirring occasionally. Remove from heat. Add chicken, cheese, pimentos, green pepper, cream of celery soup, cream of mushroom soup, salt and pepper; mix well. Pour into greased casserole. Bake, covered, at 325 degrees for 35 minutes. Remove cover. Bake for 10 minutes longer. Yield: 10 servings.

Approx Per Serving: Cal 398; Prot 25 g; Carbo 33 g; Fiber 1 g;
   T Fat 18 g; 41% Calories from Fat; Chol 128 mg; Sod 1603 mg.

Hazel Donovan, Matador

CHICKEN AND STUFFING CASSEROLE

6 cups stuffing mix
¼ cup finely chopped celery
1 cup chopped onions
Hot water
¼ cup margarine
¼ cup flour

1   10-ounce can chicken broth
1   10-ounce can cream of chicken
   soup
1 soup can milk
Salt and pepper to taste
2 cups chopped cooked chicken

Combine stuffing mix, celery and onions in bowl; mix well. Add enough hot water to moisten. Spread in greased 9x13-inch baking dish. Melt margarine in saucepan. Stir in flour until mixed. Add chicken broth, soup and milk; mix well. Cook until thickened, stirring constantly. Add salt, pepper and cooked chicken. Pour over dressing. Bake, covered, at 350 degrees for 40 minutes. Yield: 8 servings.

Approx Per Serving: Cal 394; Prot 21 g; Carbo 47 g; Fiber 1 g;
   T Fat 14 g; 32% Calories from Fat; Chol 39 mg; Sod 1206 mg.

Vickie Miller, Idalou

CHICKEN AND PINEAPPLE

1   2½ to 3 pound chicken, cut up
⅓ cup cornstarch
2 teaspoons paprika
3 to 4 tablespoons oil
1   15-ounce can pineapple chunks
1 cup sliced celery

1 green bell pepper, sliced
1 tablespoon cornstarch
3 tablespoons brown sugar
2 tablespoons soy sauce
1 cup uncooked rice

Rinse chicken; pat dry. Coat chicken with mixture of ⅓ cup cornstarch and paprika. Brown chicken in hot oil in skillet. Reduce heat. Cook, covered, for 15 minutes, stirring occasionally. Drain pineapple, reserving syrup. Add pineapple, celery and green pepper to chicken. Cook, covered, over low heat for 5 minutes, stirring occasionally. Mix 1 tablespoon cornstarch, brown sugar, soy sauce and reserved pineapple syrup together in bowl. Add to chicken mixture. Cook over low heat for 15 minutes, stirring occasionally. Cook rice using package directions. Serve chicken over hot cooked rice. May add chopped walnuts and raisins to rice. Yield: 4 servings.

Approx Per Serving: Cal 795; Prot 54 g; Carbo 83 g; Fiber 3 g;
   T Fat 27 g; 31% Calories from Fat; Chol 152 mg; Sod 696 mg.

Dell Jones, Idalou

CHICKEN POTPIE

1 2½ to 3-pound chicken, cut up
1 teaspoon salt
4 small onions, cut into quarters
3 potatoes, peeled, cubed
3 carrots, peeled, sliced
1½ cups chopped celery
¼ cup butter

½ cup flour
2 cups half and half
1 teaspoon poultry seasoning
½ teaspoon salt
½ teaspoon pepper
1 recipe 2-crust pie pastry

Rinse chicken. Combine chicken, salt and water to cover in large saucepan. Bring to a boil. Reduce heat. Simmer, covered, for 1 hour or until chicken is tender, stirring occasionally. Drain, reserving broth. Cool chicken. Debone; chop chicken. Combine vegetables and reserved broth in saucepan. Cook over low heat until vegetables are tender. Drain vegetables, reserving 3 cups broth. Melt butter in heavy saucepan over low heat. Add flour, stirring until mixed. Cook for 1 minute, stirring constantly. Add reserved broth, half and half, poultry seasoning, salt and pepper gradually, stirring until well mixed. Cook over medium heat until thickened, stirring constantly. Remove from heat. Add chicken and vegetables; mix well. Spoon into greased 9x13-inch baking dish. Roll pastry into 10x14-inch rectangle on floured surface. Spread over pie; trim. Seal and flute edges; cut steam vents. Bake at 400 degrees for 30 to 35 minutes or until brown. Yield: 8 servings.

Approx Per Serving: Cal 602; Prot 32 g; Carbo 44 g; Fiber 4 g;
    T Fat 33 g; 49% Calories from Fat; Chol 114 mg; Sod 854 mg.

Laverne McAllister, New Home

CHILI-CHICKEN CASSEROLE

½ cup chopped onion
½ cup chopped green bell pepper
5 boneless cooked chicken breasts, chopped
1 10-ounce can cream of mushroom soup

1 10-ounce can cream of chicken soup
1 10-ounce can chicken broth
1 4-ounce can chopped green chilies
5 large flour tortillas
1 to 1½ cups shredded Cheddar cheese

Sauté onion and green pepper in skillet until tender. Combine sautéed vegetables, chopped chicken, soups, chicken broth and green chilies in bowl; mix well. Cut tortillas into 1x2-inch strips. Layer tortilla strips and chicken mixture ½ at a time in greased 8x12-inch baking dish. Sprinkle with cheese. Bake at 300 degrees for 30 to 45 minutes or until hot and bubbly. Yield: 8 servings.

Approx Per Serving: Cal 361; Prot 27 g; Carbo 27 g; Fiber 1 g;
    T Fat 17 g; 41% Calories from Fat; Chol 71 mg; Sod 1085 mg.

Julia Kern, Morton

EASY OVEN-FRIED CHICKEN

6 chicken breast filets
³/₄ cup melted margarine

1 cup crushed club crackers

Rinse chicken; pat dry. Dip in margarine; coat with cracker crumbs. Place in greased baking dish. Bake at 350 degrees for 1 hour or until tender. Yield: 6 servings.

Approx Per Serving: Cal 426; Prot 28 g; Carbo 12 g; Fiber 0 g;
    T Fat 29 g; 62% Calories from Fat; Chol 72 mg; Sod 517 mg.

Carol Huggins, Lockney

FRIED AND BAKED CHICKEN

1   2¹/₂ to 3 pound chicken, cut up
Juice of ¹/₂ lime
¹/₂ teaspoon salt
Pepper to taste

¹/₂ teaspoon curry powder
1 cup flour
2 cups oil

Rinse chicken in water with lime juice added; pat dry. Combine salt, pepper, curry powder and flour in bowl; mix well. Dip chicken in mixture to coat. Brown chicken in hot oil in skillet. Place in 2-quart baking dish. Bake at 375 degrees for 20 to 25 minutes or until chicken is tender. Yield: 6 servings.

Approx Per Serving: Cal 292; Prot 35 g; Carbo 16 g; Fiber 1 g;
    T Fat 9 g; 28% Calories from Fat; Chol 101 mg; Sod 275 mg.
    Nutritional information does not include oil for frying.

Doreen Vernon, Lubbock

LITTLE RED HEN

1   2¹/₂-pound chicken, cut up, skinned
1   10-ounce can tomato soup
2 tablespoons brown sugar
1 tablespoon seasoned salt
1 tablespoon pepper
¹/₄ cup vinegar

1 tablespoon Worcestershire sauce
¹/₂ cup chopped green bell pepper
¹/₂ cup chopped onion
1   6-ounce can mushrooms
¹/₂ cup chopped celery

Rinse chicken; pat dry. Place in greased 3-quart baking dish. Combine remaining ingredients in bowl. Pour over chicken. Bake at 325 degrees for 1¹/₂ hours or until chicken is tender. Yield: 6 servings.

Approx Per Serving: Cal 248; Prot 29 g; Carbo 15 g; Fiber 1 g;
    T Fat 8 g; 29% Calories from Fat; Chol 84 mg; Sod 1216 mg.

Susan Watkins, Levelland

NANNIE'S SWEET AND SOUR CHICKEN

4 chicken breasts, skinned
Salt and pepper to taste
Garlic powder to taste
1 to 1½ cups flour
3 tablespoons butter-flavored
   shortening

3 or 4 medium potatoes, peeled
1 or 2 medium onions
1 pint apricot juice
½ cup apricot preserves
3 tablespoons chili sauce
2 tablespoons mustard

Rinse chicken; pat dry. Season with salt, pepper and garlic powder. Roll in flour to coat. Brown in hot shortening in skillet. Arrange chicken, potatoes and onions in 3-quart casserole. Pour apricot juice over mixture. Mix apricot preserves, chili sauce and mustard in bowl. Spread over top of mixture. Bake, covered, at 350 degrees for 1 hour or until chicken is tender. Yield: 4 servings.

Approx Per Serving: Cal 766; Prot 37 g; Carbo 125 g; Fiber 6 g;
   T Fat 14 g; 16% Calories from Fat; Chol 72 mg; Sod 351 mg.

My grandmother loves to cook. She took a chicken recipe
and added her own ingredients.

Tammy Owens, Lubbock

SQUASH-CHICKEN CASSEROLE

½ cup melted margarine
4 cups cooked yellow squash
1   4-ounce jar chopped pimentos
2 tablespoons grated carrot
1   10-ounce can cream of mushroom
   soup

¼ cup grated onion
1 cup sour cream
2 cups chopped cooked chicken
Salt and pepper to taste
¾ cup stuffing mix

Combine margarine, squash, pimentos, carrot, soup, onion and sour cream in bowl; mix well. Stir in chicken, salt and pepper. Spoon into greased casserole; top with stuffing mix. Bake at 350 degrees for 30 minutes. Yield: 6 servings.

Approx Per Serving: Cal 422; Prot 18 g; Carbo 19 g; Fiber 3 g;
   T Fat 31 g; 65% Calories from Fat; Chol 59 mg; Sod 740 mg.

This can be made without the chicken for a vegetable dish.

Jane Davis, Post

BLACKENED REDFISH

1 tablespoon paprika
2¹/₂ teaspoons salt
1 teaspoon onion powder
1 teaspoon red pepper
1 teaspoon garlic powder
³/₄ teaspoon white pepper

³/₄ teaspoon black pepper
¹/₂ teaspoon thyme
¹/₂ teaspoon oregano
3 pounds redfish, fileted
¹/₂ cup melted butter

Combine paprika, salt, onion powder, red pepper, garlic powder, white pepper, black pepper, thyme and oregano in shallow bowl. Dip redfish in melted butter; coat with seasoning mixture. Heat cast-iron skillet over high heat until very hot. Sear fish for 2 minutes on one side; turn. Sear for 1 minute on other side or until fish flakes easily. Yield: 4 servings.

Approx Per Serving: Cal 520; Prot 66 g; Carbo <1 g; Fiber 0 g;
    T Fat 27 g; 48% Calories from Fat; Chol 248 mg; Sod 1811 mg.

*This dish is very smoky to prepare; it cooks well
outside on a grill or camp stove.*

First Lady Barbara Bush

POACHED SALMON IN CHAMPAGNE-ROSEMARY SAUCE

¹/₄ cup sour cream
¹/₄ cup whipping cream
2 teaspoons Dijon mustard
2 tablespoons sugar
1 teaspoon dried rosemary
6 tablespoons unsalted butter, melted

3 tablespoons lemon juice
¹/₂ cup Champagne
3 tablespoons finely chopped green
    onions
6   1-inch thick salmon filets

Whisk first 5 ingredients in bowl until smooth. Chill in refrigerator. Combine butter, lemon juice, Champagne and green onions in skillet. Add salmon; baste with mixture. Cook, covered, over low heat for 30 minutes. Serve with chilled sauce. Yield: 6 servings.

Approx Per Serving: Cal 388; Prot 26 g; Carbo 6 g; Fiber <1 g;
    T Fat 27 g; 66% Calories from Fat; Chol 128 mg; Sod 211 mg.

Susan McDonald, Ransom Canyon

SALMON PATTIES

1 16-ounce can salmon
1 egg, beaten
1/2 cup chopped onion

1/8 teaspoon salt
1/2 cup potato flakes
1/4 cup oil

Pour undrained salmon into bowl, removing bones. Mix in egg. Add onion, salt and potato flakes, stirring well. Shape mixture into patties. Fry in hot oil in skillet for 2 to 3 minutes on each side or until browned; drain. Serve with cole slaw, potato salad or chips. Yield: 12 servings.

Approx Per Serving: Cal 132; Prot 9 g; Carbo 7 g; Fiber 1 g;
    T Fat 7 g; 51% Calories from Fat; Chol 37 mg; Sod 249 mg.

Easy to prepare on camping trips and also good in box lunches.

Joyce W. Williams, Floydada

TUNA-NOODLE CRISP

1/3 cup chopped onion
3 tablespoons chopped green bell
    pepper
1/4 cup shortening
1 10-ounce can cheese soup
1/2 cup milk

1 tablespoon chopped pimento
1 teaspoon salt
1/8 teaspoon pepper
4 ounces noodles, cooked
1 6-ounce can tuna, drained
1/2 cup bread crumbs

Sauté onion and green pepper in shortening in skillet until tender. Add soup, milk, pimento, salt and pepper; mix well. Bring to a boil. Add noodles and tuna. Pour into 1 1/2-quart casserole. Sprinkle with bread crumbs. Bake at 350 degrees for 20 minutes. Yield: 6 servings.

Approx Per Serving: Cal 292; Prot 15 g; Carbo 25 g; Fiber 1 g;
    T Fat 15 g; 45% Calories from Fat; Chol 63 mg; Sod 882 mg.

Imogene Suttle, Hale Center

DEVILED EGGS AND SHRIMP CASSEROLE

6 hard-boiled eggs
1/2 teaspoon salt
1 teaspoon dry mustard
1/4 teaspoon Worcestershire sauce
1/4 teaspoon cayenne pepper
1 1/2 teaspoons vinegar
1/4 cup melted butter
1 1/2 pounds shrimp, cooked, peeled
8 ounces mushrooms, sliced
2 tablespoons butter
1 tablespoon lemon juice

1 cup butter
4 1/2 tablespoons flour
1 1/2 cups milk
1 1/2 teaspoons prepared mustard
1 tablespoon Worcestershire sauce
8 ounces sharp Cheddar cheese, shredded
1 1/2 teaspoons onion juice
Cayenne pepper, paprika and Tabasco sauce to taste

Slice eggs lengthwise into halves; remove yolks. Combine yolks with salt, dry mustard, 1/4 teaspoon Worcestershire sauce, 1/4 teaspoon cayenne pepper, vinegar and melted butter in small bowl; mix well. Spoon mixture into egg whites. Place in 9x13-inch casserole; layer with cooked shrimp. Sauté mushrooms in 2 tablespoons butter in skillet; drizzle with lemon juice to prevent browning. Spoon over shrimp. Melt 1 cup butter in saucepan. Stir in flour until blended. Add milk slowly. Cook over low heat until smooth, stirring constantly. Add remaining ingredients; mix well. Cook until cheese is melted, stirring constantly. Pour over shrimp and mushroom mixture. Bake at 300 degrees for 20 to 30 minutes or until sauce bubbles and browns around edges. Yield: 12 servings.

Approx Per Serving: Cal 384; Prot 19 g; Carbo 6 g; Fiber <1 g;
T Fat 32 g; 74% Calories from Fat; Chol 276 mg; Sod 553 mg.

Betty Anne Kyle, Lubbock

SHRIMP CREOLE

1 large onion, chopped
1 small green bell pepper, chopped
1/2 cup butter
1 8-ounce can tomato sauce
1 10-ounce can cream of mushroom soup
1 10-ounce can cream of celery soup

1 4-ounce can chopped black olives, drained
1 2-ounce jar chopped pimento
1/2 teaspoon chili powder
1 teaspoon garlic powder
Salt and pepper to taste
1 1/2 pounds peeled shrimp

Sauté onion and green pepper in butter in large skillet until tender. Add next 9 ingredients. Simmer over low heat for 1 hour, stirring occasionally. Add shrimp. Simmer for 5 minutes longer. Serve over hot cooked rice. Yield: 6 servings.

Approx Per Serving: Cal 364; Prot 22 g; Carbo 13 g; Fiber 2 g;
T Fat 26 g; 63% Calories from Fat; Chol 224 mg; Sod 1444 mg.

Martha Beach, Lubbock

SHRIMP-FRIED RICE

1 cup uncooked long grain white rice
1 clove of garlic, peeled
1 tablespoon oil
1¼ pounds peeled shrimp
1 egg, beaten
1 bay leaf

1½ cups water
½ teaspoon soy sauce
½ medium onion, chopped
2 green onions, chopped
Salt, pepper and curry powder to taste

Cook rice using package directions; set aside. Saute garlic clove in hot oil in skillet for 3 minutes or until blackened; discard garlic clove. Stir in rice. Cook for 5 minutes or until slightly golden. Boil shrimp in large saucepan for 5 minutes or until pink; drain. Fry egg in small skillet. Add egg, shrimp, bay leaf and water to rice. Simmer until liquid evaporates. Stir in soy sauce, onion, green onions, salt, pepper and curry powder. Simmer for 5 to 10 minutes to blend flavors, stirring occasionally. Remove bay leaf before serving. Yield: 6 servings.

Approx Per Serving: Cal 246; Prot 19 g; Carbo 26 g; Fiber 1 g;
  T Fat 7 g; 24% Calories from Fat; Chol 183 mg; Sod 211 mg.

Doreen Vernon, Lubbock

SHRIMP OLIVER

2 tablespoons finely chopped onion
3 cloves of garlic, minced
¼ cup melted butter
1 pound peeled shrimp
1 tablespoon chopped parsley
Paprika to taste

¼ teaspoon Tabasco sauce
¼ teaspoon cayenne pepper
1 tablespoon flour
1 tablespoon water
2 tablespoons white wine
1½ teaspoons salt

Sauté onion and garlic in melted butter in 2-quart saucepan over high heat for 2 minutes, stirring frequently. Add shrimp, parsley, paprika, Tabasco sauce and cayenne pepper. Cook, covered, over high heat for 7 minutes or until shrimp are pink and tender, stirring occasionally. Stir in flour, water, wine and salt. Cook over high heat for 2 minutes or until thickened, stirring constantly. Serve over hot cooked rice. Yield: 4 servings.

Approx Per Serving: Cal 209; Prot 20 g; Carbo 3 g; Fiber <1 g;
  T Fat 13 g; 56% Calories from Fat; Chol 208 mg; Sod 1102 mg.

Mrs. Roland Hunter, Houston

SHRIMP AND SCALLOP CASSEROLE

1 pound peeled shrimp	1 cup drained bean sprouts, rinsed
8 ounces scallops	1/2 cup melted butter
1/2 cup soy sauce	1 tablespoon fresh chopped parsley
8 ounces fresh mushrooms, thinly sliced	6 cloves of garlic, crushed
1 8-ounce can sliced water chestnuts, drained	

Marinate shrimp and scallops in soy sauce in shallow dish for 15 minutes, turning occasionally to coat. Drain and place in shallow baking dish. Layer with mushrooms, water chestnuts and bean sprouts. Combine melted butter, parsley and garlic in small bowl; mix well. Pour over top layer. Bake at 350 degrees for 25 minutes. Yield: 4 servings.

Approx Per Serving: Cal 416; Prot 34 g; Carbo 16 g; Fiber 3 g;
     T Fat 25 g; 53% Calories from Fat; Chol 259 mg; Sod 2555 mg.

Maria V. Cavazos, Lubbock

BETHANY SHRIMP-STUFFED PEPPERS

4 green bell peppers, cut into halves, seeded	1/2 cup fine dry bread crumbs
1 onion, chopped	1 teaspoon salt
2 tablespoons butter	1/2 teaspoon pepper
1 clove of garlic, minced	1 egg, beaten
1 teaspoon minced parsley	1 cup chopped cooked shrimp
1 20-ounce can tomatoes, drained	1/2 cup bread crumbs
	2 teaspoons butter

Parboil green pepper halves in salted water to cover for 5 minutes; drain and set aside. Sauté onion in 2 tablespoons butter in skillet until tender and golden. Add garlic, parsley, tomatoes and 1/2 cup bread crumbs; mix well. Cook until tomatoes are tender, stirring often. Remove from heat; season with salt and pepper. Stir 1 tablespoon of mixture into beaten egg. Add egg mixture to skillet mixture, stirring constantly. Stir in shrimp. Spoon mixture into pepper halves; arrange in 9x13-inch baking dish. Sprinkle with remaining bread crumbs; dot with butter. Bake at 350 degrees for 20 minutes. Yield: 6 servings.

Approx Per Serving: Cal 201; Prot 13 g; Carbo 21 g; Fiber 3 g;
     T Fat 8 g; 34% Calories from Fat; Chol 124 mg; Sod 773 mg.

Yolonda Kelly, Lubbock

Game

Cochran County

Rubbing shoulders with New Mexico.

Cattle country.

Land of the gentle Whiteface and sweet smelling summer sorghums.

A peaceful prairie.

R.S.

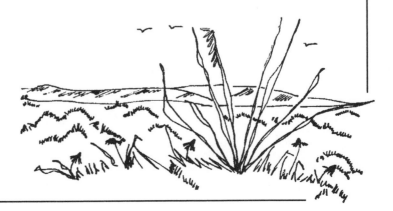

HASENPFEFFER (RABBIT STEW)

1 rabbit, cut up	Oil for frying
Salt to taste	1 tablespoon vinegar
1 cup flour	1/2 cup raisins

Soak rabbit in salted cold water to cover in bowl for 2 hours or longer. Rinse well. Sprinkle with salt; coat with flour. Fry in oil in skillet until golden brown on both sides. Drain most of the drippings from skillet; return rabbit to skillet. Drizzle with vinegar. Add enough warm water to cover. Simmer for 2 to 3 hours or until very tender, adding raisins during last hour of cooking time. Yield: 4 servings.

Approx Per Serving: Cal 511; Prot 52 g; Carbo 40 g; Fiber 2 g;
    T Fat 13 g; 23% Calories from Fat; Chol 154 mg; Sod 65 mg.
    Nutritional information does not include oil for frying.

Yolanda Kelly, Lubbock

VENISON CHILI

1 large onion, sliced	1/2 teaspoon garlic powder
1/2 green bell pepper, chopped	2 tablespoons chili powder
1/4 cup corn oil	1 teaspoon cumin
2 pounds cubed venison	1 teaspoon oregano
1 cup flour	8 coriander seeds
1 28-ounce can tomatoes	1 tablespoon salt

Sauté onion and green pepper in oil in heavy saucepan. Rinse venison; coat with flour. Add to saucepan. Cook until brown, stirring frequently. Add tomatoes, garlic powder, chili powder, cumin, oregano, coriander seeds and salt; mix well. Simmer for 1 hour. May add 1 can pinto beans if desired. Yield: 6 servings.

Approx Per Serving: Cal 323; Prot 30 g; Carbo 24 g; Fiber 2 g;
    T Fat 12 g; 33% Calories from Fat; Chol 58 mg; Sod 1345 mg.

Pat Henry, Levelland

ROAST VENISON

1   3-pound venison roast
Salt and pepper to taste
2 tablespoons oil
1 tablespoon vinegar
2 tablespoons flour

1½ cups boiling water
1 sprig of parsley
½ bay leaf
2 slices onion
2 carrots, sliced

Rinse venison and pat dry. Season with salt and pepper. Rub with oil and vinegar; sprinkle with flour. Place in roasting pan. Roast at 480 degrees until flour is brown. Add boiling water, parsley, bay leaf, onion and carrots. Roast, covered, until tender; discard bay leaf. Serve with sweet potatoes. Yield: 6 servings.

Approx Per Serving: Cal 256; Prot 40 g; Carbo 5 g; Fiber 1 g;
    T Fat 8 g; 28% Calories from Fat; Chol 87 mg; Sod 102 mg.

Sylvia Pena, Lubbock

DOVE À LA DUSTY

½ cup bread crumbs
¼ cup grated Parmesan cheese
¼ cup wheat germ
1 teaspoon salt
5 medium potatoes, peeled

2 tablespoons melted margarine
5 slices bacon
10 dove breasts
Pepper to taste

Combine bread crumbs, cheese, wheat germ and salt in bowl. Cut potatoes into halves lengthwise. Dip in melted margarine; coat with bread crumb mixture. Arrange cut side down in large cooking bag. Cut bacon slices into halves. Rinse dove breasts and pat dry. Wrap 1 bacon piece around each dove breast. Coat with bread crumb mixture. Arrange over potatoes. Season with pepper. Bake at 350 degrees for 1 hour. Yield: 5 servings.

Approx Per Serving: Cal 377; Prot 22 g; Carbo 43 g; Fiber 3 g;
    T Fat 11 g; 28% Calories from Fat; Chol 63 mg; Sod 738 mg.

This recipe was published by the County Extension Agent.

Ann Noble, Post

DOVE À LA LOUIE

Doves	Milk
Salt	Worster sauce
Pepper	Bacon
Flour	

Take a nice plump dove and pluck its feathers off (or skin it, if preferred). Then ensinerate it (singe feathers off) — wash and clean — salt and pepper, flour to taste (make it a little on the salty side). Do not use self-rising flour — dip the bird in a bowl of milk — roll in flour and fry — (Then eat) — or — marinate your dove in Worster sauce, salt and pepper 2 or 3 hours — wrap a slice of bacon around him — put in pan and put on grill or oven. Baste with juice to keep moist — mmm good. Cook at 325 degrees if cooked in oven. Yield: variable.

Nutritional information for this recipe is not available.

This recipe came word for word from my daddy—Lewis A. Young—who passed away in 1990. Looking back on recipes such as this reminds me of the wonderful sense of humor my daddy had and his love of cooking.

Debbie Greenwood, Lubbock

DOVE PIE

1 recipe 2-crust pie pastry	4 cups water
6 dove	2 tablespoons flour
1 onion, chopped	2 tablespoons melted butter
1 small bunch parsley, chopped	Salt and pepper to taste
3 whole cloves	

Line baking dish with half the pastry. Clean and split dove. Combine with onion, parsley, cloves and water in saucepan. Cook until dove are tender. Remove dove to prepared baking dish. Skim cooking liquid. Stir in mixture of flour and butter. Cook until thickened, stirring constantly. Season with salt and pepper; discard cloves. Spoon over dove. Top with remaining pastry, sealing edges; cut vents. Bake at 350 degrees for 1 hour or until golden brown. Garnish with additional parsley. Yield: 6 servings.

Approx Per Serving: Cal 409; Prot 17 g; Carbo 28 g; Fiber 2 g;
T Fat 23 g; 53% Calories from Fat; Chol 65 mg; Sod 403 mg.

The County Extension Agent published this recipe.

Ann Noble, Post

POTTED DOVE

12 dove
Salt to taste
2 cups flour
6 tablespoons butter
6 tablespoons bacon drippings

1/2 cup chopped onion
1 cup mushrooms
1/4 cup chopped parsley
1 cup white cooking wine
1/2 cup cream

Rinse dove and pat dry. Sprinkle with salt; shake in bag with flour to coat. Brown in mixture of butter and bacon drippings in large cast-iron skillet. Remove to warm plate. Add onion, mushrooms and parsley to drippings in skillet. Return dove to skillet. Add wine. Simmer, covered, for 45 minutes or until dove are tender, basting frequently. Stir in 1/2 cup cream. Cook just until heated through. Garnish with additional parsley. Serve with brown rice and a tart jam. May bake at 350 degrees if preferred. Yield: 6 servings.

Approx Per Serving: Cal 650; Prot 32 g; Carbo 34 g; Fiber 2 g;
    T Fat 35 g; 49% Calories from Fat; Chol 251 mg; Sod 248 mg.

This recipe is from Hazel White on the Yellow House Ranch, southwest of Littlefield.

Judy White, Littlefield

BAKED PHEASANT

2 pheasant, cut into quarters
1 cup flour
Oil for browning
8 slices onion

8 slices lemon
8 slices bacon
1 14-ounce can chicken broth

Rinse pheasant; coat with flour. Brown in a small amount of oil in skillet; remove to 9x13-inch baking dish. Place 1 slice onion, 1 slice lemon and 1 slice bacon across each piece of pheasant. Add chicken broth to dish. Bake, covered with foil, at 350 degrees for 1 hour. Serve with rice pilaf. Yield: 8 servings.

Approx Per Serving: Cal 301; Prot 29 g; Carbo 14 g; Fiber 1 g;
    T Fat 14 g; 41% Calories from Fat; Chol 85 mg; Sod 302 mg.
    Nutritional information does not include oil for browning.

Lelloine Waits, Abernathy

BROILED PHEASANT

1 pheasant
1 12-ounce bottle of Durkee's
  Famous Sauce

¼ cup melted margarine
Juice of 1 lemon

Cut pheasant into halves; rinse and pat dry. Combine Durkee's Famous Sauce, margarine and lemon juice in shallow dish. Add pheasant, coating well. Marinate in refrigerator overnight. Place pheasant skin side down on rack in roasting pan. Roast at 250 degrees for 1½ to 2 hours or until tender, basting frequently. May rub pheasant with Sugar-Cure prior to marinating if desired. Yield: 4 servings.

Approx Per Serving: Cal 490; Prot 24 g; Carbo 18 g; Fiber <1 g;
    T Fat 32 g; 63% Calories from Fat; Chol 107 mg; Sod 646 mg.
    Nutritional information includes entire amount of marinade.

Pheasant is abundant in Castro County.

N. A. Bryson, Dimmitt

PHEASANT STEAKS

2 boned pheasant breasts
Salt and pepper to taste
½ cup flour
¼ cup butter

2 cups cooked rice
1 cup fresh mushrooms
¼ cup sliced green onion tops

Rinse pheasant and pat dry. Pound thin with meat mallet; cut into serving pieces. Sprinkle with salt and pepper; coat with flour. Brown on both sides in butter in skillet. Arrange over rice on serving plate. Sauté mushrooms and green onion tops in drippings in skillet for 5 minutes. Spoon over pheasant. Yield: 2 servings.

Approx Per Serving: Cal 808; Prot 41 g; Carbo 76 g; Fiber 3 g;
    T Fat 37 g; 42% Calories from Fat; Chol 168 mg; Sod 253 mg.

Margaret Mary Leicht, Perryton

Pheasant with Rice Stuffing

2 2¹/₂-pound pheasant
2 teaspoons salt
1¹/₂ cups uncooked long grain rice
3 cups water
1 teaspoon salt
1 cup finely chopped celery
3 tablespoons minced onion

¹/₂ cup sliced mushrooms
¹/₂ cup butter
¹/₈ teaspoon sage
¹/₈ teaspoon thyme
¹/₈ teaspoon savory
2 tablespoons melted butter
6 slices bacon

Rinse pheasant inside and out. Sprinkle 1 teaspoon salt into cavity of each. Brown rice in nonstick skillet. Combine with water and 1 teaspoon salt in saucepan. Cook until rice is tender. Sauté celery, onion and mushrooms in ¹/₂ cup butter in skillet for 10 minutes. Add rice, sage, thyme and savory; mix well. Stuff lightly into pheasant; truss with cord. Place on rack in roasting pan. Brush with 2 tablespoons melted butter; top with bacon. Roast, covered, at 350 degrees for 2 hours or until tender. May bake any extra stuffing in greased baking dish at 350 degrees for 30 minutes. Yield: 8 servings.

Approx Per Serving: Cal 477; Prot 28 g; Carbo 29 g; Fiber 1 g;
     T Fat 27 g; 51% Calories from Fat; Chol 123 mg; Sod 1053 mg.

Ann Noble, Post

Farm Wife's Quail

4 quail, split
Salt and pepper to taste
1 cup flour
¹/₂ cup oil

1 10-ounce can cream of mushroom
   soup
1 10-ounce can onion soup
1 soup can milk

Rinse quail and pat dry. Sprinkle with salt and pepper; coat with flour. Fry in oil in skillet until golden brown on both sides. Remove to 9x13-inch baking dish. Spoon mixture of soups and milk over top. Bake at 350 degrees for 1 hour. May thicken cooking sauce for gravy. Yield: 4 servings.

Approx Per Serving: Cal 831; Prot 42 g; Carbo 37 g; Fiber 1 g;
     T Fat 57 g; 62% Calories from Fat; Chol 10 mg; Sod 1304 mg.

Jan Kennedy, Lubbock

QUAIL WITH WILD RICE

10 quail
1½ pounds chicken livers
½ cup butter
2 large onions, chopped
1 green bell pepper, chopped

2 cloves of garlic, minced
¾ cup butter
2½ cups cooked wild rice
2 cups chicken broth
1½ cups Port

Rinse quail and chicken livers; pat dry. Sew quail cavities together. Brown quail in ½ cup butter in skillet; remove to baking dish. Bake, covered, at 225 degrees for 30 minutes. Sauté livers, onions, green pepper and garlic in ¾ cup butter in skillet until vegetables are tender but not brown. Stir in rice, chicken broth and wine. Spoon into 3-quart baking dish. Bake at 325 degrees for 20 minutes or until liquid is absorbed. Arrange quail over rice to serve. Yield: 10 servings.

Approx Per Serving: Cal 715; Prot 47 g; Carbo 17 g; Fiber 2 g;
    T Fat 46 g; 62% Calories from Fat; Chol 316 mg; Sod 465 mg.

Credit for this recipe goes to the County Extension Agent.

Ann Noble, Post

ROASTED WILD TURKEY

1   8 to 10-pound turkey
Salt and pepper to taste
8 cups stale bread cubes
¾ cup finely chopped celery
½ cup chopped walnuts
2 to 3 teaspoons sage
1 teaspoon salt

¼ teaspoon pepper
1½ cups chopped onion
¼ cup butter
¼ cup water
6 slices bacon
2 tablespoons bacon drippings

Rinse turkey and pat dry; sprinkle inside and out with salt and pepper to taste. Mix bread cubes, celery, walnuts, sage, 1 teaspoon salt and ¼ teaspoon pepper in bowl. Sauté onion in butter in skillet until tender but not brown. Add to bread mixture. Add water; toss lightly. Spoon lightly into turkey cavity; spoon any leftover stuffing into greased baking dish. Truss turkey; place breast side up on rack in roasting pan. Cover with bacon slices and cheesecloth soaked in bacon drippings. Roast at 325 degrees for 20 to 25 minutes per pound or until tender, basting frequently. Bake extra stuffing for 30 minutes. Remove cheesecloth, skewers and string from turkey. Serve with extra stuffing. Yield: 10 servings.

Approx Per Serving: Cal 616; Prot 76 g; Carbo 15 g; Fiber 1 g;
    T Fat 26 g; 39% Calories from Fat; Chol 220 mg; Sod 646 mg.

The County Extension Agent published this recipe.

Ann Noble, Post

International

Lubbock County

Prairie stage manager,
Centro del Llano Estacado,
General store to the plains,
Oasis from the struggle,
Showcase of perseverance.

R.S.

HUMMOS BI TAHEENI (CHICK-PEA DIP)

1   16-ounce can chick-peas
1 or 2 cloves of garlic
¼ cup (or more) tahini

⅓ cup (or more) lemon juice
½ teaspoon salt
2 tablespoons olive oil

Drain chick-peas, reserving ¼ cup liquid. Combine chick-peas, reserved liquid, garlic, tahini, lemon juice and salt in blender container. Process until smooth. Adjust tahini and lemon juice to suit individual taste; consistency will be thin. Spread in oval platter; drizzle with olive oil. Garnish as desired. Yield: 8 servings.

Approx Per Serving: Cal 146; Prot 4 g; Carbo 15 g; Fiber 1 g;
    T Fat 8 g; 49% Calories from Fat; Chol 0 mg; Sod 306 mg.

Hummos bi Taheeni, a Syrian dish, is served at room temperature with pita bread. The secret is finding the correct relationship of lemon juice and tahini, a paste made from sesame seed. Creative cooks garnish the top with decorative arrangements of pimento, olives, parsley, seasonings and whole chick-peas.

Joni Lynch Wilson, Lubbock

TABOULI

¾ cup fine-grain bulgur
3 cups minced fresh parsley
2 or 3 large tomatoes, chopped
4 or 5 green onions, minced
15 fresh mint leaves, minced
10 pimento-stuffed green olives,
    minced

½ cup lemon juice
½ cup olive oil
1 clove of garlic, minced
1 teaspoon hot pickle juice
Salt to taste

Rinse bulgur several times. Soak in water in bowl for 20 minutes or longer. Combine parsley with tomatoes, green onions, mint leaves and olives in bowl. Squeeze moisture from bulgur. Add bulgur to salad; mix well. Combine lemon juice, olive oil, garlic, pickle juice and salt in bowl; mix well. Add to salad; mix well. Chill for 15 minutes or longer, stirring occasionally. Serve in lettuce-lined salad bowl with crisp romaine lettuce leaves for dipping. May add finely chopped cucumber or allspice if desired. Yield: 12 servings.

Approx Per Serving: Cal 136; Prot 2 g; Carbo 12 g; Fiber 3 g;
    T Fat 10 g; 62% Calories from Fat; Chol 0 mg; Sod 87 mg.

This Arabic salad is a must for every dinner party, but it is also served to celebrate the arrival of spring. The proportions of bulgur and parsley can be varied to suit individual taste.

Joni Lynch Wilson, Lubbock

Red Cabbage

1 yellow or white onion, chopped
3 tablespoons oil
1 head red cabbage, finely shredded
2 tablespoons vinegar
4 apples, peeled, sliced

3 tablespoons thawed frozen apple
  juice concentrate
1 tablespoon brown sugar
1/4 teaspoon ground cloves
1 teaspoon salt

Sauté onion in oil in Dutch oven or enamel pot until tender. Add cabbage. Sauté for several minutes. Add vinegar, apples, apple juice concentrate, brown sugar, cloves and salt; mix well. Bake, covered, at 325 degrees for 30 to 35 minutes or until cabbage is tender. May simmer on stove top if preferred, adding water if needed to prevent sticking. Yield: 6 servings.

Approx Per Serving: Cal 152; Prot 1 g; Carbo 23 g; Fiber 3 g;
  T Fat 7 g; 40% Calories from Fat; Chol 0 mg; Sod 367 mg.

This is a family recipe from Germany.

Margie Jakobsmeier, Lubbock

Avocado and Chicken Tacos

4 large avocados
1 teaspoon lemon juice
1/4 cup minced onion
1 clove of garlic, minced

1/4 teaspoon Mexican seasoning
2 cups chopped cooked chicken
12 corn tortillas
Oil for frying

Mash avocados in large bowl. Add lemon juice, onion, garlic and Mexican seasoning; mix well. Chill, covered, for 30 minutes. Add chicken; mix well. Fry tortillas in hot oil in skillet. Shape into taco shells; drain well. Spoon chicken mixture into tacos. Serve immediately. Yield: 12 (1-taco) servings.

Approx Per Serving: Cal 219; Prot 10 g; Carbo 18 g; Fiber 9 g;
  T Fat 13 g; 51% Calories from Fat; Chol 21 mg; Sod 28 mg.
  Nutritional information does not include oil for frying.

My grandmother brought this recipe from her mother in Mexico.

Connie Ontiveros, Springlake

BÖREK

1 pound shredded beef	Salt and pepper to taste
1 cup chopped onion	4 cups flour
2 tablespoons oil	1¹/₂ teaspoons salt
¹/₂ cup chopped parsley	1 cup water
1 clove of garlic, minced	Oil for frying
1 egg, beaten	

Sauté beef with onion in 2 tablespoons oil in skillet; drain. Stir in next 5 ingredients. Sift flour and 1¹/₂ teaspoons salt into bowl. Add water gradually, stirring to form dough. Knead on floured surface until smooth. Shape by ¹/₃ cupfuls into balls. Roll each into thin oval on floured surface. Cut into 4x8-inch strips. Place 1 teaspoon filling at end of each; roll up. Fry in hot oil in skillet until brown. Yield: 6 servings.

Approx Per Serving: Cal 467; Prot 24 g; Carbo 66 g; Fiber 3 g;
T Fat 11 g; 21% Calories from Fat; Chol 78 mg; Sod 572 mg.
Nutritional information does not include oil for frying.

We were frequently served this appetizer dish when we were stationed at Incirlik Air Force Base in Turkey.

Jan Kennedy, Lubbock

CAVATINI

16 ounces uncooked spaghetti	1 16-ounce can tomatoes
2 pounds sausage	1¹/₂ cups water
1 tablespoon olive oil	¹/₂ teaspoon salt
1 tablespoon basil	1 4-ounce can grated Parmesan
1 teaspoon oregano	cheese
2 teaspoons minced garlic	8 ounces pepperoni cheese, shredded
1 6-ounce can tomato paste	8 ounces mozzarella cheese, sliced
1 10-ounce can tomato soup	

Cook spaghetti using package directions; drain. Brown sausage in skillet, stirring until crumbly; drain. Combine olive oil, basil, oregano and garlic in large saucepan. Simmer over low heat for 1 minute. Add tomato paste, soup, tomatoes, water, salt and sausage; mix well. Simmer for 30 minutes or longer. Stir in 3 tablespoons Parmesan cheese. Alternate layers of spaghetti, meat sauce, remaining Parmesan cheese and pepperoni cheese in large baking dish until all ingredients are used, ending with meat sauce. Bake at 350 degrees for 30 minutes. Top with mozzarella cheese. Bake for 15 minutes longer or until cheese melts. Yield: 15 servings.

Approx Per Serving: Cal 388; Prot 20 g; Carbo 30 g; Fiber 2 g;
T Fat 21 g; 48% Calories from Fat; Chol 55 mg; Sod 1046 mg.

Janis Cowley, Earth

ITALIAN CASSEROLE

8 ounces uncooked fettucini
1 pound mild Italian sausage
1/4 cup chopped onion
1 4-ounce can sliced mushrooms
1 8-ounce can pizza sauce

2 tablespoons chopped pimento-
 stuffed green olives
2 cups shredded Cheddar cheese
1/2 cup grated Parmesan cheese

Cook pasta using package directions; rinse and drain. Remove sausage from casing. Cook with onion in skillet over low heat until brown, stirring to break into pieces; drain. Combine pasta, sausage mixture, undrained mushrooms, pizza sauce, olives and 1³/4 cups Cheddar cheese in bowl; mix gently. Spoon into 2-quart baking dish. Bake at 350 degrees for 10 to 15 minutes or until heated through. Sprinkle with remaining 1/4 cup Cheddar cheese and Parmesan cheese. Bake for 10 minutes longer or until heated through. Yield: 6 servings.

Approx Per Serving: Cal 485; Prot 25 g; Carbo 34 g; Fiber 2 g;
 T Fat 28 g; 51% Calories from Fat; Chol 74 mg; Sod 1154 mg.

Janice Lientz, New Deal

SICILIAN MEAT ROLL

2 eggs, beaten
³/4 cup bread crumbs
1/2 cup tomato juice
2 tablespoons chopped parsley
1 clove of garlic, minced
1/2 teaspoon oregano
1/4 teaspoon salt

1/4 teaspoon pepper
2 pounds ground beef
8 thin slices boiled ham
6 ounces mozzarella cheese, shredded
3 slices mozzarella cheese, cut into
 halves

Combine eggs, bread crumbs, tomato juice, parsley, garlic, oregano, salt and pepper in bowl. Add ground beef; mix well. Pat into 10x12-inch rectangle on foil or waxed paper. Arrange ham slices over beef mixture, leaving narrow edge. Sprinkle with shredded cheese. Roll up ground beef from shorter side to enclose filling; seal ends and edges. Place seam side down in 9x13-inch baking dish. Bake at 350 degrees for 1¹/4 hours. Top with sliced cheese. Bake for 5 minutes longer or until cheese melts. Yield: 8 servings.

Approx Per Serving: Cal 424; Prot 37 g; Carbo 9 g; Fiber 1 g;
 T Fat 26 g; 56% Calories from Fat; Chol 168 mg; Sod 769 mg.

Ann Marie Dobmeier, Lubbock

JAVANESE MEAL

8 3-ounce cans chow mein noodles
Curried Rice (page 103)
8 large chickens, cooked, chopped
Gravy (page 103)
2 onions, chopped
2 stalks celery, chopped
8 tomatoes, chopped

8 16-ounce cans pineapple chunks,
   drained
3 pounds cheese, shredded
3 packages slivered almonds
2 packages shredded coconut
Cranberry Chutney (page 103)
Javanese Meal Cards (below)

Place each ingredient in separate serving bowl. Arrange in order listed on serving table. Place Javanese Meal Cards on table (see below) to instruct guests on the protocol. Serve with soy sauce. Yield: 50 servings.

Nutritional information for this recipe is not available.

JAVANESE MEAL CARDS

- *You are about to partake of a Javanese meal. Make a nice nest of noodles in the middle of your plate.*
- *Each ingredient is essential for a delectable dish. Inside your nest place a gracious serving of rice.*
- *Meat is a must, so add two serving spoons or more of chicken.*
- *A sauce is needed so our meal will not be dry. Cover with gravy the meal this far.*
- *Seasoning is the spice of life. Two teaspoons of onion will add just the right spice.*
- *A little crunch will add variety. Two teaspoons of celery should do the trick.*
- *Color is a must for an appetizing appeal. Two tablespoons of tomatoes should make this a deal.*
- *Minerals, vegetables and protein are involved, so our vitamins will be next, with two tablespoons of pineapple added to our dish.*
- *A sharpness to please is obtained by adding two tablespoons of cheese.*
- *Chicken would be flat without two teaspoons of almonds to our nest.*
- *Cheer up! Two tablespoons of coconut and cranberry chutney will do the rest.*

Evelyn Verden, Earth

CURRIED RICE

3 cups chopped onions
1/2 cup margarine
12 cups uncooked rice
24 cups pineapple juice

1/2 cup curry powder
1/2 cup mixed herbs
Salt and pepper to taste

Sauté onions in margarine in large saucepan until tender. Add rice, pineapple juice, curry powder, herbs, salt and pepper. Cook until rice is tender. May add yellow food coloring if desired. Yield: 50 servings.

Approx Per Serving: Cal 248; Prot 3 g; Carbo 53 g; Fiber 1 g;
T Fat 2 g; 8% Calories from Fat; Chol 0 mg; Sod 25 mg.

Evelyn Verden, Earth

GRAVY

1 cup flour
1 tablespoon salt
1 tablespoon pepper

1 cup oil
1 gallon chicken broth
1 tablespoon chopped parsley

Blend flour, salt and pepper into oil in saucepan. Stir in chicken broth. Cook until thickened, stirring constantly. Add parsley. Yield: 50 servings.

Approx Per Serving: Cal 60; Prot 2 g; Carbo 2 g; Fiber <1 g;
T Fat 4 g; 60% Calories from Fat; Chol <1 mg; Sod 376 mg.

Evelyn Verden, Earth

CRANBERRY CHUTNEY

1 pound cranberries
2 cups sugar
1/2 cup orange juice
4 oranges, peeled, chopped
2 apples, peeled, chopped

2 pears, peeled, chopped
1 tablespoon grated orange rind
1 teaspoon Tabasco sauce
2 teaspoons curry powder
1/4 teaspoon ginger

Combine cranberries, sugar and orange juice in saucepan. Cook until cranberries pop, stirring occasionally. Add oranges, apples, pears, orange rind, Tabasco sauce, curry powder and ginger; mix well. Cook for 2 to 3 minutes. Spoon into 6 hot sterilized 1-pint jars; seal with 2-piece lids. Yield: 50 servings.

Approx Per Serving: Cal 50; Prot <1 g; Carbo 13 g; Fiber 1 g;
T Fat <1 g; 1% Calories from Fat; Chol 0 mg; Sod 1 mg.

Evelyn Verden, Earth

Honey Puffs

³/₄ teaspoon dry yeast
³/₄ cup warm water
1 cup flour

¹/₂ teaspoon salt
Oil for deep frying

Dissolve yeast in warm water in bowl. Add flour and salt; mix well. Let rise, covered, for 30 minutes or until doubled in bulk. Drop from wet spoon into hot oil in deep fryer. Deep-fry until golden brown. Drain on paper towel. Serve warm with honey and cinnamon. Yield: 8 servings.

Approx Per Serving: Cal 58; Prot 2 g; Carbo 12 g; Fiber <1 g;
T Fat <1 g; 3% Calories from Fat; Chol 0 mg; Sod 134 mg.
Nutritional information does not include oil for deep frying.

These are known as Loukoumades in Saudi Arabia.

Joni Lynch Wilson, Lubbock

Sopapillas

2¹/₂ tablespoons sugar
2 tablespoons cornstarch
1   20-ounce can crushed pineapple,
     drained
2 cups flour
1 tablespoon baking powder

1 teaspoon salt
1 tablespoon oil
³/₄ cup (about) water
Oil for frying
¹/₂ cup confectioners' sugar

Mix sugar and cornstarch in saucepan. Stir in pineapple. Bring to a boil over medium heat. Cook for 1 minute, stirring constantly. Cool to room temperature. Mix flour, baking powder and salt in bowl; make well in center. Add 1 tablespoon oil and water; mix well with fork. Divide into 4 portions. Knead 4 or 5 times. Roll on floured surface. Cut into 2¹/₂x4-inch pieces. Let rest for several minutes. Heat 3 inches oil to 385 degrees in saucepan. Fry sopapillas a few at a time in hot oil for 1 minute or until puffed and brown, turning once. Drain well. Slit and fill with pineapple mixture. Sprinkle with confectioners' sugar. Yield: 12 servings.

Approx Per Serving: Cal 146; Prot 2 g; Carbo 31 g; Fiber 1 g;
T Fat 1 g; 9% Calories from Fat; Chol 0 mg; Sod 261 mg.
Nutritional information does not include oil for frying.

Jan Kennedy, Lubbock

TEA CAKES

1 pound butter, softened
1½ cups sugar
1½ cups packed brown sugar
3 eggs, beaten
1 8-ounce package dates, chopped

1½ cups chopped pecans
Juice of ½ lemon
6 cups flour
1 teaspoon baking soda
2 teaspoons cinnamon

Cream butter, sugar and brown sugar in mixer bowl until light and fluffy. Beat in eggs. Add dates and pecans. Stir in lemon juice. Sift flour, baking soda and cinnamon together twice. Add to creamed mixture; mix to form stiff dough. Divide into 4 portions. Shape into 12-inch rolls. Chill, wrapped in waxed paper or foil, overnight. Cut into ¼-inch slices; place on cookie sheet. Bake at 325 degrees for 12 minutes. Remove to wire rack to cool. Yield: 192 servings.

Approx Per Serving: Cal 56; Prot 1 g; Carbo 8 g; Fiber <1 g;
    T Fat 3 g; 42% Calories from Fat; Chol 9 mg; Sod 23 mg.

This is an old family recipe from Germany. It was originally made
with burnt deer horn instead of baking soda.

Ruth Efird, Denver City

BAKLAVA

2 cups sugar
1½ cups water
Juice of ½ lemon
2 tablespoons honey
1 cup ground walnuts

2 teaspoons sugar
2 teaspoons cinnamon-sugar
1 16-ounce package phyllo dough
1 cup melted unsalted butter

Combine 2 cups sugar, water, lemon juice and honey in saucepan. Boil for 10 minutes. Chill in refrigerator. Mix walnuts, 2 teaspoons sugar and cinnamon-sugar in bowl. Reserve 6 sheets of phyllo dough. Layer 6 sheets of phyllo dough in 9x13-inch baking pan, brushing each sheet with butter. Layer remaining phyllo dough in pan, sprinkling every other sheet with walnut mixture. Layer 5 reserved sheets of phyllo dough in pan, brushing each sheet with butter. Top with remaining reserved sheet of dough. Cut into diamonds with sharp knife, cutting ¾ of the way through. Bake at 350 degrees for 30 minutes. Pour cold syrup over hot baklava. Chill overnight to improve flavor. Yield: 24 servings.

Approx Per Serving: Cal 226; Prot 3 g; Carbo 32 g; Fiber 1 g;
    T Fat 11 g; 41% Calories from Fat; Chol 21 mg; Sod 53 mg.

Joni Lynch Wilson, Lubbock

Easy Quito Fudge

1 400-gram (about 14 ounces) bittersweet chocolate bar
1 14-ounce can sweetened condensed milk
1 teaspoon vanilla extract
Salt to taste
1 cup chopped pecans

Melt chocolate in double boiler. Combine with condensed milk, vanilla, salt and pecans in bowl; mix well. Spoon into pan lined with waxed paper. Chill for 2 hours or until firm. Cut into squares. May add raisins or coconut if desired. Yield: 24 servings.

Approx Per Serving: Cal 169; Prot 3 g; Carbo 19 g; Fiber 1 g; T Fat 11 g; 52% Calories from Fat; Chol 6 mg; Sod 22 mg.

This easy no-cook fudge recipe is from Ecuador.

Mercedes Williams, Friona

Christmas Plum Pudding

4 eggs
1 cup suet
1 cup toasted bread crumbs
1 cup chopped citron
2 cups finely chopped apples
2 cups seedless raisins
1/2 cup currants
Juice of 1 lemon
1/2 teaspoon allspice
1/2 cup cider
1/4 cup sorghum molasses

Beat eggs in mixer bowl. Add suet and bread crumbs; mix well. Stir in citron, apples, raisins, currants, lemon juice and allspice. Add mixture of cider and molasses. Fill large pudding mold 3/4 full. Steam over hot water in steamer for 3 hours. Serve with brandy sauce or hard sauce; garnish with Christmas greens. May steam in smaller molds for 2 hours if preferred. Yield: 16 servings.

Approx Per Serving: Cal 248; Prot 3 g; Carbo 42 g; Fiber 2 g; T Fat 9 g; 30% Calories from Fat; Chol 58 mg; Sod 108 mg.

This is a traditional Christmas dessert from Scotland.

Georgia Mae Ericson, Crosbyton

Scottish Melting Dreams

1¹/₄ cups sifted flour
¹/₄ cup cornstarch

¹/₂ cup confectioners' sugar
³/₄ cup butter

Sift flour, cornstarch and confectioners' sugar into bowl. Cut in butter with pastry blender or fork. Mix to form dough. Shape by tablespoonfuls into balls. Place 1¹/₂ inches apart on ungreased cookie sheet. Press with fork in crisscross design. Bake at 300 degrees for 20 to 25 minutes or until light brown. Remove to wire rack to cool. Yield: 24 servings.

Approx Per Serving: Cal 87; Prot 1 g; Carbo 8 g; Fiber <1 g;
    T Fat 6 g; 60% Calories from Fat; Chol 16 mg; Sod 49 mg.

Georgia Mae Ericson, Crosbyton

Humboldt Torte

7 egg yolks
10 tablespoons sugar
6 ounces pecans, finely ground

5 ounces bitter chocolate, grated
7 egg whites
1¹/₂ cups whipping cream, whipped

Beat egg yolks with sugar in mixer bowl until thick and lemon-colored. Add pecans and chocolate. Beat egg whites in mixer bowl until stiff peaks form. Fold into egg yolk mixture. Spoon into oiled and floured 10 or 11-inch springform pan. Bake at 300 degrees for 30 minutes. Cool on wire rack; remove side of pan. Split into 2 layers with string or long knife. Spread whipped cream between layers and over top of torte. Yield: 12 servings.

Approx Per Serving: Cal 342; Prot 6 g; Carbo 21 g; Fiber 1 g;
    T Fat 28 g; 70% Calories from Fat; Chol 165 mg; Sod 46 mg.

Germany is the origin of this family recipe.

Margie Jakobsmeier, Lubbock

ICELANDIC CHRISTMAS CAKE

2 pounds dried prunes	2 eggs
1 cup sugar	4 cups flour
1 teaspoon vanilla extract	2 teaspoons baking powder
1/4 teaspoon salt	1/2 teaspoon salt
1 cup butter, softened	1 teaspoon vanilla extract
1 cup sugar	1/4 cup milk

Cook prunes in water in saucepan until tender. Drain, reserving 1/2 cup liquid. Combine prunes, reserved liquid, 1 cup sugar, 1 teaspoon vanilla and 1/4 teaspoon salt in saucepan. Cook until thickened to consistency of jam. Cream butter and 1 cup sugar in mixer bowl until light and fluffy. Beat in eggs. Add flour, baking powder, 1/2 teaspoon salt, 1 teaspoon vanilla and milk; mix well. Chill in refrigerator. Divide into 7 portions. Roll into 8-inch circles on floured surface. Place on bottoms of 8-inch cake pans. Bake at 350 degrees for 20 minutes. Remove to wire rack to cool. Spread prune mixture between layers. Chill, wrapped in plastic wrap, overnight or longer. Cut into thin slices to serve. Yield: 16 servings.

Approx Per Serving: Cal 460; Prot 6 g; Carbo 85 g; Fiber 6 g;
T Fat 13 g; 24% Calories from Fat; Chol 58 mg; Sod 251 mg.

Brenda Farr, Lubbock

ARABIAN WALNUT CAKE

3 1/2 cups water	1 teaspoon baking powder
3 cups sugar	2 cups finely chopped walnuts
1 cinnamon stick	Grated rind of 1 lemon
2 whole cloves	1 tablespoon ground cinnamon
15 egg yolks	1/2 teaspoon ground cloves
15 tablespoons sugar	1/4 cup Cognac
15 tablespoons semolina	15 egg whites

Bring water, 3 cups sugar, cinnamon stick and cloves to a boil in saucepan. Boil for 2 or 3 minutes; discard cinnamon stick and cloves. Cool to room temperature. Beat egg yolks with 15 tablespoons sugar in mixer bowl until thick and lemon-colored. Add mixture of semolina and baking powder; mix well. Mix walnuts, lemon rind, ground cinnamon and ground cloves in small bowl. Add to batter with Cognac; mix well. Beat egg whites in mixer bowl until stiff peaks form. Fold into batter. Spoon into greased 10x14-inch cake pan. Bake at 350 degrees for 1 hour. Drizzle cool syrup over hot cake. Yield: 16 servings.

Approx Per Serving: Cal 396; Prot 9 g; Carbo 59 g; Fiber 1 g;
T Fat 15 g; 33% Calories from Fat; Chol 200 mg; Sod 78 mg.

Joni Lynch Wilson, Lubbock

Breads

Hale County

The settlers came to Plainview
to stand toe to toe with the prairie sea.
They came to wrestle prosperity from Hale County,
with big dreams and the plow.

R.S.

CORN LIGHT BREAD

2 cups boiling water	1/2 teaspoon baking soda
2 cups cornmeal	1 teaspoon salt
2 cups cold water	1/2 cup sugar
1/2 teaspoon baking soda	1 egg, beaten
1 teaspoon salt	1/2 cup lard
1 cup buttermilk	1/4 cup cornmeal

Combine boiling water and 2 cups cornmeal in bowl; mix well. Add cold water, 1/2 teaspoon baking soda and 1 teaspoon salt, stirring until thickened. Let stand, covered, in warm place overnight. Stir in buttermilk, 1/2 teaspoon baking soda, 1 teaspoon salt, sugar, egg, lard and 1/4 cup cornmeal, mixing well. Pour into hot greased 5x6-inch loaf pan. Bake at 325 degrees for 30 minutes. Remove to wire rack to cool. Yield: 12 servings.

Approx Per Serving: Cal 218; Prot 3 g; Carbo 30 g; Fiber 2 g;
    T Fat 10 g; 39% Calories from Fat; Chol 27 mg; Sod 451 mg.

This recipe is 125 years old; it was given to me by
a schoolmate's great-grandmother.

Ann Marie Dobmeier, Lubbock

COACH'S FAVORITE JALAPEÑO CORN BREAD

1 cup buttermilk	1/2 teaspoon baking soda
1 cup yellow cornmeal	1 egg, beaten
1 cup sifted flour	1/4 cup melted shortening
3 tablespoons sugar	1 16-ounce can corn, drained
1 teaspoon salt	8 ounces Cheddar cheese, shredded
1 teaspoon baking powder	3 jalapeño peppers, chopped

Combine buttermilk, cornmeal and flour in bowl; mix well. Add sugar, salt, baking powder, baking soda, egg, shortening, corn, cheese and jalapeño peppers; mix well. Pour into greased 9x13-inch baking pan. Bake at 375 degrees for 30 minutes. May substitute other cheese for Cheddar. Yield: 15 servings.

Approx Per Serving: Cal 200; Prot 7 g; Carbo 23 g; Fiber 1 g;
    T Fat 9 g; 42% Calories from Fat; Chol 31 mg; Sod 377 mg.

Sharon Dykes, Wife of Texas Tech football coach Spike Dykes, Lubbock

6666 CORN BREAD

1 cup flour
1 cup cornmeal
1 egg, beaten
4 teaspoons baking powder
1 teaspoon salt
1/4 cup sugar

1 cup milk
2 cups shredded Cheddar cheese
1   4-ounce can chopped green chilies,
    drained
1/4 cup bacon drippings

Combine flour and cornmeal in large bowl. Add egg, baking powder, salt, sugar, milk, cheese, chilies and bacon drippings; mix well. Pour into greased and heated cast-iron skillet. Bake at 425 degrees for 25 minutes. Yield: 8 servings.

Approx Per Serving: Cal 355; Prot 12 g; Carbo 35 g; Fiber 2 g;
    T Fat 19 g; 47% Calories from Fat; Chol 102 mg; Sod 799 mg.

From the famous 6666 and Triangle Hereford ranches in Guthrie, Texas.

Karen Blodgett, First Lady of the 6666 Ranch, Guthrie

WAYLON'S CORN BREAD

2 eggs
1 1/2 cups buttermilk
1/2 cup sugar
1/4 teaspoon baking soda
1 cup white cornmeal

1 cup flour
1 tablespoon baking powder
1 teaspoon salt
1/2 cup melted butter

Beat eggs with buttermilk in large bowl. Add sugar, baking soda, cornmeal, flour, baking powder and salt; mix well. Batter should be thin for lighter corn bread. Stir in melted butter. Grease cast-iron skillet; sprinkle with a small amount of cornmeal to prevent corn bread from sticking. Pour in batter. Bake at 450 degrees for 20 to 25 minutes or until golden brown. Cut into slices to serve. May increase sugar to 3/4 cup or use 2 cups buttermilk instead of 1 1/2 cups. Yield: 8 servings.

Approx Per Serving: Cal 310; Prot 6 g; Carbo 41 g; Fiber 2 g;
    T Fat 14 g; 40% Calories from Fat; Chol 86 mg; Sod 578 mg.

Waylon Jennings, Nashville, Tennessee

APRICOT BREAD

1 6-ounce package dried apricots	2 cups flour
1 cup sugar	2 teaspoons baking powder
2 tablespoons margarine, softened	1/4 teaspoon baking soda
1 egg, beaten	1 teaspoon salt
1/4 cup cold water	1/2 cup chopped pecans
1/2 cup orange juice	

Soak apricots in warm water for 30 minutes; drain. Combine sugar, margarine, egg, cold water, orange juice and apricots in bowl; mix well. Stir in flour, baking powder, baking soda and salt until moistened. Fold in pecans. Pour into greased and floured loaf pan. Bake at 350 degrees for 55 to 65 minutes or until golden brown. Remove to wire rack to cool. Yield: 12 servings.

Approx Per Serving: Cal 236; Prot 4 g; Carbo 43 g; Fiber 2 g;
T Fat 6 g; 22% Calories from Fat; Chol 18 mg; Sod 307 mg.

This recipe has been handed down through several generations.

Berta Simmons, Lubbock

BANANA-NUT BREAD

1/2 cup shortening	2 cups flour
1 cup sugar	1 teaspoon baking soda
2 eggs, beaten	1/2 cup chopped pecans
3 bananas, mashed	

Cream shortening and sugar in mixer bowl until light and fluffy. Add eggs and bananas, mixing well. Sift flour and baking soda together. Stir into creamed mixture. Fold in pecans. Pour into greased and floured bundt pan or 2 loaf pans. Bake at 350 degrees for 40 minutes or until bread tests done. May use 5 mashed bananas and 1 teaspoon vanilla extract and substitute 2 cups chopped walnuts for pecans. Yield: 14 servings.

Approx Per Serving: Cal 247; Prot 3 g; Carbo 34 g; Fiber 1 g;
T Fat 11 g; 40% Calories from Fat; Chol 30 mg; Sod 70 mg.

Jaquita Blevins, Post, and Jessie Amerson, Abernathy

CASSEROLE DILL BREAD

1 cup cottage cheese
1/4 cup warm water
1 envelope dry yeast
1 egg, beaten
2 tablespoons sugar
2 teaspoons dill seed
1 tablespoon dried minced onion

1 tablespoon oil
1 teaspoon salt
1/2 teaspoon dillweed
1/4 teaspoon baking soda
2 1/4 to 2 1/2 cups flour
1 tablespoon butter, softened
1 teaspoon onion salt

Heat cottage cheese in small saucepan; remove from heat. Combine warm water and yeast in bowl. Stir in cottage cheese. Add egg, sugar, dill seed, onion, oil, salt, dillweed and baking soda; mix well. Stir in flour gradually. Knead 4 or 5 times on lightly floured surface. Let rise, covered, until doubled in bulk. Punch dough down; knead 4 or 5 times. Place in greased 2-quart casserole or loaf pan. Let rise, covered, until doubled in bulk. Bake at 350 degrees for 40 to 50 minutes or until bread tests done. Remove to wire rack. Brush with butter; dust with onion salt. Yield: 16 servings.

Approx Per Serving: Cal 111; Prot 4 g; Carbo 17 g; Fiber 1 g;
    T Fat 3 g; 22% Calories from Fat; Chol 17 mg; Sod 310 mg.

Martha Beach, Lubbock

JALAPEÑO BREAD

2 envelopes dry yeast
1 cup lukewarm water
1/3 cup sugar
1 cup scalded milk
2 eggs, beaten
1 teaspoon salt

1/2 cup margarine, softened
1 tablespoon shortening
5 to 6 cups flour
2 cups shredded longhorn cheese
1 onion, chopped
1/2 cup chopped jalapeño peppers

Dissolve yeast in water with 1 tablespoon sugar in small bowl; set aside. Mix remaining sugar, scalded milk, eggs, salt, margarine and shortening in large bowl. Let cool for 5 minutes. Stir in yeast mixture. Add flour 1 cup at a time, beating well after each addition. Place dough into buttered bowl, turning to grease surface. Let rise until doubled in bulk; punch dough down. Let rise for 30 minutes longer. Knead on lightly floured surface until smooth and elastic. Divide dough into two equal portions. Roll out to 1/4-inch thickness. Sprinkle with cheese, onion and peppers. Roll up tightly, sealing edges. Place on greased baking sheet. Let rise for 30 minutes. Bake at 325 degrees for 45 minutes. Slice and serve hot. Yield: 24 servings.

Approx Per Serving: Cal 218; Prot 7 g; Carbo 28 g; Fiber 1 g;
    T Fat 9 g; 36% Calories from Fat; Chol 29 mg; Sod 244 mg.

Linda Moorhouse, Pitchfork Ranch, Guthrie

PEPPERONI CHEESE BREAD

3/4 cup Italian salad dressing
1/2 cup milk
1   5-ounce jar Old English cheese
    spread
2 eggs, beaten
2³/4 cups flour

2 tablespoons sugar
1¹/2 teaspoons dry mustard
1/4 teaspoon baking soda
1   4-ounce package sliced pepperoni,
    chopped
1/4 to 1/2 cup chopped green bell pepper

Combine salad dressing, milk, cheese and eggs in bowl; mix well. Add flour, sugar, mustard and baking soda, stirring until moistened. Fold in pepperoni and green pepper. Pour into greased 5x9-inch loaf pan. Bake at 350 degrees for 50 to 55 minutes or until bread tests done. Remove to wire rack to cool. Yield: 12 servings.

Approx Per Serving: Cal 286; Prot 9 g; Carbo 27 g; Fiber 1 g;
    T Fat 18 g; 53% Calories from Fat; Chol 49 mg; Sod 438 mg.

This recipe was submitted by Diana Phillips.

Frankie Mills, Abernathy

QUICK YEAST BREAD

1 cup warm water
2 tablespoons sugar
1 teaspoon salt
1 envelope dry yeast

1¹/2 tablespoons oil
1¹/2 cups flour
1 egg, beaten

Combine water, sugar, salt and yeast in bowl; let stand for 5 minutes. Add oil, flour and egg. Beat until dough is stiff. Knead on lightly floured surface until dough is smooth and elastic. Let rise until doubled in bulk. Place in greased loaf pan. Bake at 350 degrees for 45 minutes or until loaf tests done. Yield: 12 servings.

Approx Per Serving: Cal 87; Prot 2 g; Carbo 14 g; Fiber <1 g;
    T Fat 2 g; 24% Calories from Fat; Chol 18 mg; Sod 184 mg.

Pat Henry, Levelland

YEAST BREAD

2 envelopes dry yeast
2 cups warm water
2/3 cup dry milk powder
1/2 cup sugar

1 tablespoon salt
1 egg, beaten
5 tablespoons oil
6 cups flour

Dissolve yeast in warm water in bowl. Add milk powder, sugar, salt, egg and oil; mix well. Stir in half the flour. Add remaining flour to form stiff dough. Place in greased bowl, turning to grease surface. Let rise until doubled in bulk; punch dough down. Let rise again until doubled in bulk. Punch down; place in 2 greased loaf pans. Let rise until doubled in bulk. Bake at 350 degrees for 45 minutes. Remove to wire racks to cool. Yield: 24 servings.

Approx Per Serving: Cal 167; Prot 4 g; Carbo 29 g; Fiber 1 g;
T Fat 3 g; 19% Calories from Fat; Chol 9 mg; Sod 281 mg.

LaVerne Stolle, Slaton

ANGEL BISCUITS

1 envelope dry yeast
1/4 cup warm water
5 cups flour
1 teaspoon baking soda
5 teaspoons baking powder

1 teaspoon salt
5 tablespoons sugar
1 cup shortening
2 cups buttermilk
3/4 cup melted margarine

Dissolve yeast in warm water in small bowl; set aside. Sift flour, baking soda, baking powder, salt and sugar into large bowl. Cut in shortening until mixture is crumbly. Stir in buttermilk and yeast mixture. Turn out onto floured surface. Roll out to 1/4- to 1/2-inch thickness; cut with biscuit cutter. Brush with melted margarine. Fold over; brush tops with melted margarine. Place on greased baking sheet. Let rise for 1 1/2 to 2 hours or until doubled in bulk. Bake at 400 degrees for 15 minutes. May place dough in tightly covered bowl in refrigerator for up to 10 days. May freeze on baking sheet before baking. Let frozen biscuits rise for 2 to 4 hours before baking. Yield: 48 servings.

Approx Per Serving: Cal 122; Prot 2 g; Carbo 12 g; Fiber <1 g;
T Fat 7 g; 54% Calories from Fat; Chol <1 mg; Sod 120 mg.

Joan Blackmon, Lubbock

QUICK BUNS

1 envelope dry yeast
1 cup warm water
2 tablespoons sugar
2¼ cups flour

1 teaspoon salt
1 egg, slightly beaten
2 tablespoons oil

Dissolve yeast in warm water in large bowl. Add sugar, half the flour and salt into yeast mixture, beating until smooth. Stir in egg and oil. Beat in remaining flour until dough is stiff and smooth. Let rise, covered, in warm place until doubled in bulk. Punch dough down. Spoon mixture into greased muffin cups, filling half full. Let rise for 20 to 30 minutes in warm place. Bake at 400 degrees for 15 to 20 minutes. Yield: 12 servings.

Approx Per Serving: Cal 122; Prot 3 g; Carbo 20 g; Fiber 1 g;
    T Fat 3 g; 22% Calories from Fat; Chol 18 mg; Sod 184 mg.

Barbara Amerson, Abernathy

BUTTER DIPS

2¼ cups sifted flour
1 tablespoon sugar
3½ teaspoons baking powder

1½ teaspoons salt
1 cup milk
⅓ cup butter

Sift flour, sugar, baking powder and salt into large bowl. Add milk, stirring to form stiff dough. Turn out onto well-floured surface. Knead lightly 10 times. Roll out to an 8x12-inch rectangle, ½ inch thick. Cut into halves lengthwise; cut into 16 strips crosswise. Melt butter in 9x13-inch baking pan. Dip strips in butter, turning to coat. Arrange in 2 rows in pan. Bake at 400 degrees for 10 to 20 minutes or until brown. May add ½ cup shredded cheese or sprinkle with mixture of 2 tablespoons sugar and ½ teaspoon cinnamon. Yield: 16 servings.

Approx Per Serving: Cal 106; Prot 2 g; Carbo 14 g; Fiber <1 g;
    T Fat 4 g; 38% Calories from Fat; Chol 12 mg; Sod 310 mg.

Terri Cox, Friona

DINNER ROLLS

4 cups milk
1 cup sugar
1 cup shortening
3 envelopes dry yeast
3/4 cup warm water
3 1/2 cups flour

1 1/2 cups whole wheat flour
3 cups sifted flour
1 tablespoon salt
2 teaspoons baking powder
1 teaspoon baking soda

Combine milk, sugar and shortening in saucepan. Cook until heated through; remove from heat. Dissolve yeast in warm water; add to milk mixture. Combine 3 1/2 cups flour, 1 1/2 cups wheat flour and milk mixture in large bowl, stirring until smooth. Let rise, covered, for 2 hours. Add 3 cups sifted flour, salt, baking powder and baking soda; mix well. Knead on floured surface until smooth and elastic. Roll out to desired thickness; cut out as for biscuits. Place on greased baking sheet. Bake at 350 degrees for 20 minutes. May freeze and store in plastic bags before baking. Yield: 36 servings.

Approx Per Serving: Cal 186; Prot 4 g; Carbo 27 g; Fiber 1 g;
T Fat 7 g; 33% Calories from Fat; Chol 4 mg; Sod 231 mg.

Billie Martin, Levelland

GRANNY'S BREAD ROLLS

1 envelope dry yeast
1/4 cup warm water
1 teaspoon sugar
1/4 cup shortening
1 teaspoon salt

2 tablespoons sugar
1 cup boiling water
1 egg, beaten
3 cups flour

Dissolve yeast in warm water with 1 teaspoon sugar; let stand for 10 minutes. Combine shortening, salt and 2 tablespoons sugar in large bowl. Pour in boiling water, stirring well. Let stand until lukewarm. Add yeast mixture, egg and flour; mix well. Let rise, covered, for 3 hours. Shape dough into rolls; place on baking sheet. Let rise, covered, until doubled in bulk. Bake at 350 degrees for 15 to 30 minutes or until light brown. Yield: 12 servings.

Approx Per Serving: Cal 169; Prot 4 g; Carbo 27 g; Fiber 1 g;
T Fat 5 g; 27% Calories from Fat; Chol 18 mg; Sod 184 mg.

Leigh Anne Stephenson, Springlake

ICEBOX ROLLS

1 envelope dry yeast
1/2 cup sugar
2 cups warm water

2 tablespoons oil
1 teaspoon salt
6 cups flour

Combine yeast and sugar in large bowl. Pour in warm water mixed with oil and salt. Let stand until yeast is dissolved. Add flour, stirring until dough is stiff. Shape into rolls; place on baking sheet. Bake at 400 degrees for 25 to 30 minutes or until light brown. May keep dough in refrigerator for several days before baking. Yield: 36 servings.

Approx Per Serving: Cal 94; Prot 2 g; Carbo 19 g; Fiber 1 g;
    T Fat 1 g; 9% Calories from Fat; Chol 0 mg; Sod 60 mg.

Leta Kelley, Earth

REFRIGERATOR ROLLS

2 envelopes dry yeast
2 cups warm water
1/2 cup sugar
1 teaspoon salt

6 1/2 to 7 cups flour
1 egg, beaten
1/4 cup shortening

Dissolve yeast in warm water in mixer bowl. Add sugar, salt and half the flour. Beat for 2 minutes. Add egg and shortening, beating well. Stir in enough remaining flour to form stiff dough. Place in greased bowl, turning to grease surface. Let rise in refrigerator, punching dough down occasionally. Remove from refrigerator 2 1/2 hours before baking. Shape desired amount into rolls; place on baking sheet. Let rise until doubled in bulk. Bake at 400 degrees for 12 to 15 minutes. Store remaining dough in refrigerator. Yield: 36 servings.

Approx Per Serving: Cal 115; Prot 3 g; Carbo 21 g; Fiber 1 g;
    T Fat 2 g; 14% Calories from Fat; Chol 6 mg; Sod 62 mg.

Sherry White, Farwell

LUNCH ROLLS

1 cake yeast
1 tablespoon sugar
1½ cups milk, scalded and cooled

2 tablespoons melted shortening
3 cups flour
1 teaspoon salt

Dissolve yeast and sugar in lukewarm milk in bowl. Add shortening. Stir in mixture of flour and salt gradually to form soft dough. Turn onto floured surface, kneading until dough is stiff. Place in greased bowl, turning to grease surface. Let rise, covered, in warm place until doubled in bulk; punch dough down. Shape into small rolls; place on baking sheet. Let rise until doubled in bulk. Bake at 375 degrees for 12 to 15 minutes or until light brown. May shape into loaves and bake in loaf pan. May double recipe for 3 loaves of bread. Yield: 12 servings.

Approx Per Serving: Cal 157; Prot 5 g; Carbo 27 g; Fiber 1 g;
    T Fat 3 g; 20% Calories from Fat; Chol 4 mg; Sod 191 mg.

This recipe from a 1912 Post cookbook was used on the OS Ranch and the Connell Ranch for many years. It never fails.

Elizabeth Connell, Colorado City

MORE ROLLS

1 cake yeast
1½ cups lukewarm water
1 teaspoon salt
1½ tablespoons shortening

1 tablespoon (heaping) sugar
3 to 4 cups flour
2 teaspoons melted shortening

Dissolve yeast in lukewarm water in large bowl. Add salt, shortening, sugar and enough flour to make soft dough; mix well. Let rise, covered, in warm place for 1 hour. Roll out to ½ inch thick on floured surface. Brush with melted shortening. Cut out with medium-sized cutter. Fold greased sides together. Place on baking sheet. Let rise, covered, for 2 hours. Bake at 375 degrees for 12 to 15 minutes or until golden brown. Yield: 12 rolls.

Approx Per Roll: Cal 178; Prot 5 g; Carbo 33 g; Fiber 1 g;
    T Fat 3 g; 14% Calories from Fat; Chol 0 mg; Sod 179 mg.

These rolls were made and served with family-style meals at the Golightly Hotel in O'Donnell, Texas. A pleasant memory for people far and near, including our claim to fame, Bobby Dan Blocker (Hoss Cartwright). When you ate at the Hotel it was "More rolls, Mrs. Golightly."

Mary Frances Gardenhire, O'Donnell

Flour Tortillas

3 cups flour
2 teaspoons baking powder
1/4 teaspoon salt

1 teaspoon shortening
1 cup warm water

Combine flour, baking powder and salt in bowl. Cut in shortening. Add warm water all at once. Stir for 1 minute; let stand for 1 minute. Divide dough into 12 equal portions. Roll out thinly on floured surface. Bake on medium-hot griddle for 17 seconds on first side and 8 seconds on remaining side. Yield: 12 servings.

Approx Per Serving: Cal 118; Prot 3 g; Carbo 24 g; Fiber 1 g;
 T Fat 1 g; 5% Calories from Fat; Chol 0 mg; Sod 100 mg.

*I have been making tortillas since I was 8 years old and
I taught my son to make them when he was 8.*

Ruth Torres-Naron, Abernathy

Croutons

8 slices white bread, cut into 1/2-inch
  cubes
1/2 cup butter

1/2 teaspoon garlic powder
1/4 cup grated Parmesan cheese
2 teaspoons fresh minced parsley

Place bread cubes in 10-inch round glass dish. Combine butter and garlic powder in 1-cup glass measure. Microwave on High for 1 minute or until melted; stir well. Drizzle butter mixture over bread cubes. Sprinkle with cheese and parsley, tossing gently. Microwave on High for 5 1/2 to 6 minutes or until crisp, stirring after 2 minutes. Yield: 8 servings.

Approx Per Serving: Cal 189; Prot 4 g; Carbo 14 g; Fiber 1 g;
 T Fat 13 g; 63% Calories from Fat; Chol 33 mg; Sod 288 mg.

Lee Ruth Krieg, Lubbock

Outdoor & Picnic

Parmer
County

Trade gate to the West,

Borderland cowhands,

How many catfish in Catfish Draw?

The sun sinks like a giant egg yolk

Westward toward California.

Sage fills the night wind in Parmer County.

R.S.

WALKING SALAD

1 apple	1 tablespoon peanut butter
1 teaspoon lemon juice	1 teaspoon raisins

Slice off top of apple; core center. Brush center with lemon juice. Mix peanut butter and raisins together; spoon into center. May substitute cole slaw, pineapple and cream cheese or tuna salad for peanut butter mixture. Yield: 1 serving.

Approx Per Serving: Cal 187; Prot 5 g; Carbo 27 g; Fiber 5 g;
    T Fat 9 g; 38% Calories from Fat; Chol 0 mg; Sod 66 mg.

Mrs. T. Kinder Farris, Floydada

BEEF TERIYAKI

1½ pounds flank steak	1 small onion, sliced
6 tablespoons soy sauce	½ teaspoon ground ginger
6 tablespoons dry sherry	Salt and pepper to taste
¼ cup oil	

Pound meat between waxed paper to tenderize; cut into 4 serving portions. Place in large shallow dish. Mix remaining ingredients in bowl. Pour over steak. Marinate in refrigerator overnight. Drain, discarding marinade. Grill over hot coals for 3 to 4 minutes or until desired degree of doneness. Yield: 4 servings.

Approx Per Serving: Cal 394; Prot 34 g; Carbo 5 g; Fiber <1 g;
    T Fat 23 g; 53% Calories from Fat; Chol 96 mg; Sod 1598 mg.

Susan McDonald, Ransom Canyon

CAMP PACKS

1 pound ground beef	1 10-ounce can cream of mushroom
4 potatoes, sliced ½ inch thick	soup
1 onion, sliced ¼ inch thick	½ cup milk
4 carrots, peeled, halved lengthwise	Salt and pepper to taste

Shape ground beef into 8 thin patties. Place half the patties on 8x8-inch squares of foil. Layer with potatoes, onion and carrot halves. Top each with ¼ cup soup, 2 tablespoons milk, salt and pepper. Place remaining patties on top. Wrap tightly in foil. Grill over campfire for 20 minutes on each side. May bake in 350-degree oven for 45 minutes. Yield: 4 servings.

Approx Per Serving: Cal 594; Prot 29 g; Carbo 70 g; Fiber 8 g;
    T Fat 23 g; 34% Calories from Fat; Chol 79 mg; Sod 700 mg.

Alice Allen, Friona

CHICKEN AND VEGETABLE FOIL-PACKET DINNERS

4 chicken breast filets
Salt and pepper to taste
Lemon-pepper seasoning to taste
1 onion, sliced

4 ounces mushrooms, sliced
1 large yellow squash, sliced
1 large zucchini, sliced

Rinse chicken and pat dry; season with salt, pepper and lemon-pepper seasoning. Place onion slices in center of 4 large squares of foil. Layer with chicken, mushrooms, squash and zucchini. Wrap tightly in foil. Place over hot coals on campfire or grill. Cook for 20 to 30 minutes, turning frequently to prevent burning. May substitute other vegetables as desired. May also cook in box oven. Yield: 4 servings.

Approx Per Serving: Cal 184; Prot 29 g; Carbo 9 g; Fiber 3 g;
    T Fat 3 g; 17% Calories from Fat; Chol 72 mg; Sod 68 mg.

Debbie Greenwood, Lubbock

SPICE CHICKEN

1 3-pound chicken
Cumin, garlic powder, MSG and
    paprika to taste

Seasoned salt and lemon-pepper to
    taste

Rinse chicken and pat dry. Skin and cut into serving pieces. Place in shallow pan. Sprinkle both sides with seasonings. Cover and chill for 5 hours. Grill over medium hot coals for 50 minutes, turning every 10 minutes. Yield: 6 servings.

Approx Per Serving: Cal 215; Prot 33 g; Carbo 0 g; Fiber 0 g;
    T Fat 8 g; 37% Calories from Fat; Chol 101 mg; Sod 97 mg.

Judy Anderson, Earth

GRILLED ORANGE ROUGHY

4 orange roughy
    filets

1 8-ounce bottle of Italian salad
    dressing

Marinate fish in salad dressing in shallow dish for 30 minutes; drain. Grill fish over hot coals for 8 minutes or until fish flakes easily, basting with dressing occasionally. Serve with hot cooked rice or buttered noodles. Yield: 4 servings.

Approx Per Serving: Cal 371; Prot 22 g; Carbo 6 g; Fiber <1 g;
    T Fat 35 g; 74% Calories from Fat; Chol 62 mg; Sod 372 mg.

Jan Kennedy, Lubbock

Banana-Dijon Grilled Shrimp

½ cup mashed ripe banana
¼ cup reduced-calorie mayonnaise
1 tablespoon lime juice
1 tablespoon Dijon mustard
1 tablespoon honey

1 teaspoon grated lime rind
¼ teaspoon ground red pepper
1 cup plain nonfat yogurt
1½ pounds large unpeeled shrimp

Combine banana, mayonnaise, lime juice, mustard, honey, lime rind and red pepper in food processor container. Process at High speed for 5 seconds, scraping sides with rubber spatula. Process for 5 seconds longer or until smooth. Pour into bowl; stir in yogurt. Spoon 1 cup banana sauce into shallow flat dish. Cover and chill remaining sauce. Peel and devein shrimp, leaving tails. Thread 6 shrimp onto eight 10-inch skewers. Place in banana sauce. Marinate in refrigerator for 4 hours, turning occasionally. Drain, discarding sauce. Spray grill rack with nonstick cooking spray. Grill shrimp over medium hot coals for 4 minutes on each side. Serve with chilled banana sauce. Yield: 4 servings.

Approx Per Serving: Cal 251; Prot 32 g; Carbo 18 g; Fiber 1 g;
　　T Fat 5 g; 19% Calories from Fat; Chol 270 mg; Sod 524 mg.

*This recipe appeared in **Cooking Light Magazine**.*

Susan McDonald, Ransom Canyon

Barbecue Sauce

1 cup margarine
¾ cup flour
2 cups vinegar

1 cup water
Salt and pepper to taste

Combine margarine, flour, vinegar and water in saucepan. Cook over medium heat until thickened, stirring frequently. Season with salt and pepper. Use for basting chicken on grill. Yield: 46 ounces.

Approx Per Ounce: Cal 44; Prot <1 g; Carbo 2 g; Fiber <1 g;
　　T Fat 4 g; 78% Calories from Fat; Chol 0 mg; Sod 47 mg.

N. A. Bryson, Dimmitt

CAJUN SPICE RECIPE

1 tablespoon paprika
2 teaspoons salt
1 teaspoon onion powder
1 teaspoon garlic powder
1 teaspoon cayenne pepper

3/4 teaspoon white pepper
3/4 teaspoon black pepper
1/2 teaspoon thyme
1/2 teaspoon oregano

Combine paprika, salt, onion powder, garlic powder, cayenne pepper, white pepper, black pepper, thyme and oregano in shaker container. Shake well to mix. Sprinkle over chicken or fish for grilling. Yield: 10½ teaspoons.

Nutritional information for this recipe is not available.

Diana Phillips, Abernathy

ITALIAN POTATOES

4 medium potatoes
1/2 cup Italian salad dressing

1 teaspoon salt
1/4 teaspoon pepper

Cook unpeeled potatoes in 1 inch boiling salted water in saucepan until tender. Slice diagonally into ½-inch slices. Place in shallow glass dish. Pour salad dressing over slices. Let stand for 1 hour, turning once. Place slices on grill 3 inches from hot coals. Cook for 8 to 10 minutes on each side or until golden brown. Season with salt and pepper after turning. Yield: 6 servings.

Approx Per Serving: Cal 238; Prot 3 g; Carbo 36 g; Fiber 3 g;
    T Fat 12 g; 41% Calories from Fat; Chol 0 mg; Sod 462 mg.

Lee Ruth Krieg, Lubbock

VEGETABLE CARE PACKAGES

12 ounces fresh or frozen peas
8 ounces fresh whole kernel corn
1 green bell pepper, finely chopped
1 red bell pepper, finely chopped

1/4 cup butter
1 teaspoon tarragon
Salt and pepper to taste

Cut heavy-duty foil into four 6x6-inch squares. Layer each square with an equal portion of peas, corn, green pepper and red pepper. Dot each layer with 1 tablespoon butter, ¼ teaspoon tarragon, salt and pepper. Wrap tightly in foil. Grill over medium-hot coals for 20 to 30 minutes. Yield: 4 servings.

Approx Per Serving: Cal 228; Prot 7 g; Carbo 25 g; Fiber 7 g;
    T Fat 13 g; 47% Calories from Fat; Chol 31 mg; Sod 110 mg.

Susan McDonald, Ransom Canyon

GRILLED STUFFED MUSHROOMS

8 large whole mushrooms
2 tablespoons fresh bread crumbs
1 green onion, finely chopped
1 tomato, peeled, chopped
1 teaspoon tomato paste

1 teaspoon lemon juice
$1/2$ teaspoon dried thyme
$1/4$ teaspoon dried oregano
Salt and pepper to taste

Remove mushroom caps and set aside. Chop stems finely. Combine with remaining ingredients in small bowl; mix well. Spoon mixture into mushroom caps. Butter double thickness of heavy-duty foil on shiny side. Arrange mushrooms on foil; fold up, securing edges. Grill over medium-hot coals for 5 to 6 minutes. Yield: 8 servings.

Approx Per Serving: Cal 15; Prot 1 g; Carbo 3 g; Fiber 1 g;
    T Fat <1 g; 11% Calories from Fat; Chol <1 mg; Sod 14 mg.

Susan McDonald, Ransom Canyon

BARBECUED APPLES

4 small Granny Smith apples
$1/4$ cup packed dark brown sugar
2 tablespoons raisins

1 teaspoon grated lemon rind
$1/2$ teaspoon cinnamon

Core and cut ring around each apple with knife. Mix brown sugar, raisins, lemon rind and cinnamon in small bowl. Spoon mixture into cored centers. Wrap each apple in heavy-duty foil with shiny side against the apple. Grill over warm coals for 40 minutes, turning occasionally. Unwrap carefully to serve. Yield: 4 servings.

Approx Per Serving: Cal 140; Prot <1 g; Carbo 37 g; Fiber 3 g;
    T Fat <1 g; 2% Calories from Fat; Chol 0 mg; Sod 9 mg.

Susan McDonald, Ransom Canyon

GRILLED PINEAPPLE RINGS WITH KIRSCH

1 large fresh pineapple
$1/4$ cup apricot jam

2 tablespoons Kirsch

Cut pineapple into 8 slices, removing outer peel and inner core. Spread each side of slices with apricot jam; sprinkle with Kirsch. Grill over warm coals for 3 to 4 minutes on each side or until jam begins to bubble and brown. Yield: 8 servings.

Approx Per Serving: Cal 80; Prot <1 g; Carbo 19 g; Fiber 1 g;
    T Fat <1 g; 4% Calories from Fat; Chol 0 mg; Sod 2 mg.

Susan McDonald, Ransom Canyon

BARBECUED BANANAS FLAMBÉ

4 ripe unpeeled bananas
2 tablespoons dark brown sugar

6 tablespoons dark rum

Grill bananas over warm coals for 10 minutes on each side. Cut into halves lengthwise. Place on serving plates. Sprinkle with brown sugar and rum. Ignite and serve immediately. Yield: 8 servings.

Approx Per Serving: Cal 89; Prot 1 g; Carbo 17 g; Fiber 1 g;
    T Fat <1 g; 3% Calories from Fat; Chol 0 mg; Sod 2 mg.

Susan McDonald, Ransom Canyon

BUFFALO CHIPS

2 cups sugar
1/2 cup margarine
5 tablespoons baking cocoa
1/2 cup sweetened condensed milk

1/2 cup peanut butter
3 cups quick-cooking oats
Vanilla extract to taste

Combine first 4 ingredients in saucepan. Bring to a boil, stirring constantly; remove from heat. Stir in peanut butter, oats and vanilla. Drop by tablespoonfuls onto waxed paper-lined tray. Let stand until cool. Yield: 48 servings.

Approx Per Serving: Cal 96; Prot 2 g; Carbo 14 g; Fiber 1 g;
    T Fat 4 g; 36% Calories from Fat; Chol 1 mg; Sod 38 mg.

Mrs. James Lattimore, Levelland

BANANA PUDDING ICE CREAM

3 cups milk
2 cups whipping cream
1 cup sugar
1 tablespoon vanilla extract
3 rennet tablets, crushed

2 tablespoons water
3 bananas, chopped
2   12-ounce cans evaporated milk
2 cups coarsely crushed vanilla wafers
5 1/3 ounces banana instant drink mix

Heat first 4 ingredients in saucepan to 110 degrees on candy thermometer, stirring constantly. Dissolve rennet in water. Add to milk mixture, stirring well. Pour into 1-gallon ice cream freezer. Let stand for 10 minutes or until thickened. Do not stir. Add remaining ingredients; mix well. Freeze mixture using manufacturer's directions. Yield: 16 (1-cup) servings.

Approx Per Serving: Cal 342; Prot 8 g; Carbo 39 g; Fiber <1 g;
    T Fat 18 g; 46% Calories from Fat; Chol 67 mg; Sod 168 mg.

Carol Tobias, Post

BUTTER PECAN ICE CREAM

1 cup chopped pecans	2 teaspoons vanilla extract
5 eggs	2 teaspoons butter extract
2 cups sugar	2 teaspoons maple extract
1 14-ounce can sweetened	2 cups whipping cream, whipped
condensed milk	4 to 5 cups milk

Spread pecans on baking sheet. Roast at 300 degrees for 10 minutes, stirring occasionally; set aside. Beat eggs with sugar in large bowl. Add sweetened condensed milk, vanilla, butter extract and maple extract; beat well. Fold in pecans and whipped cream. Pour into 1 gallon ice cream freezer, adding enough milk to fill canister. Freeze using manufacturer's directions. Yield: 16 (1-cup) servings.

Approx Per Serving: Cal 400; Prot 8 g; Carbo 44 g; Fiber <1 g;
    T Fat 23 g; 49% Calories from Fat; Chol 126 mg; Sod 97 mg.

Sherry White, Farwell

STRAWBERRY ICE CREAM

2 3-ounce packages vanilla instant	1 cup sugar
pudding mix	2 16-ounce packages frozen
4 cups milk	strawberries
1 tablespoon vanilla extract	Food coloring
1 cup sweetened condensed milk	5 to 6 cups milk

Combine pudding mix with 4 cups milk in large bowl; mix well. Stir in vanilla, condensed milk, sugar and strawberries. Add food coloring to obtain desired tint. Pour into 1-gallon ice cream freezer, adding enough remaining milk to fill canister. Freeze using manufacturer's directions. Yield: 16 (1-cup) servings.

Approx Per Serving: Cal 262; Prot 7 g; Carbo 45 g; Fiber 2 g;
    T Fat 7 g; 23% Calories from Fat; Chol 27 mg; Sod 161 mg.

Monda Daniel, Earth

VANILLA ICE CREAM

8 eggs
4 cups sugar
¹/₈ teaspoon salt
1 12-ounce can evaporated milk

1 14-ounce can sweetened
   condensed milk
2 tablespoons vanilla extract
3 to 4 quarts milk

Beat eggs at high speed in mixer bowl until lemon-colored. Add sugar and salt. Beat until thickened. Stir in evaporated milk, condensed milk and vanilla. Pour into 2-gallon ice cream freezer, adding enough milk to make 1¹/₂ gallons. Freeze using manufacturer's directions. Yield: 24 (1-cup) servings.

Approx Per Serving: Cal 330; Prot 10 g; Carbo 52 g; Fiber 0 g;
    T Fat 9 g; 27% Calories from Fat; Chol 103 mg; Sod 139 mg.

Mary Frances Gardenhire, O'Donnell

OLD-FASHIONED VANILLA ICE CREAM

5 egg yolks
1¹/₂ cups sugar
1 cup whipping cream
1 12-ounce can evaporated milk

2 teaspoons vanilla extract
¹/₈ teaspoon salt
8 to 10 cups milk
5 egg whites

Beat egg yolks in bowl until frothy. Add sugar, whipping cream and evaporated milk. Beat well until sugar is dissolved. Add vanilla, salt and half the milk; mix well. Beat egg whites in mixer bowl until stiff peaks form. Fold into milk mixture. Pour into ice cream freezer, adding enough remaining milk to make 1 gallon. Freeze using manufacturer's directions. Yield: 16 (1-cup) servings.

Approx Per Serving: Cal 271; Prot 9 g; Carbo 28 g; Fiber 0 g;
    T Fat 14 g; 46% Calories from Fat; Chol 114 mg; Sod 127 mg.

This was my Grandmother Bearden's recipe.

Linda Duckworth, Olton

CARAMELIZED APRICOT-APPLE KABOBS

12 ripe apricots, cut into halves
Juice of 1 orange
2 tart apples, peeled, cut into chunks

Juice of 1 lemon
12 large grapes
2 tablespoons sugar

Combine apricots and orange juice in bowl. Combine apples and lemon juice in bowl. Let stand for 30 minutes. Thread fruit onto skewers. Coat with sugar. Grill over medium coals for 5 to 6 minutes or until sugar caramelizes. Yield: 4 servings.

Approx Per Serving: Cal 142; Prot 2 g; Carbo 35 g; Fiber 3 g;
T Fat 1 g; 5% Calories from Fat; Chol 0 mg; Sod 1 mg.

Susan McDonald, Ransom Canyon

GRILLED PEAR AND BANANA KABOBS

2 pears, peeled, cut into chunks
2 bananas, peeled, cut into chunks
16 large strawberries, hulled

Juice of 2 lemons
3 tablespoons sugar

Combine fruit in bowl. Sprinkle with lemon juice and 1½ tablespoons sugar. Let stand for 30 minutes. Thread onto skewers; coat with remaining sugar. Grill over medium coals for 5 to 6 minutes or until sugar caramelizes. Yield: 4 servings.

Approx Per Serving: Cal 134; Prot 1 g; Carbo 41 g; Fiber 4 g;
T Fat 1 g; 6% Calories from Fat; Chol 0 mg; Sod 1 mg.

Susan McDonald, Ransom Canyon

SOME MORE SOME-MORES

8 1½-ounce plain milk chocolate
bars, broken into thirds

48 graham crackers
24 marshmallows, toasted

Make sandwich of 1 piece of chocolate and 2 crackers. Place marshmallow between chocolate and crackers. Press gently together. Yield: 24 servings.

Approx Per Serving: Cal 164; Prot 2 g; Carbo 3 g; Fiber 0 g;
T Fat 5 g; 26% Calories from Fat; Chol 0 mg; Sod 129 mg.

Robinson Crusoes: Spread crackers with peanut butter instead of chocolate.

Apple Some-Mores: Use round apple slices for crackers.

Girl Scouts of the USA

Cooking for-a-Crowd

Motley
County

Liquid silver slices Motley County.

The Pease River rumbles in spring thunderstorms,

Rancher's county,

Just enough yesterday to flavor today.

R.S.

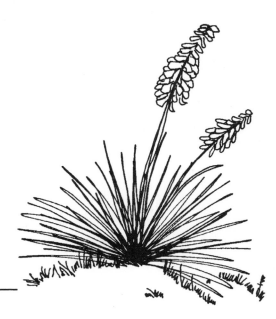

One-Two-Three Slaw

1 head cabbage, chopped
1/2 cup crushed pineapple
1/2 cup raisins
1/2 cup shredded carrot
1/2 cup chopped apple

1/2 cup chopped walnuts
1/2 cup vinegar
1 cup mayonnaise
1 1/2 cups sugar

Combine first 6 ingredients in large bowl; mix well. Mix vinegar, mayonnaise and sugar in bowl. Add to salad; toss to mix. Chill until serving time. Yield: 24 servings.

Approx Per Serving: Cal 150; Prot 1 g; Carbo 18 g; Fiber 1 g;
   T Fat 9 g; 51% Calories from Fat; Chol 6 mg; Sod 56 mg.

Suzzie Hubble, Dimmitt

Cherry Frozen Salad

1   21-ounce can cherry pie filling
1   20-ounce can crushed pineapple
1 cup chopped pecans

1   14-ounce can sweetened
   condensed milk
32 ounces whipped topping

Mix first 4 ingredients in bowl. Fold in whipped topping. Spoon into freezer containers or paper-lined muffin cups. Freeze until firm. Yield: 24 servings.

Approx Per Serving: Cal 249; Prot 2 g; Carbo 30 g; Fiber 1 g;
   T Fat 14 g; 50% Calories from Fat; Chol 6 mg; Sod 38 mg.

Darla Cloud, Lubbock

Perfection Salad

4 envelopes unflavored gelatin
1 cup cold water
6 cups boiling water
1 1/2 cups sugar
2 teaspoons salt
1 cup cider vinegar

1/4 cup lemon juice
1 pound cabbage, shredded
12 ounces celery, finely chopped
2 ounces green bell pepper, chopped
1   3-ounce can chopped pimento,
   drained

Soften gelatin in cold water in bowl. Add boiling water, sugar and salt, stirring until gelatin and sugar dissolve. Cool to room temperature. Add cider vinegar and lemon juice. Chill until thickened but not set. Fold in remaining ingredients. Spoon into salad mold. Chill until set. Unmold onto serving plate. Yield: 25 servings.

Approx Per Serving: Cal 60; Prot 1 g; Carbo 14 g; Fiber 1 g;
   T Fat <1 g; 1% Calories from Fat; Chol 0 mg; Sod 187 mg.

Betty Anne Kyle, Lubbock

RICH AND CHARLIE'S SALAD

1 head romaine lettuce, torn
1 head iceberg lettuce, torn
1 9-ounce jar artichoke hearts,
   drained
1 4-ounce jar chopped pimentos,
   drained

1 large red onion, chopped
Salt and pepper to taste
1 envelope Italian salad dressing mix
½ cup grated Parmesan cheese
⅓ cup vinegar
½ cup oil

Combine lettuces, artichokes, pimentos, onion, salt and pepper in salad bowl. Sprinkle with dry salad dressing mix and cheese; toss to mix. Add vinegar and oil at serving time; toss lightly. Yield: 12 servings.

Approx Per Serving: Cal 118; Prot 3 g; Carbo 4 g; Fiber 1 g;
T Fat 10 g; 77% Calories from Fat; Chol 3 mg; Sod 200 mg.

Jan Kennedy, Lubbock

BARBECUED BRISKET

2 tablespoons liquid smoke
2 tablespoons Worcestershire sauce
½ teaspoon salt
1 teaspoon garlic salt

1 teaspoon celery salt
1 to 2 teaspoons pepper
1 6 to 7-pound beef brisket
1 18-ounce bottle of barbecue sauce

Combine first 6 ingredients in shallow baking dish; mix well. Add beef, coating well. Marinate in refrigerator overnight, turning once. Cover tightly with foil. Bake at 250 degrees for 5 hours. Pour barbecue sauce over beef. Bake, uncovered, for 1 hour longer. Yield: 16 servings.

Approx Per Serving: Cal 289; Prot 37 g; Carbo <1 g; Fiber 0 g;
T Fat 11 g; 34% Calories from Fat; Chol 112 mg; Sod 653 mg.

Debbie Bergen, Lubbock

BEST BRISKET

1 14 to 16-pound brisket

2 jars Woody's Brisket Sauce

Combine brisket with brisket sauce in shallow dish. Marinate in refrigerator for 24 hours. Place brisket fat side up in baking pan. Add marinade. Bake, covered, at 350 degrees for 6 to 8 hours or until very tender, removing cover during last 2 hours of cooking time. Yield: 30 servings.

Nutritional information for this recipe is not available.

Roger Fields, Friona

BEST-EVER CHILI

9 pounds lean beef, chopped
3 quarts water
3 16-ounce cans tomatoes
6 medium onions, chopped
3 tablespoons sugar
1 tablespoon garlic powder
10 tablespoons chili powder

1 tablespoon cumin
1 tablespoon marjoram
9 tablespoons paprika
3 tablespoons salt
1 tablespoon black pepper
1 tablespoon cayenne pepper
6 to 12 tablespoons cornmeal

Brown beef lightly in large nonstick saucepan; drain. Add water, tomatoes and onions. Simmer for 1 to 1½ hours. Add sugar, garlic powder, chili powder, cumin, marjoram, paprika, salt, black pepper and cayenne pepper; mix well. Simmer for 45 minutes. Stir in cornmeal 1 tablespoon at a time, simmering until of desired consistency. Yield: 30 servings.

Approx Per Serving: Cal 325; Prot 27 g; Carbo 10 g; Fiber 2 g;
     T Fat 20 g; 55% Calories from Fat; Chol 89 mg; Sod 818 mg.

This old family-favorite recipe has been used for church suppers and youth meetings for years. A copy of it is taped to the kitchen of Leonard's Cafe in Floydada, where it has been served for 20 years.

Mrs. T. Kinder Farris, Floydada

"AND TWO LITTLE FISHES"

3 pounds ground beef
2 teaspoons onion powder
½ teaspoon garlic powder
2 teaspoons salt
1 teaspoon pepper

2 16-ounce cans tomatoes
2 16-ounce cans ranch-style beans
1 16-ounce package corn chips
1 pound Cheddar cheese, shredded

Brown ground beef with onion powder, garlic powder, salt and pepper in saucepan, stirring until crumbly; drain. Stir in tomatoes and beans. Layer corn chips, meat sauce and cheese ½ at a time in large baking pan or two 14-inch baking dishes. Bake, covered with foil, at 425 degrees for 20 minutes or until heated through. Yield: 16 servings.

Approx Per Serving: Cal 511; Prot 28 g; Carbo 28 g; Fiber 2 g;
     T Fat 32 g; 56% Calories from Fat; Chol 85 mg; Sod 995 mg.

Like the parable of the loaves and fishes in the Bible, this recipe feeds any number of hungry people.

Lorene Thompson, O'Donnell

BARBECUED MEATBALLS

2 cups catsup
1 cup packed brown sugar
2 tablespoons liquid smoke
1/4 cup dried onion flakes
3 pounds ground beef
1   13-ounce can evaporated milk
1 cup quick-cooking oats

1 cup cracker crumbs
2 eggs
1/2 cup chopped onion
1/2 teaspoon garlic powder
2 teaspoons chili powder
2 teaspoons salt
1/2 teaspoon pepper

Combine catsup, brown sugar, liquid smoke and onion flakes in bowl; mix well. Combine ground beef, evaporated milk, oats, cracker crumbs, eggs, chopped onion, garlic powder, chili powder, salt and pepper in bowl; mix well. Shape into 1-inch balls. Place in baking pan. Pour barbecue sauce over top. Bake at 350 degrees for 1 hour. May store meatballs in freezer and use as needed. Yield: 16 servings.

Approx Per Serving: Cal 360; Prot 20 g; Carbo 36 g; Fiber 1 g;
    T Fat 16 g; 38% Calories from Fat; Chol 91 mg; Sod 780 mg.

Louisa Wilson, Friona

MEXICAN FIESTA

4 pounds ground beef
3 large onions, chopped
2   16-ounce cans whole tomatoes
1   16-ounce can tomato sauce

2   6-ounce cans tomato purée
1   28-ounce can ranch-style beans
1 tablespoon chili powder
1 tablespoon garlic salt

Brown ground beef with onions in large saucepan, stirring until ground beef is crumbly; drain. Add tomatoes, tomato sauce, tomato purée, beans, chili powder and garlic salt; mix well. Simmer for 1 hour or until of desired consistency. Spoon into serving bowl. Arrange on table with separate bowls of crushed chips, cooked rice, sliced olives, shredded cheese, picante sauce, coconut, chopped onions, ground pecans, chopped tomatoes, shredded lettuce and shoestring potatoes. Allow guests to layer desired ingredients on plates. Yield: 20 servings.

Approx Per Serving: Cal 254; Prot 20 g; Carbo 13 g; Fiber 1 g;
    T Fat 14 g; 49% Calories from Fat; Chol 59 mg; Sod 699 mg.
    Nutritional information is for meat sauce only.

Jaquita Blevins, Post

Hillbilly Cabbage Rolls

1 large head cabbage
5 pounds ground pork
2 cups cooked rice
Sage, salt and pepper to taste

1   32-ounce can tomato juice
3   16-ounce cans whole tomatoes
2   8-ounce cans tomato sauce

Soak cabbage in large bowl of hot water, removing leaves as they become flexible. Combine ground pork with rice, sage, salt and pepper in bowl; mix well. Pour tomato juice into large saucepan. Spoon a small amount of pork mixture onto each cabbage leaf. Roll to enclose fillings, securing with wooden picks if necessary. Layer rolls in prepared saucepan, pouring 1 can of tomatoes over each layer. Top with tomato sauce. May add water if needed for desired consistency. Simmer, covered, over low to medium heat for 4 to 5 hours or until pork is cooked through. Yield: 20 servings.

Approx Per Serving: Cal 249; Prot 29 g; Carbo 12 g; Fiber 2 g;
    T Fat 9 g; 33% Calories from Fat; Chol 84 mg; Sod 480 mg.

This recipe from Germany is a family favorite from my grandmother;
we always have it on New Year's Day.

Jim Gross, El Paso

Serve-A-Dozen Lasagna

8 ounces Italian sausage
8 ounces ground beef
1/2 cup chopped onion
1/2 cup chopped celery
1/2 cup chopped carrot
1 clove of garlic, chopped
1   16-ounce can tomatoes, chopped
1   6-ounce can tomato paste

1 teaspoon sugar
2 teaspoons Italian seasoning
2 eggs, beaten
2 cups ricotta cheese
1/2 cup grated Parmesan cheese
2 tablespoons chopped parsley
8 lasagna noodles, cooked
8 ounces mozzarella cheese, shredded

Brown sausage and ground beef in 10-inch skillet, stirring until ground beef is crumbly; drain. Add onion, celery, carrot, garlic, tomatoes, tomato paste, sugar and Italian seasoning; mix well. Combine eggs, ricotta cheese, Parmesan cheese and parsley in bowl; mix well. Layer half the noodles, ricotta cheese mixture, remaining noodles, meat sauce and mozzarella cheese in baking dish. Bake at 350 degrees for 45 minutes to 1 hour or until bubbly. Yield: 12 servings.

Approx Per Serving: Cal 321; Prot 20 g; Carbo 22 g; Fiber 1 g;
    T Fat 17 g; 48% Calories from Fat; Chol 93 mg; Sod 383 mg.

Martha Beach, Lubbock

STROMBOLI

3 pounds sausage
6 loaves frozen bread dough, thawed
3 cups shredded Cheddar cheese

1½ pounds thinly sliced ham
3 cups shredded mozzarella cheese
2 tablespoons melted butter

Brown sausage in skillet, stirring until crumbly; drain. Roll dough into large rectangle on lightly floured surface. Spread sausage down middle third of dough; sprinkle with Cheddar cheese. Fold over 1 side to cover filling. Arrange ham on folded section; sprinkle with mozzarella cheese. Fold over remaining dough to cover filling. Press edges to seal. Brush with butter. Place on baking sheet. Bake at 400 degrees for 20 minutes. Yield: 24 servings.

Approx Per Serving: Cal 532; Prot 27 g; Carbo 62 g; Fiber 0 g;
    T Fat 22 g; 36% Calories from Fat; Chol 66 mg; Sod 1558 mg.

Diana Phillips, Abernathy

CHICKEN SPAGHETTI

6 pounds cut-up chicken
2 bay leaves
1 green bell pepper, chopped
1 clove of garlic, chopped
1 onion, chopped
1 cup chopped celery
¼ cup butter

2 pounds uncooked spaghetti
6 hard-boiled eggs, sliced
1 cup stuffed green olives
2 teaspoons Worcestershire sauce
2   10-ounce cans cream of mushroom
    soup
1 pound American cheese, shredded

Rinse chicken and pat dry. Combine with bay leaves and water to cover in large saucepan. Cook until tender. Drain, reserving broth; discard bay leaves. Cut chicken into bite-sized pieces, discarding skin and bone. Sauté green pepper, garlic, onion and celery in butter in skillet. Cook spaghetti *al dente* in water in saucepan; drain. Combine chicken, sautéed vegetables, spaghetti, eggs, olives, Worcestershire sauce, soup and ⅓ of the cheese in large bowl. Add 2 soup cans reserved broth; mix well. Spoon into large baking pan. Top with remaining cheese. Bake at 375 degrees for 1 hour. May cook in slow cooker or electric roaster if preferred. Yield: 30 servings.

Approx Per Serving: Cal 310; Prot 22 g; Carbo 25 g; Fiber 2 g;
    T Fat 13 g; 38% Calories from Fat; Chol 102 mg; Sod 510 mg.

Gail Threet, Lubbock

BARBECUE SAUCE

1½ cups oil
⅓ cup vinegar
2 cups catsup
1 cup prepared mustard
1 cup Worcestershire sauce

Tabasco sauce to taste
⅓ cup sugar
1 clove of garlic, finely chopped
Juice of 1 lemon

Combine oil, vinegar, catsup, mustard, Worcestershire sauce, Tabasco sauce, sugar, garlic and lemon juice in large saucepan; mix well. Simmer for 30 minutes, stirring frequently. May substitute cooking wine or garlic vinegar for vinegar. Yield: 24 servings.

Approx Per Serving: Cal 172; Prot 1 g; Carbo 11 g; Fiber <1 g;
　　T Fat 14 g; 72% Calories from Fat; Chol 0 mg; Sod 466 mg.

*This recipe came from Vinson Boring, a foreman on
George Littlefield White's Yellow House Ranch.*

Judy White, Littlefield

NANNIE'S DRESSING

3　7-ounce packages corn bread mix
1 gallon turkey broth
1　8-ounce package herb-seasoned
　 croutons
5 medium onions, chopped
2 stalks celery, chopped
4 medium apples, chopped

18 hard-boiled eggs, chopped
1½ cups chopped pecans
½ cup melted butter
1 cup half and half
1½ teaspoons sage
1 teaspoon poultry seasoning
Salt and pepper to taste

Prepare and bake corn bread mix using package directions. Cool corn bread and crumble into large bowl. Add turkey broth, croutons, onions, celery, apples, eggs, pecans, butter, half and half, sage, poultry seasoning, salt and pepper; mix well. Spoon into 9x13-inch baking dish sprayed with nonstick cooking spray. Bake at 350 degrees for 45 minutes. May add 1 can of cream of mushroom, chicken or celery soup if desired. Yield: 20 servings.

Approx Per Serving: Cal 438; Prot 16 g; Carbo 42 g; Fiber 2 g;
　　T Fat 24 g; 48% Calories from Fat; Chol 231 mg; Sod 3203 mg.

*My grandmother serves this to our family every
Thanksgiving and Christmas holiday. It is her modern version
of a recipe she got from her mother.*

Tammy Owens, Lubbock

APPLE RINGS

2 gallons sliced cucumbers
2 gallons water
2 cups lime
1 teaspoon alum
2 or 3 ounces red food coloring
3 cups vinegar

2 cups water
10 cups sugar
8 cinnamon sticks
1½ 3-ounce packages red hot
 cinnamon candies

Combine cucumbers with 2 gallons water and lime in blue enamel pan. Soak for 24 hours. Rinse well. Cover with fresh cold water in crock. Soak for 3 hours; drain. Add alum, food coloring, 1 cup vinegar and water to cover. Soak for 24 hours. Simmer for 2 hours; drain. Combine 2 cups vinegar, 2 cups water, sugar, cinnamon sticks and candies in saucepan. Bring to a boil. Pour over cucumbers in enamel pan. Soak for 24 hours. Repeat process twice, draining, reheating and soaking cucumbers. Drain liquid into saucepan. Bring to a boil. Pack cucumbers into 9 hot sterilized 1-pint jars. Fill with hot liquid, leaving ½ inch head space; seal with 2-piece lids. Yield: 9 pints.

Nutritional information for this recipe is not available.

This is my Aunt Betty's recipe. It takes several days, but the result is worth it.

Betty Bell, Levelland

PEACH CONSERVE

9 cups sliced firm peaches
Fruit-Fresh
¾ cup water
6 cups sugar

1 10-ounce jar maraschino cherries,
 drained, sliced
1 cup coarsely chopped pecans

Soak peaches in water to cover and Fruit-Fresh in bowl; drain. Combine with ¾ cup water and sugar in large heavy saucepan. Cook to desired consistency, stirring frequently. Add cherries and pecans. Cook for 5 minutes longer. Let cool in saucepan. Return to a boil. Spoon into 5 hot sterilized 1-pint jars, leaving ½ inch head space; seal with 2-piece lids. Process in boiling water bath for 5 minutes. Yield: 5 pints (160 tablespoons).

Approx Per Tablespoon: Cal 40; Prot <1 g; Carbo 9 g; Fiber <1 g;
 T Fat 1 g; 11% Calories from Fat; Chol 0 mg; Sod <1 mg.
 Nutritional information does not include Fruit-Fresh.

This was my Grandmother Dorsett's recipe.

Mickey Hall, Lubbock

Jalapeño Jelly

12 jalapeño peppers, seeded
1¹/₂ green bell peppers, seeded
6 cups sugar

1¹/₂ cups white vinegar
1   6-ounce bottle of liquid pectin
Green food coloring

Grind peppers in food grinder. Heat sugar in vinegar in saucepan until dissolved. Add peppers. Simmer for 10 minutes. Stir in pectin and food coloring. Spoon into hot sterilized jars, leaving ¹/₂ inch headspace; seal with 2-piece lids. Serve with cream cheese and wheat crackers or pork or chicken. Yield: 4 pints (128 tablespoons).

Approx Per Tablespoon: Cal 38; Prot <1 g; Carbo 8 g; Fiber <1 g;
    T Fat <1 g; 0% Calories from Fat; Chol 0 mg; Sod <1 mg.

Diana Phillips, Abernathy

Best Pickles on Earth

3¹/₂ cups sugar
¹/₂ cup each flour and dry mustard
¹/₄ cup each turmeric and salt
¹/₄ cup each mustard and celery seed
1 tablespoon pepper
¹/₄ cup olive oil

1 quart vinegar
1 cup dill pickle juice
5 pounds cabbage, finely chopped
12 dill pickles, finely chopped
4 large strong onions, finely chopped
3 cloves of garlic, minced

Mix first 8 ingredients in saucepan. Stir in liquids. Add vegetables. Bring to a boil. Cook for 15 to 20 minutes. Spoon into hot sterilized jars, leaving ¹/₂ inch headspace; seal with 2-piece lids. Yield: 6 pints (48 servings).

Approx Per Serving: Cal 106; Prot 2 g; Carbo 22 g; Fiber 2 g;
    T Fat 2 g; 18% Calories from Fat; Chol 0 mg; Sod 728 mg.

Joyce Nash, Lubbock

Green Tomato Pickles

¹/₂ gallon apple cider vinegar
6 cups sugar
1 cup salt

2 gallons green tomato quarters
¹/₂ gallon onion quarters
2 cups chopped hot peppers

Bring vinegar, sugar and salt to a boil in large saucepan. Add vegetables. Cook just until tomatoes and peppers change color; do not boil. Pack into hot sterilized jars, leaving ¹/₂ inch headspace; seal with 2-piece lids. Yield: 6 quarts (96 servings).

Approx Per Serving: Cal 63; Prot 1 g; Carbo 16 g; Fiber <1 g;
    T Fat <1 g; 0% Calories from Fat; Chol 0 mg; Sod 1070 mg.

Diana Phillips, Abernathy

WATERMELON RIND PICKLE

Thick watermelon rind
Green food coloring
Sugar
White vinegar

Whole allspice
Whole cloves
Cinnamon sticks

Scrape and cut away pink portion of watermelon from thick rind portions. Peel outer skin. Cut rind into thin pieces. Combine with water to cover and food coloring in large saucepan. Cook until tender; drain. Add ice water or crushed ice to cover. Let stand for 1 hour; drain. Weigh rind. Add 1 pound sugar and 1 cup vinegar for each pound of rind; mix well. Let stand for 12 hours. Cook for 1 hour. Place 12 allspice, 12 cloves and 1 cinnamon stick for each pound of pickle in hot sterilized jars. Add pickles, leaving 1/2 inch headspace; seal with 2-piece lids. Let stand for 1 week or longer before serving. Yield: variable.

Nutritional information for this recipe is not available.

Anne S. Glover, Lubbock

GREEN TOMATO MINCEMEAT

3 lemons
4 quarts sliced green tomatoes
2 quarts chopped apples
1   15-ounce package seedless raisins
4 pounds sugar

2 tablespoons cinnamon
2 tablespoons nutmeg
1 tablespoon salt
1 cup water

Grate yellow zest of lemons. Chop lemons and remaining rinds into small pieces. Combine lemon and zest with tomatoes, apples, raisins, sugar, cinnamon, nutmeg, salt and water in saucepan. Cook until thickened to desired consistency. Pack into 4 hot sterilized 1-quart jars, leaving 1/2 inch headspace; seal with 2-piece lids. Process in boiling water bath for 20 minutes. Yield: 4 quarts (64 servings).

Approx Per Serving: Cal 166; Prot 2 g; Carbo 42 g; Fiber 1 g;
     T Fat <1 g; 0% Calories from Fat; Chol 0 mg; Sod 113 mg.

Penny Morin, Lubbock

Green Tomato Relish

8 quarts green tomatoes
1 medium head cabbage
6 red bell peppers
6 cups vinegar

8 cups sugar
1/2 cup salt
2 teaspoons mixed pickling spices

Grind tomatoes, cabbage and bell peppers. Combine with vinegar, sugar and salt in saucepan. Add pickling spices tied in cheesecloth bag. Cook for 30 minutes; remove spices. Pack into hot sterilized jars, leaving 1/2 inch headspace; seal with 2-piece lids. Yield: 7 pints (56 servings).

Approx Per Serving: Cal 142; Prot 1 g; Carbo 36 g; Fiber <1 g;
    T Fat <1 g; 0% Calories from Fat; Chol 0 mg; Sod 929 mg.

Linda Quarles, Lubbock

Fresh Relish

Onions, finely chopped
Cucumbers, finely chopped
Sugar

Vinegar
Water

Combine onions and cucumbers in bowl. Add equal parts sugar, vinegar and water; mix to dissolve sugar completely. Store in refrigerator. Serve with red beans or black-eyed peas and corn bread. May heat mixture of sugar, vinegar and water and pour over vegetables in jars to preserve relish. Yield: variable.

Nutritional information for this recipe is not available.

Suzzie Hubble, Dimmitt

Pepper Relish

12 green bell peppers, coarsely ground
12 red bell peppers, coarsely ground
5 hot peppers, ground
5 large onions, ground

2 cups sugar
3 cups vinegar
1 teaspoon celery seed
1 tablespoon salt

Pour boiling water over bell peppers in bowl. Let stand for 10 minutes; drain. Repeat process; drain. Combine with hot peppers, onions, sugar, vinegar, celery seed and salt in saucepan. Cook for 15 minutes. Spoon into hot sterilized jars, leaving 1/2 inch headspace; seal with 2-piece lids. Yield: 4 quarts (64 servings).

Approx Per Serving: Cal 38; Prot 1 g; Carbo 10 g; Fiber 1 g;
    T Fat <1 g; 0% Calories from Fat; Chol 0 mg; Sod 101 mg.

Anne S. Glover, Lubbock

Breakfast & Brunch

Hockley County

Wildcatters and roughnecks,

Black Gold in Sundown,

Sunflowers following the sun.

Tractors floating on the spring soil

like ships in a brown sea in Hockley County.

R.S.

B.B.'s Morning Casserole

1 pound sausage
6 to 8 slices buttered bread
1   10-ounce can cream of mushroom
   soup

12 eggs, slightly beaten
1   4-ounce can chopped green chilies
1½ cups shredded Cheddar cheese

Brown sausage in skillet, stirring until crumbly; drain. Layer bread buttered side down and sausage in baking dish. Combine soup, eggs and chilies in bowl; mix well. Pour over sausage layer. Sprinkle cheese over top. Bake at 350 degrees for 30 minutes. May refrigerate overnight before baking. Yield: 12 servings.

Approx Per Serving: Cal 301; Prot 15 g; Carbo 12 g; Fiber <1 g;
   T Fat 21 g; 63% Calories from Fat; Chol 250 mg; Sod 762 mg.

Barbara Babb, Post

Breakfast Pizza

1   8-count can crescent rolls
6 eggs, beaten
½ cup cooked sausage
¼ cup chopped green bell pepper

1 cup hashed brown potatoes
½ cup Cheddar cheese
½ cup mozzarella cheese

Spread roll dough to cover bottom of 9x16-inch baking pan coated with nonstick cooking spray. Layer eggs, sausage, green pepper and potatoes in prepared pan. Sprinkle with cheeses. Bake at 350 degrees for 20 to 25 minutes. Yield: 8 servings.

Approx Per Serving: Cal 274; Prot 11 g; Carbo 17 g; Fiber <1 g;
   T Fat 18 g; 58% Calories from Fat; Chol 178 mg; Sod 439 mg.

Pat Cruse, Post

Chicken Rolls

½   12-ounce can evaporated milk
½ cup Cheddar cheese
1   8-count can crescent rolls

1   6-ounce can chunk chicken
½ cup shredded Cheddar cheese

Heat evaporated milk and ½ cup cheese in saucepan over low heat until cheese melts, stirring frequently. Pour into 8x8-inch baking dish. Separate roll dough into triangles. Spoon chicken and ½ cup cheese on each. Roll up. Arrange rolls in sauce. Bake at 350 degrees for 30 minutes. Yield: 8 servings.

Approx Per Serving: Cal 211; Prot 11 g; Carbo 14 g; Fiber 0 g;
   T Fat 12 g; 53% Calories from Fat; Chol 21 mg; Sod 415 mg.

Betty Wagnon, Muleshoe

Breakfast Casserole

2 tablespoons butter, softened
3 English muffins, cut into halves
1 pound mild pork sausage
1 4-ounce can chopped green chilies

3 cups shredded Cheddar cheese
1½ cups sour cream
12 eggs, beaten

Spread butter on muffins. Place buttered side down in 9x13-inch baking dish. Brown sausage in skillet, stirring until crumbly; drain. Layer half the sausage, half the drained chilies and half the cheese over muffins. Mix sour cream and eggs in bowl. Pour over layers. Repeat layers with remaining ingredients. Chill, covered, for 8 hours. Let stand at room temperature for 30 minutes. Bake, uncovered, at 350 degrees for 35 to 40 minutes. Yield: 10 servings.

Approx Per Serving: Cal 449; Prot 23 g; Carbo 11 g; Fiber <1 g;
    T Fat 35 g; 70% Calories from Fat; Chol 330 mg; Sod 800 mg.

Linda Thompson, Olton

Egg Casserole

1 pound sausage
12 eggs, beaten
2 cups milk

6 slices white bread, crumbled
2 cups shredded Cheddar cheese

Brown sausage in skillet, stirring until crumbly; drain. Combine with beaten eggs and milk in bowl; mix well. Spread bread crumbs in greased 9x13-inch baking dish. Pour egg mixture over bread. Sprinkle with cheese. Bake at 350 degrees for 1 hour. Yield: 10 servings.

Approx Per Serving: Cal 340; Prot 20 g; Carbo 12 g; Fiber <1 g;
    T Fat 23 g; 62% Calories from Fat; Chol 303 mg; Sod 605 mg.

*My son, Barry Corbin, star of TV's Northern Exposure, was raised
in Lubbock, Texas. This is one of his favorite recipes.*

Mrs. Kilmer Corbin, Lubbock

HOT HOMINY

1 16-ounce can white hominy, drained
½ cup each chopped onion and celery
½ cup hot chilies

1 10-ounce can cream of mushroom
   soup
6 to 8 slices Velveeta cheese

Mix first 5 ingredients in bowl. Spoon into greased 2-quart baking dish. Cover with cheese. Bake at 350 degrees for 30 minutes, stirring 2 times. Yield: 4 servings.

Approx Per Serving: Cal 365; Prot 16 g; Carbo 24 g; Fiber 1 g;
    T Fat 24 g; 57% Calories from Fat; Chol 55 mg; Sod 1728 mg.

Joann Rackler, Springlake

HUEVOS RANCHEROS

4 slices bacon, chopped
½ small onion, chopped
2 hot peppers, chopped
½ cup water

1 16-ounce can peeled whole
   tomatoes, crushed
4 ounces Velveeta cheese, chopped
6 fried eggs

Fry bacon with onion in skillet until bacon is crisp; drain. Stir in next 4 ingredients. Cook until cheese melts, stirring frequently. Serve over eggs. Yield: 6 servings.

Approx Per Serving: Cal 202; Prot 12 g; Carbo 6 g; Fiber 1 g;
    T Fat 14 g; 62% Calories from Fat; Chol 268 mg; Sod 606 mg.

Josie DeAnda, Abernathy

MUSHROOM QUICHE

1¼ pounds mushrooms, sliced
3 green onions, finely chopped
1 clove of garlic, minced
3 shallots, minced
3 tablespoons margarine
1¾ teaspoons each oregano and basil
¾ teaspoon marjoram

¼ teaspoon thyme
1¼ teaspoons salt
¼ teaspoon pepper
½ teaspoon dry mustard
4 eggs or egg substitute
¾ cup skim milk
1 unbaked 9-inch pie shell

Sauté first 4 ingredients in margarine in large skillet. Add seasonings; mix well. Cook for 2 minutes, stirring frequently. Let stand for 5 minutes. Beat eggs and milk in mixer bowl. Stir in mushroom mixture. Pour into pie shell. Bake at 375 degrees for 35 to 45 minutes or until golden brown and puffy. Yield: 6 servings.

Approx Per Serving: Cal 196; Prot 9 g; Carbo 20 g; Fiber 2 g;
    T Fat 10 g; 43% Calories from Fat; Chol 142 mg; Sod 585 mg.

First Lady Barbara Bush

SAUSAGE PINWHEELS

3 tablespoons shortening
2 cups flour
1/2 teaspoon salt

3 tablespoons baking powder
2/3 cup milk
1 pound pork sausage

Cut shortening into mixture of sifted dry ingredients until crumbly. Add milk; stir until soft dough forms. Roll into two 5x8-inch rectangles. Spread half the sausage on each rectangle. Roll up. Chill, wrapped, for 2 hours to overnight. Cut into slices. Place on baking sheet. Bake at 400 degrees for 10 to 15 minutes. Yield: 20 servings.

Approx Per Serving: Cal 109; Prot 4 g; Carbo 10 g; Fiber <1 g;
T Fat 6 g; 47% Calories from Fat; Chol 10 mg; Sod 343 mg.

Shirley Burress, Earth

ZUCCHINI-CHEESE SOUFFLÉ

4 eggs, beaten
1 cup baking mix
1/2 cup oil
3 cups shredded zucchini

1 teaspoon chopped parsley
1/2 cup finely chopped onion
1 cup shredded Cheddar cheese
Salt and pepper to taste

Mix eggs, baking mix and oil in bowl. Stir in remaining ingredients. Spoon into greased 8x8-inch baking dish. Bake at 350 degrees for 40 minutes. Yield: 4 servings.

Approx Per Serving: Cal 605; Prot 18 g; Carbo 29 g; Fiber 2 g;
T Fat 47 g; 69% Calories from Fat; Chol 243 mg; Sod 646 mg.

Brenda Parker, Lubbock

MEXICAN CHEESE GRITS

1 cup uncooked grits
1 teaspoon salt
4 cups boiling water
1 1/2 cups shredded Cheddar cheese
1/2 cup butter

1/2 cup milk
2 eggs, beaten
8 ounces jalapeño Velveeta cheese,
cubed
3 tablespoons picante sauce

Stir grits into salted boiling water in heavy saucepan. Bring to a boil again. Boil for 2 1/2 to 5 minutes, stirring occasionally. Add Cheddar cheese, butter, milk, eggs, jalapeño cheese and picante sauce, stirring until cheese melts. Spoon into greased 2-quart baking dish. Bake at 350 degrees for 1 hour. Yield: 6 servings.

Approx Per Serving: Cal 529; Prot 21 g; Carbo 23 g; Fiber 3 g;
T Fat 39 g; 67% Calories from Fat; Chol 181 mg; Sod 1272 mg.

Joan Thompson Porter, Lubbock

BAKED APPLES

6 apples
¼ cup raisins
½ cup packed brown sugar

2 tablespoons butter, softened
¼ cup water

Core apples ¾ of the way through. Mix raisins, brown sugar and butter in bowl. Fill apples with mixture. Wrap apples in foil. Pour water in bottom of slow cooker. Place apples in cooker. Cook on Low for 6 to 8 hours or until apples are tender. Yield: 6 servings.

Approx Per Serving: Cal 215; Prot 1 g; Carbo 47 g; Fiber 4 g;
    T Fat 4 g; 17% Calories from Fat; Chol 10 mg; Sod 43 mg.

Lee Ruth Krieg, Lubbock

THAT'S GOOD PEACHES

⅓ cup baking mix
⅔ cup oats
¼ teaspoon cinnamon

½ cup sugar
½ cup packed brown sugar
4 cups sliced peaches

Combine baking mix, oats, cinnamon, sugar and brown sugar in bowl; mix well. Stir in peaches. Spoon into slow cooker coated with nonstick cooking spray. Cook on Low for 4 to 6 hours. Yield: 6 servings.

Approx Per Serving: Cal 263; Prot 3 g; Carbo 62 g; Fiber 3 g;
    T Fat 2 g; 6% Calories from Fat; Chol 0 mg; Sod 99 mg.

Lee Ruth Krieg, Lubbock

SUNDAY BREAKFAST CAKE

½ cup milk
1 egg
¼ cup butter, melted
½ cup sugar
1 cup (scant) flour

1 tablespoon baking powder
¼ teaspoon cinnamon
½ teaspoon salt
2 tablespoons sugar
Cinnamon to taste

Stir milk and egg into slightly cooled butter in bowl. Sift in sugar, flour, baking powder, ¼ teaspoon cinnamon and salt, stirring just until smooth. Spoon into greased 8-inch baking dish. Sprinkle with mixture of 2 tablespoons sugar and cinnamon. Bake at 350 degrees for 25 minutes. Yield: 6 servings.

Approx Per Serving: Cal 252; Prot 4 g; Carbo 38 g; Fiber 1 g;
    T Fat 9 g; 34% Calories from Fat; Chol 59 mg; Sod 428 mg.

Barbara Babb, Post

CREAM CHEESE COFFEE CAKE

1½ cups butter, softened
½ cup flour
2 envelopes dry yeast
¼ cup warm water
1 cup warm milk
1 egg, slightly beaten

3 tablespoons sugar
½ teaspoon salt
4 cups flour
Cream Cheese Filling
Confectioners' Sugar Icing

Cream butter with ½ cup flour in bowl until light and fluffy. Chill for 45 minutes. Dissolve yeast in warm water. Add warm milk, egg, sugar and salt. Stir in 2 cups flour. Beat with spoon until smooth and elastic. Beat in remaining flour until blended. Shape dough into ball on floured surface; dust with additional flour. Roll into 16-inch square. Place chilled butter mixture on floured surface. Roll into 8x16-inch rectangle. Place on half the dough; fold up other half to enclose, sealing edges. Pound lightly with rolling pin to 12x16-inches. Fold ⅓ of dough over center. Fold remaining ⅓ over center. Chill for 30 minutes. Pound dough lightly into rectangle. Roll into 16-inch square. Repeat the folding over process. Roll into 16-inch square. Spread Cream Cheese Filling over dough. Repeat the folding porcess again, sealing edges. Cut into halves. Place sealed edges down in 2 greased 9-inch round baking pans. Slice into dough at 1-inch intervals. Let rise for 45 to 60 minutes or until almost doubled in bulk. Bake at 375 degrees for 25 minutes. Drizzle with Confectioners' Sugar Icing. Garnish with pecans. Yield: 12 servings.

Cream Cheese Filling

8 ounces cream cheese, softened
1 egg
1 tablespoon lemon juice
1 teaspoon grated lemon rind

¾ cup flour
2½ cups confectioners' sugar
¼ cup sour cream
½ cup pecans

Combine cream cheese, egg, lemon juice, lemon rind, flour, confectioners' sugar, sour cream and pecans in bowl; mix well.

Confectioners' Sugar Icing

2 cups sifted confectioners' sugar
½ teaspoon vanilla extract

3 tablespoons milk

Combine confectioners' sugar, vanilla and milk in bowl; stir until smooth.

Approx Per Serving: Cal 716; Prot 10 g; Carbo 90 g; Fiber 2 g;
    T Fat 36 g; 45% Calories from Fat; Chol 124 mg; Sod 365 mg.

*This is a recipe I learned to make as a teenager. I won first place
with it in the Texas 4-H food show.*

Connie Burt, Lubbock

Mom's Easy Coffee Cake

1 2-layer package yellow cake mix
1 envelope dry yeast
1 cup flour
2 eggs
2/3 cup water

1 21-ounce can cherry pie filling
5 tablespoons melted butter
1 cup confectioners' sugar
1 tablespoon corn syrup
1 tablespoon water

Beat 1 1/2 cups cake mix and next 4 ingredients in mixer bowl for 2 minutes. Spread in greased 9x13-inch baking pan. Spoon pie filling over dough. Sprinkle mixture of remaining cake mix and butter over top. Bake at 375 degrees for 30 minutes. Drizzle with mixture of remaining ingredients. Yield: 12 servings.

Approx Per Serving: Cal 372; Prot 3 g; Carbo 67 g; Fiber 1 g;
    T Fat 9 g; 22% Calories from Fat; Chol 48 mg; Sod 330 mg.

Linda Thompson, Olton

Peanut Butter Breakfast Cookies

3/4 cup margarine, softened
2/3 cup peanut butter
2/3 cup packed brown sugar
2 eggs, beaten

1 1/4 cups flour
1 teaspoon baking soda
1/4 teaspoon salt
3 cups cornflakes cereal

Beat first 3 ingredients in bowl. Add eggs. Beat until light and fluffy. Add mixture of flour, baking soda and salt; mix well. Stir in cereal. Drop by heaping tablespoonfuls onto ungreased cookie sheet. Bake at 350 degrees for 10 minutes or until golden brown. Yield: 36 (1-cookie) servings.

Approx Per Serving: Cal 111; Prot 2 g; Carbo 11 g; Fiber <1 g;
    T Fat 7 g; 52% Calories from Fat; Chol 12 mg; Sod 131 mg.

Mrs. T. Kinder Farris, Floydada

Chili-Cheese Bread

2 cups pancake mix
1 cup milk
2 eggs

1 4-ounce can chopped green chilies
1 cup shredded longhorn cheese

Mix first 3 ingredients in bowl. Spread chilies in 8x8-inch baking pan coated with nonstick cooking spray. Layer cheese and prepared pancake mixture over top. Bake at 400 degrees for 15 to 20 minutes or until golden brown. Yield: 9 servings.

Approx Per Serving: Cal 205; Prot 9 g; Carbo 25 g; Fiber 0 g;
    T Fat 8 g; 34% Calories from Fat; Chol 64 mg; Sod 575 mg.

Connie Dominguez, Muleshoe

PECAN BISCUITS

½ cup margarine
½ cup chopped pecans
1 cup packed brown sugar

2 tablespoons water
2 10-ounce cans flaky biscuits

Melt margarine in small saucepan. Stir in pecans, brown sugar and water. Bring to a boil, stirring occasionally. Remove from heat. Cut biscuits into halves. Shape each half into a ball. Place 20 balls in bottom of 12-cup bundt pan. Drizzle half the sauce over top. Layer remaining biscuit balls and sauce over top. Bake at 375 degrees for 20 minutes or until biscuits test done. Invert onto serving plate. Yield: 10 servings.

Approx Per Serving: Cal 354; Prot 3 g; Carbo 47 g; Fiber 1 g;
    T Fat 17 g; 44% Calories from Fat; Chol 2 mg; Sod 617 mg.

Lauren Busby, Springlake

BISCUITS

2 cups flour
1½ teaspoons baking powder
¼ teaspoon baking soda

⅛ teaspoon salt
½ cup buttermilk
2 tablespoons oil

Sift first 4 ingredients together into bowl. Add buttermilk and 2 tablespoons oil; stir until moistened. Pat dough ½ inch thick on floured surface. Cut with biscuit cutter. Place in oiled 9-inch round baking dish; turn biscuits to coat with oil. Bake at 450 degrees for 15 minutes or until golden brown. Yield: 8 servings.

Approx Per Serving: Cal 151; Prot 4 g; Carbo 25 g; Fiber 1 g;
    T Fat 4 g; 23% Calories from Fat; Chol 1 mg; Sod 137 mg.

Carol Huggins, Lockney

MONKEY BREAD

3 10-ounce cans biscuits, cut into
    fourths
½ cup sugar

1 tablespoon cinnamon
½ cup margarine
½ cup packed brown sugar

Shake biscuits in mixture of sugar and cinnamon in plastic bag. Arrange in bundt pan. Melt margarine and brown sugar in small saucepan over low heat, stirring frequently. Pour over biscuits. Bake at 350 degrees for 30 minutes. Invert onto serving plate immediately. Yield: 10 servings.

Approx Per Serving: Cal 367; Prot 4 g; Carbo 52 g; Fiber 1 g;
    T Fat 15 g; 38% Calories from Fat; Chol 3 mg; Sod 860 mg.

Jan Kennedy, Lubbock

BANANA-NUT MUFFINS

1½ cups sugar
½ cup shortening
2 eggs
2 cups flour
⅛ teaspoon salt

1 teaspoon baking soda
¼ cup buttermilk
4 bananas, mashed
½ cup chopped pecans

Cream sugar, shortening and eggs in bowl until light and fluffy. Add flour, salt, baking soda, buttermilk, bananas and pecans in order listed, mixing well after each addition. Spoon into greased miniature muffin cups. Bake at 350 degrees for 12 minutes or until muffins test done. Yield: 96 (1-muffin) servings.

Approx Per Serving: Cal 41; Prot 1 g; Carbo 6 g; Fiber <1 g;
    T Fat 2 g; 35% Calories from Fat; Chol 4 mg; Sod 14 mg.

Beth Mims, Muleshoe

ENGLISH MUFFINS

1 cake yeast
1¼ cups lukewarm water
1 tablespoon sugar

¾ teaspoon salt
3 tablespoons shortening
3½ to 3¾ cups sifted flour

Dissolve yeast, sugar and salt in water in large bowl. Stir in shortening. Add flour ½ at a time, mixing with wooden spoon until mixture forms a ball. Knead on lightly floured surface until dough is smooth and elastic. Place in greased bowl, turning to grease surface. Let rise, covered with damp towel, in warm place for about 2 hours or until doubled in bulk. Punch dough down. Roll 1 inch thick; cut with 2½-inch round cutter dipped in flour. Place 1 inch apart on lightly greased and cornmeal-coated baking sheet. Let rise, covered with damp towel, for 50 minutes; remove towel. Let rise for 10 minutes longer. Place ungreased lightweight baking sheet on top of muffins. Bake at 375 degrees for 25 minutes. Yield: 12 servings.

Approx Per Serving: Cal 165; Prot 4 g; Carbo 29 g; Fiber 1 g;
    T Fat 4 g; 20% Calories from Fat; Chol 0 mg; Sod 134 mg.

Anne Thompson, Lubbock

AUNT NAN'S HOMINY MUFFINS

1 cup cooked hominy grits	4 teaspoons baking powder
¼ cup shortening, melted	1 tablespoon sugar
1 cup milk	2 eggs, well beaten
1 cup flour	½ teaspoon salt

Mix grits and shortening in bowl. Stir in milk. Add flour gradually, mixing well after each addition. Add baking powder, sugar, eggs and salt; mix well. Spoon into muffin cups. Bake at 350 degrees for 25 to 30 minutes. Note: Muffins will appear soggy. Yield: 12 servings.

Approx Per Serving: Cal 119; Prot 3 g; Carbo 13 g; Fiber 1 g;
    T Fat 6 g; 46% Calories from Fat; Chol 38 mg; Sod 219 mg.

*This, along with baked ham and scrambled eggs, was breakfast at my
Aunt Nelly Gadsden's almost every morning.*

Myra G. Burris, Lubbock

MYSTERY MUFFINS

1 cup self-rising flour	½ cup milk
3 tablespoons mayonnaise	

Combine flour, mayonnaise and milk in bowl; mix well. Spoon into greased muffin cups. Bake at 425 degrees for 15 to 20 minutes or until muffins test done. Do not substitute mayonnaise-type salad dressing for mayonnaise. Yield: 6 servings.

Approx Per Serving: Cal 135; Prot 3 g; Carbo 17 g; Fiber 1 g;
    T Fat 6 g; 42% Calories from Fat; Chol 7 mg; Sod 272 mg.

Myra G. Burris, Lubbock

APPLE-CINNAMON PANCAKES

1 egg, lightly beaten	1 7-ounce package apple-cinnamon
¾ cup milk	muffin mix

Combine egg, milk and muffin mix in bowl; stir just until moistened. Pour onto hot lightly greased griddle. Bake until brown on both sides, turning once. Yield: 8 servings.

Approx Per Serving: Cal 136; Prot 3 g; Carbo 18 g; Fiber 0 g;
    T Fat 6 g; 37% Calories from Fat; Chol 30 mg; Sod 252 mg.

Sylvia Gonzalez, Lubbock

Maple Syrup

4 cups sugar
1/2 cup packed brown sugar
2 cups water

1 teaspoon vanilla extract
1 teaspoon maple extract

Stir sugars and water in saucepan until dissolved. Bring to a boil over medium-high heat. Boil gently, covered, for 10 minutes. Do not stir. Cool slightly. Add flavorings. Store unused portion in refrigerator. Yield: 16 (2-ounce) servings.

Approx Per Serving: Cal 226; Prot 0 g; Carbo 58 g; Fiber 0 g;
T Fat 0 g; 0% Calories from Fat; Chol 0 mg; Sod 5 mg.

Kay Alexander, Brownfield

Dilly Cheese Scones

1/4 cup butter
2 cups flour
1 tablespoon baking powder
2 teaspoons dillweed
1 teaspoon salt

1/2 teaspoon dry mustard
1 cup shredded Cheddar cheese
1 cup milk
1 egg
1 teaspoon water

Cut butter into next 5 ingredients in bowl until crumbly. Add cheese. Stir in milk. Knead on floured surface 5 to 10 times. Pat dough 1/2 inch thick. Cut with 2-inch cutter. Place on ungreased baking sheet. Brush with mixture of egg and water. Bake at 425 degrees for 15 minutes or until brown. Serve warm. Yield: 18 servings.

Approx Per Serving: Cal 112; Prot 4 g; Carbo 12 g; Fiber <1 g;
T Fat 6 g; 45% Calories from Fat; Chol 27 mg; Sod 243 mg.

Abisue' Linn, Slaton

Portifield Pudding

1   10-count can biscuits
1/2 cup melted butter
3/4 cup milk

1 cup sugar
2 teaspoons cinnamon
1 1/2 teaspoons vanilla extract

Place quartered biscuits in 9x9-inch baking pan. Pour mixture of remaining ingredients over top. Bake at 350 degrees for 20 minutes. Yield: 10 servings.

Approx Per Serving: Cal 237; Prot 2 g; Carbo 31 g; Fiber <1 g;
T Fat 12 g; 45% Calories from Fat; Chol 28 mg; Sod 335 mg.

Made famous by the Portifield family of Tahoka.

Lana Banks, Springlake

Desserts

Floyd County

There is an earthiness
when the tractors turn the soil in Floyd County.
It is damp dirt, renewal, reaffirmation.
It is mother nature's baking bread smell,
a bond between farm families and the earth,
Another year of financing from the greatest banker.

R.S.

ANGEL-GELATIN DESSERT

1 6-ounce package strawberry gelatin
2 cups boiling water
1 12-ounce package frozen
  strawberries, thawed

2 bananas, sliced
2 cups whipping cream, whipped
1 12-ounce angel food cake, torn into
  chunks

Dissolve gelatin in water in bowl. Add strawberries; mix well. Chill overnight or until set. Cut into squares. Alternate layers of bananas, gelatin squares, whipped cream and cake in serving bowl until all ingredients are used. Yield: 8 servings.

Approx Per Serving: Cal 425; Prot 6 g; Carbo 54 g; Fiber 2 g;
  T Fat 22 g; 46% Calories from Fat; Chol 82 mg; Sod 307 mg.

Nelda Merriott, Muleshoe

APPLE DUMPLINGS

6 apples, cored, cut into halves
2 tablespoons brown sugar
1½ teaspoons cinnamon
2 tablespoons chopped pecans

2 unbaked 9-inch pie shells, cut into
  12 wedges
2 cups sugar
1 cup water

Place apple half, brown sugar, cinnamon and pecans on each pastry wedge; seal. Place in 9x13-inch baking dish. Bring sugar and water to a boil in saucepan. Pour over dumplings. Bake at 350 degrees for 1 hour. Yield: 12 servings.

Approx Per Serving: Cal 332; Prot 2 g; Carbo 59 g; Fiber 2 g;
  T Fat 11 g; 29% Calories from Fat; Chol 0 mg; Sod 185 mg.

Brenda Farr, Lubbock

APRICOT DELIGHT

2 cups crushed graham crackers
1 cup confectioners' sugar
1 cup chopped pecans
½ cup melted butter
16 ounces cream cheese, softened

1 cup sugar
2 eggs
1 21-ounce can apricot pie filling
1 cup whipping cream, whipped

Press mixture of first 4 ingredients into 9x13-inch baking pan. Beat cream cheese, sugar and eggs in mixer bowl. Pour over crumb mixture. Bake at 350 degrees for 20 minutes. Cool. Spread with pie filling and whipped cream. Chill. Yield: 15 servings.

Approx Per Serving: Cal 466; Prot 5 g; Carbo 46 g; Fiber 1 g;
  T Fat 30 g; 57% Calories from Fat; Chol 100 mg; Sod 267 mg.

Jenna Parish, Springlake

Banana Split Cake

2 cups graham cracker crumbs
1/2 cup melted margarine
3 cups confectioners' sugar
3 eggs
5 bananas, sliced

1   16-ounce can crushed pineapple
2 cups strawberries
8 ounces whipped topping
1/2 cup chopped pecans

Mix graham cracker crumbs and melted margarine in bowl. Press into 9x13-inch baking pan. Beat confectioners' sugar and eggs in mixer bowl for 15 minutes. Spread over crumb mixture. Cover with bananas, pineapple and strawberries. Spread whipped topping over fruit. Sprinkle with pecans. Chill overnight. Cut into squares. Yield: 15 servings.

Approx Per Serving: Cal 370; Prot 4 g; Carbo 57 g; Fiber 2 g;
T Fat 16 g; 37% Calories from Fat; Chol 43 mg; Sod 188 mg.

Joanne Flusche, Idalou

Cheesecake

1 cup graham cracker crumbs
1/4 cup melted margarine
1 tablespoon sugar
1/8 teaspoon cinnamon
1 1/3 cups sugar
40 ounces cream cheese, softened

3 tablespoons flour
5 eggs
2 egg yolks
3/4 cup milk
1 tablespoon vanilla extract
1   21-ounce can cherry pie filling

Spray chilled 9-inch springform pan with nonstick cooking spray. Mix graham cracker crumbs, melted margarine, sugar and cinnamon in bowl. Press into prepared pan. Cream sugar, cream cheese and flour in mixer bowl until light and fluffy. Add eggs, egg yolks, milk and vanilla; beat well. Pour over graham cracker mixture. Bake at 475 degrees for 13 minutes. Reduce oven temperature to 200 degrees. Bake for 1 hour. Turn off oven. Let cheesecake stand in closed oven overnight or until cooled completely. Chill until serving time. Top with pie filling. Yield: 16 servings.

Approx Per Serving: Cal 455; Prot 9 g; Carbo 37 g; Fiber 1 g;
T Fat 31 g; 61% Calories from Fat; Chol 172 mg; Sod 328 mg.

Betty Wagnon, Muleshoe

OUR FAVORITE CHEESECAKE

¾ cup sugar	1 9-inch graham cracker pie shell
12 ounces cream cheese, softened	1 cup sour cream
2 teaspoons vanilla extract	1 teaspoon vanilla extract
½ teaspoon lemon juice	4½ teaspoons sugar
2 eggs, beaten	

Cream ¾ cup sugar, cream cheese, 2 teaspoons vanilla and lemon juice in mixer bowl until light and fluffy. Add eggs; beat well. Pour into pie shell. Bake at 350 degrees for 15 to 20 minutes or until browned. Cool for 5 minutes. Combine sour cream, 1 teaspoon vanilla and 4½ teaspoons sugar in bowl; mix well. Pour over cheesecake. Bake at 350 degrees for 10 minutes. Chill overnight. Serve with fresh strawberries or peaches. Yield: 6 servings.

Approx Per Serving: Cal 694; Prot 10 g; Carbo 66 g; Fiber 1 g;
 T Fat 44 g; 57% Calories from Fat; Chol 150 mg; Sod 530 mg.

Pansy Byers, Dimmitt

PARTY CHEESECAKE

2 cups flour	3 tablespoons grated lemon rind
2 tablespoons sugar	½ to ¾ cup lemon juice
½ cup shortening	3 tablespoons flour
½ cup butter	1 cup sugar
24 ounces cream cheese, softened	2 cups sour cream
4 eggs	1 teaspoon vanilla extract
2 cups sugar	

Combine flour, 2 tablespoons sugar and shortening in bowl. Cut in butter until crumbly. Press into buttered 8x12-inch baking dish. Bake at 375 degrees for 20 minutes. Combine cream cheese and eggs in mixer bowl; beat well. Add 2 cups sugar, lemon rind, lemon juice and flour; mix well. Pour over baked crust. Bake at 375 degrees for 35 to 40 minutes or until set. Cool. Combine 1 cup sugar, sour cream and vanilla in bowl; mix well. Spread over cooled cheesecake. Yield: 15 servings.

Approx Per Serving: Cal 591; Prot 8 g; Carbo 59 g; Fiber 1 g;
 T Fat 37 g; 55% Calories from Fat; Chol 136 mg; Sod 222 mg.

This recipe comes from the 6666 Ranch which along with the Triangle Ranch spreads over a large part of the Texas range land. Together these two ranches continue to uphold the standards of quality and performance their founders established years ago.

Karen Blodgett, First Lady of 6666 Ranch, Guthrie

TRIPLE CHOCOLATE DELIGHT

1 2-layer package chocolate cake mix
2 cups sour cream
1 4-ounce package chocolate instant
   pudding mix

³/₄ cup oil
4 eggs
1 cup water
1 cup chocolate chips

Spray slow cooker with nonstick cooking spray. Mix next 6 ingredients in bowl. Stir in chocolate chips. Pour into slow cooker. Cook on Low for 6 to 8 hours or until of desired consistency. Serve over vanilla ice cream in bowl. Yield: 8 servings.

Approx Per Serving: Cal 777; Prot 9 g; Carbo 82 g; Fiber 1 g;
    T Fat 48 g; 55% Calories from Fat; Chol 132 mg; Sod 556 mg.

Lee Ruth Krieg, Lubbock

CHERRY COBBLER

1 21-ounce can cherry pie filling
¹/₂ teaspoon cinnamon
¹/₄ cup butter

1 unbaked 9-inch pie shell
¹/₄ cup milk
¹/₄ cup sugar

Spread pie filling in 8-inch square glass baking dish. Sprinkle with cinnamon; dot with butter. Top with pie shell. Pour milk over all. Sprinkle with sugar. Bake at 425 degrees for 15 minutes or until browned and bubbly. Yield: 6 servings.

Approx Per Serving: Cal 350; Prot 3 g; Carbo 47 g; Fiber 2 g;
    T Fat 18 g; 45% Calories from Fat; Chol 22 mg; Sod 282 mg.

Debi Moses, Wife of Lubbock Independent School Superintendent Mike Moses, Lubbock

QUICK COBBLER

¹/₂ cup melted butter
1 cup flour
1 cup sugar
1 teaspoon baking powder

¹/₈ teaspoon salt
1 cup milk
1 16-ounce can cherries
1 cup sugar

Pour melted butter into 9x13-inch baking pan. Combine flour, 1 cup sugar, baking powder, salt and milk in bowl; mix well. Pour into prepared pan. Combine cherries and 1 cup sugar in saucepan. Bring to a boil. Spoon over flour mixture. Bake at 350 degrees for 45 minutes. May substitute favorite fruit for cherries. Yield: 15 servings.

Approx Per Serving: Cal 223; Prot 2 g; Carbo 40 g; Fiber <1 g;
    T Fat 7 g; 27% Calories from Fat; Chol 19 mg; Sod 100 mg.

Kristi Townsen, Lubbock

QUICK FRUIT COBBLER

1/2 cup butter
2 21-ounce cans blueberry pie filling
1 cup flour
1 cup sugar

1 teaspoon baking powder
1/8 teaspoon nutmeg
1 cup (or more) milk

Melt butter in baking pan. Add pie filling. Combine flour, sugar, baking powder and nutmeg in bowl. Stir in enough milk to make of batter consistency. Pour over pie filling. Bake at 350 degrees for 1 hour. Yield: 15 servings.

Approx Per Serving: Cal 222; Prot 2 g; Carbo 40 g; Fiber 1 g;
T Fat 7 g; 27% Calories from Fat; Chol 19 mg; Sod 105 mg.

Lori Leal, Muleshoe

PEACH COBBLER

2 29-ounce cans peaches
1 1/2 cups flour
1/8 teaspoon baking powder
1/8 teaspoon salt
1/2 cup shortening

1/2 cup boiling water
1 cup sugar
1/2 cup margarine
1/3 cup sugar
Cinnamon to taste

Drain 1 can peaches, discarding juice. Mix flour, baking powder, salt and shortening in bowl with pastry blender. Add boiling water; mix quickly. Knead 2 to 3 times on lightly floured surface. Roll into 10x14-inch rectangle. Cut into 2-inch strips. Place 1/3 of the strips on baking sheet. Bake at 400 degrees for 10 minutes. Place baked strips in 9x13-inch baking pan. Combine drained peaches, undrained peaches and 1 cup sugar in saucepan. Cook until sugar is dissolved, stirring frequently. Pour over baked strips. Top with remaining pastry strips. Dot with margarine. Sprinkle with 1/3 cup sugar and cinnamon. Bake at 400 degrees for 40 minutes or until browned. Serve with whipped cream. Yield: 8 servings.

Approx Per Serving: Cal 581; Prot 4 g; Carbo 92 g; Fiber 3 g;
T Fat 25 g; 37% Calories from Fat; Chol 0 mg; Sod 186 mg.

When we work sheep, this cobbler is always a hit with the cowboys.

Betty Dennis, Gail

Easy Peach Cobbler

3 16-ounce cans sliced peaches
1/2 cup butter
1 cup baking mix

1 cup sugar
1 cup milk

Drain 1 can peaches, discarding juice. Melt butter in 9x13-inch baking pan. Combine baking mix, sugar and milk in bowl; mix well. Pour into prepared pan. Add drained and undrained peaches. Bake at 350 degrees for 1 hour or until golden brown. Serve warm or slightly cooled with ice cream or whipped topping. Yield: 8 servings.

Approx Per Serving: Cal 411; Prot 3 g; Carbo 71 g; Fiber 2 g;
   T Fat 15 g; 31% Calories from Fat; Chol 35 mg; Sod 319 mg.

This recipe was handed down from my grandmother, who got it while working in a boarding house in Claude, Texas.

Connie Ontiveros, Springlake

Ice Delight

2 cups sugar
2 cups hot water
Juice of 2 lemons
1 6-ounce can frozen orange juice
   concentrate

2 bananas, coarsely crushed
1 16-ounce can crushed pineapple
1 4-ounce bottle of maraschino
   cherries, chopped

Dissolve sugar in hot water in bowl. Add lemon juice, orange juice concentrate, bananas, pineapple and cherries; mix well. Pour into freezer-proof container. Freeze until firm, stirring several times. Let stand for 30 minutes. Serve in sherbet glasses. Yield: 12 servings.

Approx Per Serving: Cal 211; Prot 1 g; Carbo 54 g; Fiber 1 g;
   T Fat <1 g; 1% Calories from Fat; Chol 0 mg; Sod 2 mg.

This is convenient to have in the freezer when a dessert is needed.

Helen Otken, Lubbock

LEMON FREEZE

1¹/2 cups graham cracker crumbs
¹/2 cup butter, softened
3 egg yolks, beaten
Juice of 2 lemons

1 14-ounce can sweetened
   condensed milk
3 egg whites
2 tablespoons sugar

Mix graham cracker crumbs and butter in bowl. Pat into 9x12-inch glass dish, reserving ¹/2 cup crumbs. Combine egg yolks, lemon juice and condensed milk in bowl; mix well. Beat egg whites in mixer bowl. Add sugar; beat until stiff. Fold into egg yolk mixture. Pour over crumb mixture. Sprinkle with ¹/2 cup crumbs. Freeze until firm. Yield: 8 servings.

Approx Per Serving: Cal 402; Prot 8 g; Carbo 49 g; Fiber 1 g;
    T Fat 20 g; 45% Calories from Fat; Chol 128 mg; Sod 320 mg.

Mary Edna Hendrix, Dimmitt

PEACH PUDDING

¹/4 cup milk
4 cups bread cubes
1 cup butter, softened

3 eggs, beaten
2 cups sugar
1 16-ounce can peaches

Pour milk over bread cubes in large bowl. Cream butter, eggs and sugar in mixer bowl until light and fluffy. Add to milk mixture. Stir in peaches with juice. Spoon into 9x13-inch baking pan. Bake at 325 degrees for 1 hour. Yield: 12 servings.

Approx Per Serving: Cal 341; Prot 3 g; Carbo 46 g; Fiber 1 g;
    T Fat 17 g; 44% Calories from Fat; Chol 95 mg; Sod 203 mg.

Zelma Hale, Abernathy

CHOCOLATE PUDDING

3 cups sugar
2 tablespoons flour
3 tablespoons baking cocoa
2 eggs, beaten
¹/2 teaspoon salt

5 cups milk
¹/8 cup water
1 teaspoon vanilla extract
¹/4 cup butter

Combine first 7 ingredients in saucepan; mix well. Cook for 10 to 15 minutes or until thickened, stirring frequently. Beat in vanilla and butter. Yield: 16 servings.

Approx Per Serving: Cal 234; Prot 4 g; Carbo 42 g; Fiber <1 g;
    T Fat 6 g; 24% Calories from Fat; Chol 45 mg; Sod 132 mg.

Tami Bolyard, Tahoka

Rice Pudding

2 cups milk
½ cup rice
½ cup raisins
¼ cup butter
3 eggs, beaten

2 cups milk
½ cup sugar
1 teaspoon vanilla extract
½ teaspoon salt
Cinnamon to taste

Combine 2 cups milk, rice and raisins in saucepan. Bring to a boil, stirring occasionally. Simmer, covered, over low heat for 15 minutes, stirring occasionally. Stir in butter. Combine eggs, 2 cups milk, sugar, vanilla and salt in bowl; mix well. Add to rice mixture; mix well. Pour into buttered 6x10-inch baking dish. Bake at 325 degrees for 30 minutes. Sprinkle with cinnamon. Bake for 30 minutes longer. Yield: 8 servings.

Approx Per Serving: Cal 278; Prot 7 g; Carbo 36 g; Fiber 1 g;
    T Fat 12 g; 38% Calories from Fat; Chol 112 mg; Sod 261 mg.

Debbie Lovelady, Muleshoe

Punch Bowl Cake

2 21-ounce cans cherry pie filling
1 2-layer package yellow cake mix
2 4-ounce packages vanilla instant
   pudding mix, prepared

1 16-ounce can crushed pineapple
1 7-ounce can coconut
16 ounces whipped topping
2 cups chopped pecans

Reserve ½ cup pie filling for topping. Prepare and bake cake mix using package directions. Break cooled cake into pieces. Layer cake, pudding, pineapple, coconut and remaining pie filling in punch bowl. Top with whipped topping, pecans and reserved pie filling. Yield: 30 servings.

Approx Per Serving: Cal 344; Prot 4 g; Carbo 49 g; Fiber 2 g;
    T Fat 17 g; 41% Calories from Fat; Chol 4 mg; Sod 201 mg.

This is a favorite recipe at the Senior Citizens Center in Shallowater, Texas.

Joan Blackmon, Lubbock

LONG JOHNS

1 envelope yeast	¼ teaspoon salt
¼ cup warm water	2¾ cups (or more) flour
1 teaspoon sugar	Oil for deep frying
1 egg, beaten	¼ cup butter
¾ cup warm water	¼ cup milk
¼ cup shortening	⅓ cup packed brown sugar
¼ cup sugar	1 cup (or more) confectioners' sugar

Mix yeast, ¼ cup warm water and 1 teaspoon sugar in bowl. Let rise for 5 minutes. Combine egg, ¾ cup warm water, shortening, ¼ cup sugar, salt and 1¼ cups flour in large bowl; mix well. Add yeast; stir until well blended. Add enough flour to form dough. Roll into thin rectangle on lightly floured surface. Cover with wet cloth. Let rise for 30 minutes. Cut into 2x6-inch strips. Deep-fry in hot oil until lightly browned. Combine butter, milk and brown sugar in saucepan. Bring to a boil. Boil for 1 minute. Stir in enough confectioners' sugar to make of desired consistency. Spoon over cooked strips. Yield: 18 servings.

Approx Per Serving: Cal 181; Prot 3 g; Carbo 29 g; Fiber 1 g;
T Fat 6 g; 30% Calories from Fat; Chol 19 mg; Sod 59 mg.
Nutritional information does not include oil for deep frying.

Una Childress, Levelland

GERMAN SWEET RICE

1 cup long grain rice	Sugar to taste
Milk	Cinnamon to taste

Place rice in top of double boiler. Add milk to cover. Cook over hot water for 1 to 2 hours or until rice is done, adding milk as it is absorbed by rice. Add sugar to taste. Serve warm sprinkled with cinnamon. Yield: 4 servings.

Nutritional information for this recipe is not available.

Although this is a sweetened rice dish, it is very good served as a side dish.

Lee Ruth Krieg, Lubbock

Cakes

Yoakum County

Salt, sweat, and sweet Texas crude,

a code,

rooted like the wily Mesquite,

unyielding,

people and land,

A compact in Yoakum County.

R.S.

APPLESAUCE CAKE

1/2 teaspoon baking soda	1 1/4 cups sugar
1/2 teaspoon each cloves, cinnamon, nutmeg, allspice	2 eggs
	1 cup applesauce
1/2 teaspoon vanilla extract	1 1/4 cups flour
1/2 cup corn oil	1/2 cup chopped pecans

Combine baking soda, cloves, cinnamon, nutmeg and allspice in bowl. Add vanilla, oil, sugar and eggs; mix well. Add applesauce and flour; beat well. Stir in pecans. Spoon into greased and floured 5x9-inch cake loaf pan. Bake at 350 degrees for 30 minutes or until cake tests done. Cool in pan for several minutes. Remove to wire rack to cool completely. Yield: 12 servings.

Approx Per Serving: Cal 271; Prot 3 g; Carbo 36 g; Fiber 1 g;
    T Fat 14 g; 44% Calories from Fat; Chol 36 mg; Sod 47 mg.

Judy Bowman, Littlefield

APRICOT NECTAR CAKE

1 2-layer package lemon supreme cake mix	2/3 cup apricot nectar
	4 eggs
1 3-ounce package orange gelatin	2/3 cup apricot nectar
2/3 cup oil	2/3 cup sugar

Combine cake mix and orange gelatin in mixer bowl; mix well. Add oil and 2/3 cup apricot nectar; beat well. Beat in eggs 1 at a time. Spoon into greased and floured 9x13-inch cake pan. Bake at 350 degrees for 30 minutes or until cake tests done. Cool slightly. Combine 2/3 cup apricot nectar and sugar in saucepan. Bring to a boil, stirring constantly. Pierce holes in cake with fork; pour hot glaze over cake. Cool before cutting into squares. Yield: 15 servings.

Approx Per Serving: Cal 319; Prot 4 g; Carbo 46 g; Fiber <1 g;
    T Fat 14 g; 39% Calories from Fat; Chol 57 mg; Sod 247 mg.

John T. Montford, State Senator, Lubbock

APRICOT PRESERVE CAKE

1 cup butter, softened
2 cups sugar
4 eggs
1 teaspoon baking soda
1 cup buttermilk
1 teaspoon cinnamon

1/2 teaspoon cloves
1/2 teaspoon nutmeg
3 cups flour
1 cup apricot preserves
1 cup chopped walnuts

Cream butter and sugar in mixer bowl until light and fluffy. Beat in eggs 1 at a time. Stir baking soda into buttermilk. It will foam up. Mix cinnamon, cloves, nutmeg and flour together. Add flour mixture alternately with buttermilk to creamed mixture, beating well after each addition. Fold in preserves and walnuts. Spoon into greased and floured tube pan. Bake at 350 degrees for 1 hour or until cake tests done. Cool in pan for several minutes. Invert onto cake plate.
Yield: 16 servings.

Approx Per Serving: Cal 411; Prot 6 g; Carbo 59 g; Fiber 1 g;
     T Fat 18 g; 38% Calories from Fat; Chol 85 mg; Sod 185 mg.

Mickey Hall, Lubbock

CHOCOLATE-KAHLUA CAKE

1 cup chopped pecans
1   2-layer package chocolate cake mix
1   4-ounce package chocolate instant
     pudding mix
1/2 cup Kahlua
1/2 cup water

1/2 cup oil
4 eggs
1 cup sugar
1/4 cup Kahlua
1/2 cup butter
1/4 cup water

Sprinkle pecans into greased and floured tube pan. Combine cake mix and pudding mix in mixer bowl; mix well. Add 1/2 cup Kahlua, 1/2 cup water and 1/2 cup oil; beat well. Add eggs; beat for 2 minutes. Pour into tube pan. Bake at 325 degrees for 50 to 60 minutes or until cake tests done. Combine sugar, remaining Kahlua, butter and 1/4 cup water in saucepan. Bring to a boil. Cook for 2 to 3 minutes or until thickened, stirring constantly. Pour over hot cake. Cool cake in pan for 30 minutes. Invert onto cake plate. Yield: 15 servings.

Approx Per Serving: Cal 464; Prot 4 g; Carbo 57 g; Fiber 1 g;
     T Fat 23 g; 46% Calories from Fat; Chol 73 mg; Sod 332 mg.

Susan McDonald, Ransom Canyon

CHOCOLATE CAKE

1/3 cup baking cocoa	2 eggs
1 teaspoon baking soda	Salt to taste
1 cup warm water	1/2 cup sour cream
2 cups sugar	2 cups flour
1/2 cup shortening	1 teaspoon vanilla extract

Mix first 3 ingredients in bowl. Cream sugar and shortening in mixer bowl until fluffy. Beat in eggs 1 at a time. Add cocoa mixture alternately with remaining ingredients; mix well. Pour into greased and floured 9x13-inch cake pan. Bake at 350 degrees for 25 minutes or until cake tests done. Yield: 15 servings.

Approx Per Serving: Cal 257; Prot 3 g; Carbo 41 g; Fiber 1 g;
    T Fat 10 g; 33% Calories from Fat; Chol 32 mg; Sod 69 mg.

Tammy Ray, Lockney

CREAM OF COCONUT CAKE

1 2-layer package white cake mix	1 12-ounce can cream of coconut
1 14-ounce can sweetened	8 ounces whipped topping
condensed milk	1 3-ounce can coconut

Prepare and bake cake using package directions for 9x13-inch cake pan. Pierce holes in hot cake with fork. Pour condensed milk and cream of coconut over cake. Cool. Frost with whipped topping; sprinkle with coconut. Yield: 15 servings.

Approx Per Serving: Cal 451; Prot 6 g; Carbo 63 g; Fiber 1 g;
    T Fat 21 g; 41% Calories from Fat; Chol 9 mg; Sod 209 mg.

Lydia White, Farwell

EARTHQUAKE CAKE

1 cup coconut	8 ounces cream cheese, softened
1 cup chopped pecans	1/2 cup melted margarine
1 2-layer package German chocolate	1 1-pound package confectioners'
cake mix	sugar

Sprinkle coconut and pecans in greased and floured 8x14-inch cake pan. Prepare cake mix using package directions. Pour into pan. Beat cream cheese and margarine in mixer bowl. Add confectioners' sugar; mix well. Pour over batter. Bake at 350 degrees for 45 minutes or until cake tests done. Yield: 15 servings.

Approx Per Serving: Cal 530; Prot 4 g; Carbo 68 g; Fiber 1 g;
    T Fat 28 g; 46% Calories from Fat; Chol 61 mg; Sod 453 mg.

Jeanette O'Hair, Earth, and Connie Martin, Levelland

LAFAYETTE GINGERBREAD

1 cup butter, softened
1 cup packed light brown sugar
1 cup molasses
1/2 cup milk, warmed
2 tablespoons ginger
1 teaspoon cinnamon
2 tablespoons grated orange rind
1/2 teaspoon nutmeg
1/8 teaspoon mace

3 cups sifted flour
1/4 cup brandy
3 eggs, beaten
1/2 cup orange juice
1 teaspoon baking soda
1/4 cup warm water
1 cup sour cream
1 cup raisins

Cream butter and brown sugar in mixer bowl until light and fluffy. Add next 7 ingredients; mix well. Reserve 1 tablespoon flour. Add remaining flour, brandy, eggs and orange juice; mix well. Dissolve baking soda in warm water. Add to batter. Add sour cream; mix well. Stir in mixture of reserved flour and raisins. Pour into greased and floured 9x13-inch cake pan. Bake at 350 degrees for 35 minutes or until cake tests done. Serve warm or cold. This is also good with a lemon sauce. Yield: 15 servings.

Approx Per Serving: Cal 406; Prot 5 g; Carbo 59 g; Fiber 1 g;
    T Fat 17 g; 38% Calories from Fat; Chol 84 mg; Sod 197 mg.

Myra G. Burris, Lubbock

ITALIAN CREAM CAKE

1/2 cup margarine, softened
1/2 cup shortening
2 cups sugar
5 egg yolks
1 teaspoon baking soda
1 cup buttermilk
2 cups flour
1 teaspoon vanilla extract

1 cup coconut
5 egg whites, stiffly beaten
1 ounce cream cheese, softened
1/2 cup margarine, softened
1   1-pound package confectioners'
    sugar
1 teaspoon vanilla extract
1/2 cup chopped pecans

Cream first 3 ingredients in mixer bowl. Beat in egg yolks 1 at a time. Dissolve baking soda in buttermilk. Add to creamed mixture alternately with flour, beating well. Add 1 teaspoon vanilla. Stir in coconut. Fold in egg whites. Pour into 3 greased and floured 9-inch cake pans. Bake at 350 degrees for 25 minutes or until layers test done. Cool in pans for several minutes. Remove to wire rack to cool completely. Combine next 3 ingredients in mixer bowl; beat well. Add 1 teaspoon vanilla. Stir in pecans. Spread between layers and over top and side of cooled cake. Yield: 16 servings.

Approx Per Serving: Cal 528; Prot 5 g; Carbo 74 g; Fiber 1 g;
    T Fat 25 g; 41% Calories from Fat; Chol 69 mg; Sod 227 mg.

Laquita Miller, Lubbock

Lazy Daisy Cake

1½ cups flour
1 cup sugar
2 teaspoons baking powder
¾ to 1 cup milk
2 eggs

¼ cup melted shortening
1 teaspoon vanilla extract
5 tablespoons melted margarine
¼ cup heavy cream
9 tablespoons brown sugar

Sift flour, sugar and baking powder together into mixer bowl. Add enough milk to eggs to measure 1 cup. Add to flour mixture; beat well. Add shortening and vanilla; mix well. Pour into greased and floured 9x13-inch cake pan. Bake at 350 degrees for 25 minutes or until cake tests done. Combine margarine, cream and brown sugar in bowl; mix well. Spread over hot cake. Broil until bubbly.
Yield: 15 servings.

Approx Per Serving: Cal 228; Prot 3 g; Carbo 32 g; Fiber <1 g;
    T Fat 10 g; 40% Calories from Fat; Chol 36 mg; Sod 110 mg.

I got this recipe in Corsicana, Texas, in 1930.

Hazel Donovan, Matador

Grandma's Lemon Cake

1 3-ounce package lemon gelatin
1 cup boiling water
1 2-layer package lemon cake mix
⅓ cup oil

3 eggs
½ to ¾ cup lemon juice
⅓ to ½ cup confectioners' sugar

Dissolve gelatin in boiling water in mixer bowl. Add cake mix and oil; mix until slightly cooled. Add eggs; beat for 2 minutes. Pour into greased and floured bundt pan. Bake at 350 degrees for 20 to 30 minutes or until cake tests done. Cool in pan for several minutes. Invert onto serving plate. Pierce holes in hot cake with wooden pick. Add enough lemon juice to confectioners' sugar to make a thin syrup. Spoon over warm cake. Serve warm or cool. Refrigerate leftovers.
Yield: 16 servings.

Approx Per Serving: Cal 229; Prot 3 g; Carbo 36 g; Fiber <1 g;
    T Fat 8 g; 32% Calories from Fat; Chol 40 mg; Sod 226 mg.

This has been a family favorite since Grandma Sheldon started it.

Sandy Butler, Lubbock

LEMON JELLY CAKE

1 cup butter, softened
2 cups sugar
3 cups flour
2 teaspoons baking powder
1 cup milk
7 egg whites, stiffly beaten

7 egg yolks
Juice of 2 lemons
1¾ cups sugar
3 tablespoons water
½ teaspoon butter

Cream 1 cup butter and 2 cups sugar in mixer bowl until light and fluffy. Add mixture of flour and baking powder alternately with milk, beating well after each addition. Fold in egg whites. Spoon into 3 greased and floured cake pans. Bake at 375 degrees for 30 minutes or until layers test done. Cool in pans for several minutes. Remove to wire rack to cool completely. Combine egg yolks, lemon juice, 1¾ cups sugar, water and ½ teaspoon butter in double boiler. Cook over boiling water until thickened, stirring constantly. Spread between layers and on top and side of cooled cake. Yield: 15 servings.

Approx Per Serving: Cal 442; Prot 6 g; Carbo 70 g; Fiber 1 g;
    T Fat 16 g; 32% Calories from Fat; Chol 135 mg; Sod 184 mg.

Elizabeth Connell, Colorado City

HELEN'S ORANGE SLICE CAKE

1 8-ounce package chopped dates
2 cups chopped pecans
1 12-ounce package orange slice
    candy, chopped
1 3-ounce can flaked coconut
½ cup flour
1 cup butter, softened

2 cups sugar
4 eggs
3½ cups cake flour
½ cup buttermilk
2 cups confectioners' sugar
1 cup orange juice

Combine dates, pecans, orange slice candy, coconut and ½ cup flour in bowl, tossing until fruit and pecans are well coated. Cream butter and sugar in mixer bowl until light and fluffy. Beat in eggs 1 at a time. Add cake flour alternately with buttermilk, beating well after each addition. Fold in floured fruit and pecan mixture. Pour into greased and floured tube pan. Bake at 325 degrees for 1½ hours or until cake tests done. Combine confectioners' sugar and orange juice in mixer bowl; beat until well mixed. Pour over hot cake. Let stand in tube pan until liquid is absorbed. Invert onto cake plate. Yield: 16 servings.

Approx Per Serving: Cal 624; Prot 6 g; Carbo 97 g; Fiber 4 g;
    T Fat 25 g; 35% Calories from Fat; Chol 85 mg; Sod 140 mg.

Anne S. Glover, Lubbock

PLUM CAKE

1 cup oil
2 cups sugar
3 eggs
2 cups self-rising flour
Cloves to taste
1 teaspoon cinnamon

¹/₄ teaspoon allspice
2 4-ounce jars baby food plums
1 cup chopped pecans
¹/₂ 1-pound package confectioners'
  sugar
1 tablespoon milk

Cream oil and sugar in mixer bowl until light and fluffy. Beat in eggs 1 at a time. Mix flour, cloves, cinnamon and allspice together. Add to eggs mixture. Add baby food plums; mix well. Stir in pecans. Pour into greased and floured tube pan. Bake at 350 degrees for 50 to 60 minutes or until cake tests done. Cool in pan for several minutes. Invert onto serving plate to cool. Combine confectioners' sugar and milk in mixer bowl; beat until of spreading consistency. Spread over cooled cake. Yield: 16 servings.

Approx Per Serving: Cal 412; Prot 3 g; Carbo 58 g; Fiber 1 g;
    T Fat 20 g; 42% Calories from Fat; Chol 40 mg; Sod 184 mg.

Natalie Blankenship, Wilson

ANNIVERSARY POUND CAKE

1 cup margarine, softened
1 cup shortening
3 cups sugar
5 eggs
3 cups sifted flour

¹/₂ teaspoon salt
¹/₂ teaspoon baking powder
5 tablespoons baking cocoa
1 cup milk
1 tablespoon vanilla extract

Cream margarine, shortening and sugar in mixer bowl until light and fluffy. Beat in eggs 1 at a time. Sift flour, salt, baking powder and baking cocoa together. Add to creamed mixture alternately with milk and vanilla, beating well after each addition. Pour into greased and floured 10-inch tube pan. Bake at 350 degrees for 40 to 50 minutes or until cake tests done. Cool in pan for 10 to 20 minutes. Remove to serving plate. Yield: 16 servings.

Approx Per Serving: Cal 479; Prot 5 g; Carbo 56 g; Fiber 1 g;
    T Fat 27 g; 50% Calories from Fat; Chol 69 mg; Sod 240 mg.

This recipe was clipped out of the Lubbock paper about 25 years ago.

Valerie Martin, Sundown

BUTTERMILK POUND CAKE

1 cup margarine, softened
2 cups sugar
4 eggs
1/2 teaspoon salt
3 cups flour
1/4 teaspoon baking soda

1/2 teaspoon baking powder
1 cup buttermilk
1 teaspoon vanilla extract
1/2 teaspoon lemon extract
1/2 teaspoon orange extract
1/2 teaspoon butter extract

Cream margarine and sugar in mixer bowl until light and fluffy. Beat in eggs 1 at a time. Mix salt, flour, baking soda and baking powder together. Add to creamed mixture alternately with buttermilk, beating well after each addition. Add flavorings; mix well. Pour into greased and floured bundt pan. Bake at 350 degrees for 1 to 1 1/4 hours or until cake tests done. Cool in pan for several minutes. Invert onto serving plate. Yield: 16 servings.

Approx Per Serving: Cal 312; Prot 5 g; Carbo 44 g; Fiber 1 g;
T Fat 13 g; 38% Calories from Fat; Chol 54 mg; Sod 258 mg.

Janis Cowley, Earth

PEPPERMINT POUND CAKE

1 cup shortening
2 cups sugar
4 eggs
1 teaspoon peppermint extract
1/2 teaspoon salt
3 cups sifted flour

3/4 cup buttermilk
1 teaspoon baking soda
1 tablespoon vinegar
1/4 cup crushed peppermint candy
1/2 teaspoon red food coloring

Cream shortening and sugar in mixer bowl until light and fluffy. Beat in eggs 1 at a time. Add peppermint extract and salt; mix well. Add flour alternately with buttermilk, beating well after each addition. Stir baking soda into vinegar. Add to batter; beat well. Fold in crushed peppermint candy. Remove 1/3 of the batter to small bowl. Stir in red food coloring. Spoon pink batter and plain batter alternately into greased and floured 10-inch tube pan. Cut through batter with knife to marbleize. Bake at 325 degrees for 1 hour and 10 minutes or until cake tests done. Cool in pan for 10 minutes. Invert onto wire rack to cool completely. May sprinkle top of cake with additional crushed peppermint candy. Yield: 16 servings.

Approx Per Serving: Cal 327; Prot 4 g; Carbo 46 g; Fiber 1 g;
T Fat 15 g; 40% Calories from Fat; Chol 54 mg; Sod 149 mg.

This is a family favorite for Christmas time. May also be baked in individual cake loaf pans at 325 degrees for 50 to 55 minutes.

Gwen Parish, Earth

Pumpkin Cake Roll

3 eggs	1 teaspoon ginger
1 cup sugar	1/2 teaspoon nutmeg
2/3 cup cooked pumpkin	1/2 teaspoon salt
1 teaspoon lemon juice	11/2 cups confectioners' sugar
3/4 cup flour	6 ounces cream cheese, softened
1 teaspoon baking powder	1/4 cup butter, softened
2 teaspoons cinnamon	1/2 teaspoon vanilla extract

Beat eggs at high speed in mixer bowl for 5 minutes. Add sugar; beat until well blended. Add pumpkin and lemon juice; mix well. Mix flour, baking powder, cinnamon, ginger, nutmeg and salt together. Add to batter; mix well. Spread in greased and floured 10x15-inch jelly roll pan. Bake at 375 degrees for 15 minutes or until cake tests done. Dust towel with 1/2 cup confectioners' sugar. Remove cake to towel. Roll from narrow end to enclose towel and cake. Cool. Combine 1 cup confectioners' sugar, cream cheese, butter and vanilla in mixer bowl; beat until of spreading consistency. Unroll cake. Spread with filling. Roll cake to enclose filling; place on tray. Chill, covered, in refrigerator until serving time. May dust with additional confectioners' sugar. Yield: 15 servings.

Approx Per Serving: Cal 206; Prot 3 g; Carbo 31 g; Fiber <1 g;
T Fat 8 g; 35% Calories from Fat; Chol 63 mg; Sod 167 mg.

*This has become a family tradition for the holiday
season and makes a wonderful gift.*

Darla Cloud, Lubbock

Sad Cake

1 1-pound package brown sugar	1/2 teaspoon salt
11/2 cups flour	1 teaspoon vanilla extract
11/2 teaspoons baking powder	11/2 to 2 cups chopped pecans

Combine brown sugar, flour, baking powder and salt in bowl; mix well. Add vanilla and pecans; mix well. Pour into greased and floured 9x13-inch cake pan. Bake at 350 degrees for 30 minutes. Cool in pan. Cut into servings. Yield: 15 servings.

Approx Per Serving: Cal 266; Prot 3 g; Carbo 42 g; Fiber 1 g;
T Fat 11 g; 36% Calories from Fat; Chol 0 mg; Sod 118 mg.

This cake received its name because it falls when baked.

Natalie Blankenship, Wilson

SANDY'S STRAWBERRY CAKE

1 2-layer package strawberry cake mix 3 eggs 1/3 cup oil 10 to 15 frozen strawberries	1/3 to 1/2 cup water 1/2 cup margarine, softened 11/2 pounds confectioners' sugar 1/2 cup milk 1 tablespoon vanilla extract

Combine cake mix, eggs and oil in mixer bowl; mix well. Process strawberries in blender container until puréed, adding enough water to measure 1 cup. Add to cake mixture; beat for 2 minutes. Pour into 2 greased and floured 8-inch cake pans. Bake at 350 degrees for 20 to 30 minutes or until layers test done. Cool in pan for several minutes. Remove to wire rack to cool completely. Combine margarine and confectioners' sugar in mixer bowl; beat well. Add enough milk to make of spreading consistency. Add vanilla; beat well. Spread between layers and over top and side of cooled cake. Yield: 16 servings.

Approx Per Serving: Cal 453; Prot 3 g; Carbo 80 g; Fiber <1 g;
    T Fat 14 g; 28% Calories from Fat; Chol 41 mg; Sod 280 mg.

Sandy Butler, Lubbock

TEXAS TORNADO CAKE

11/2 cups sugar 2 eggs 1 teaspoon vanilla extract 2 cups drained fruit cocktail 2 tablespoons lemon or pineapple juice 2 teaspoons baking soda 1/8 teaspoon baking powder 2 cups flour	3/4 teaspoon cinnamon 1/2 teaspoon nutmeg 1/4 cup packed brown sugar 1 cup chopped pecans 1/2 cup margarine 1 cup packed brown sugar 1/2 cup evaporated milk 1 cup coconut

Combine sugar, eggs and vanilla in saucepan; mix well. Process fruit cocktail and lemon juice in blender container until puréed. Add to saucepan. Bring to a boil, stirring frequently. Mix baking soda, baking powder, flour, cinnamon and nutmeg together. Combine flour mixture and hot mixture in mixer bowl; beat well. Pour into greased and floured 9x13-inch cake pan. Mix 1/4 cup brown sugar and pecans together in bowl. Sprinkle over cake batter. Bake at 325 degrees for 40 to 45 minutes or until cake tests done. Let stand in pan on wire rack for 3 or 4 minutes to cool. Pierce 10 to 12 holes in top of hot cake with fork. Combine margarine, 1 cup brown sugar and evaporated milk in saucepan. Bring to a boil, stirring frequently. Stir in coconut. Pour over warm cake. Yield: 15 servings.

Approx Per Serving: Cal 401; Prot 4 g; Carbo 66 g; Fiber 2 g;
    T Fat 15 g; 32% Calories from Fat; Chol 31 mg; Sod 216 mg.

Carrie Tatum, Friona

WACKY CAKE

1¹/₂ cups flour
1 cup sugar
1 teaspoon baking soda
¹/₄ cup baking cocoa

1 teaspoon vanilla extract
1 teaspoon vinegar
2 tablespoons melted margarine
1 cup water

Sift flour, sugar, baking soda and baking cocoa together into ungreased 8-inch cake pan. Make 3 wells in mixture. Add vanilla to 1 well, vinegar to 1 well and margarine to 1 well. Pour water over all, stirring with fork until all ingredients are moist. Bake at 350 degrees for 30 minutes or until cake tests done. Cool in pan for several minutes. Remove to serving plate. Yield: 6 servings.

Approx Per Serving: Cal 288; Prot 4 g; Carbo 59 g; Fiber 2 g;
    T Fat 5 g; 15% Calories from Fat; Chol 0 mg; Sod 184 mg.

Megan Ashley Estrada, Abernathy

YANKEE CAKE

¹/₂ cup butter, softened
1 cup sugar
2 eggs
¹/₂ cup corn syrup
1³/₄ cups flour
1¹/₂ teaspoons baking powder
1 teaspoon cinnamon
1 teaspoon ground cloves
1 teaspoon allspice
1 teaspoon nutmeg

²/₃ cup milk
1 cup chopped raisins
1 cup chopped pecans
1 cup chopped apples
2 cups sugar
1 cup milk
1 cup chopped pecans
1 cup coconut
2 tablespoons butter
1 cup chopped dates

Cream ¹/₂ cup butter and 1 cup sugar in mixer bowl until light and fluffy. Beat in eggs 1 at a time. Add corn syrup; mix well. Mix flour, baking powder, cinnamon, cloves, allspice and nutmeg together. Add to creamed mixture. Add ²/₃ cup milk; beat well. Stir in raisins, pecans and apples. Pour into 2 greased and floured 8-inch cake pans. Bake at 325 degrees for 45 minutes or until layers test done. Cool in pans for several minutes. Remove to wire rack to cool completely. Combine 2 cups sugar, 1 cup milk, pecans and coconut in saucepan. Cook over medium heat until thickened, stirring frequently. Stir in 2 tablespoons butter and dates. Spread between layers and over top and side of cooled cake. Yield: 16 servings.

Approx Per Serving: Cal 499; Prot 5 g; Carbo 79 g; Fiber 4 g;
    T Fat 21 g; 36% Calories from Fat; Chol 50 mg; Sod 119 mg.

This old family cake recipe was a blue ribbon winner at the South Plains Fair.

Una Childress, Levelland

Candy & Cookies

Swisher County

Summer rain in the Middle Tule in Swisher County,
Washing the arroyos of the last Indian stronghold,
Cutting,
Changing the prairie like physical history.

R.S.

APRICOT STICKS

16 ounces dried apricots, ground	2 cups sugar
1 orange, ground	16 ounces chopped pecans
Juice of 1/2 orange	1 cup confectioners' sugar, sifted

Combine first 4 ingredients in saucepan; mix well. Cook over low heat until mixture begins to thicken. Let stand until cool. Stir in pecans. Drop by rounded teaspoonfuls into confectioners' sugar, turning to coat. Shape into sticks. Yield: 100 servings.

Approx Per Serving: Cal 62; Prot 1 g; Carbo 9 g; Fiber 1 g;
    T Fat 3 g; 42% Calories from Fat; Chol 0 mg; Sod 1 mg.

Shelly Livingston, Wilson

BRAN-DITS CANDY

1 1/2 cups sugar	1 cup coconut
1/4 cup butter	1 cup salted peanuts
2/3 cup evaporated milk	2 cups All-Bran cereal
1 7-ounce jar marshmallow creme	

Combine sugar, butter and evaporated milk in saucepan. Bring to a boil over medium heat, stirring constantly. Cook to 234 to 240 degrees on candy thermometer, soft-ball stage. Remove from heat. Stir in remaining ingredients. Spread in buttered 9x13-inch dish. Chill completely. Cut into squares. Yield: 36 servings.

Approx Per Serving: Cal 112; Prot 2 g; Carbo 18 g; Fiber 2 g;
    T Fat 4 g; 32% Calories from Fat; Chol 5 mg; Sod 91 mg.

Barbara Amerson, Abernathy

CARAMEL CORN

4 to 5 quarts popped popcorn	1 teaspoon salt
2 cups packed brown sugar	1/2 cup light corn syrup
1 cup margarine	1/2 teaspoon baking soda

Place popcorn in large oven-safe bowl. Keep warm in 250-degree oven. Combine next 4 ingredients in saucepan; mix well. Cook over medium heat to 250 to 268 degrees on candy thermometer, hard-ball stage. Remove from heat. Stir in baking soda. Pour over popcorn, stirring until coated. Spread on baking sheet. Bake at 250 degrees for 45 minutes, stirring every 15 minutes. Yield: 12 servings.

Approx Per Serving: Cal 395; Prot 2 g; Carbo 65 g; Fiber 2 g;
    T Fat 16 g; 35% Calories from Fat; Chol 0 mg; Sod 417 mg.

Minnie H. Struve, Abernathy

MICROWAVE CARAMEL CORN

4 to 5 quarts popped popcorn
1/2 cup margarine
1 cup packed brown sugar

1/4 cup light corn syrup
1/2 teaspoon salt
1/2 teaspoon baking soda

Place popped popcorn in large bowl. Combine margarine, brown sugar and corn syrup in glass bowl. Microwave on High until mixture boils. Boil for 2 minutes longer. Stir in salt and baking soda until light and foamy. Pour over popped popcorn. Spread on waxed paper. Let stand until cool. Yield: 16 servings.

Approx Per Serving: Cal 167; Prot 1 g; Carbo 28 g; Fiber 2 g;
    T Fat 6 g; 32% Calories from Fat; Chol 0 mg; Sod 170 mg.

Carolyne Stephens, Earth, and Doris Vandiver, Muleshoe

MRS. SMITH'S PEANUT BUTTER FUDGE

4 cups sugar
1 cup evaporated milk

1 18-ounce jar peanut butter
1 7-ounce jar marshmallow creme

Combine sugar and evaporated milk in saucepan; mix well. Bring to a boil over medium heat, stirring constantly. Cook to 238 degrees exactly. Remove from heat. Stir in peanut butter and marshmallow creme until well blended. Spread into buttered 11x16-inch dish. Let stand until set. Cut into squares. Yield: 60 servings.

Approx Per Serving: Cal 118; Prot 3 g; Carbo 18 g; Fiber 1 g;
    T Fat 5 g; 34% Calories from Fat; Chol 1 mg; Sod 41 mg.

Anne S. Glover, Lubbock

EASY WHITE FUDGE

3 ounces cream cheese, softened
1 teaspoon vanilla extract
1/8 teaspoon salt

2 3/4 cups confectioners' sugar
1/2 cup chopped walnuts

Beat cream cheese, vanilla and salt at low speed in mixer bowl until smooth. Add confectioners' sugar gradually; beat constantly, scraping side of bowl frequently. Stir in walnuts. Spoon into greased 5x9-inch dish, spreading evenly. Chill until firm. Cut into 24 pieces; wrap each in plastic wrap. Store in refrigerator. Yield: 24 servings.

Approx Per Serving: Cal 82; Prot 1 g; Carbo 14 g; Fiber <1 g;
    T Fat 3 g; 30% Calories from Fat; Chol 4 mg; Sod 22 mg.

Rhonda Bentley, Friona

VELVEETA FUDGE

8 ounces Velveeta cheese
1 cup butter
1/2 tablespoon vanilla extract

1/2 cup baking cocoa
2 pounds confectioners' sugar
3 cups chopped pecans

Melt cheese and butter in top of double boiler, stirring frequently. Stir in vanilla. Sift baking cocoa and confectioners' sugar together. Combine with cheese mixture and pecans in bowl; mix well. Mixture will be stiff. Spread in 9x13-inch dish coated with nonstick cooking spray. Chill for 1 hour. Cut into squares. Yield: 36 servings.

Approx Per Serving: Cal 255; Prot 2 g; Carbo 33 g; Fiber 1 g;
    T Fat 14 g; 47% Calories from Fat; Chol 20 mg; Sod 134 mg.

Marie Johnston, Lubbock

MILLIONAIRE CANDY

1   14-ounce package caramel candies
2 tablespoons margarine
2 tablespoons water

1 1/2 to 2 cups pecan halves
1   8-ounce chocolate candy bar
1/6 block paraffin

Melt caramels and margarine with water in top of double boiler, stirring frequently. Arrange pecans in clusters on waxed paper. Spoon caramel mixture over clusters. Let stand until cool. Melt chocolate candy bar and paraffin together in top of double boiler. Dip caramel-coated clusters into chocolate, coating completely. Place on waxed paper. Let stand until set. Yield: 36 servings.

Approx Per Serving: Cal 122; Prot 1 g; Carbo 13 g; Fiber 1 g;
    T Fat 8 g; 55% Calories from Fat; Chol 2 mg; Sod 37 mg.

Betty Curry, Post

MICROWAVE PEANUT BRITTLE

1 cup raw peanuts
1 cup sugar
1/2 cup light corn syrup

1/8 teaspoon salt
1 teaspoon each margarine, baking
    soda and vanilla extract

Combine first 4 ingredients in glass bowl; mix well. Microwave on High for 7 minutes, stirring after 4 minutes. Add margarine; mix well. Microwave for 2 minutes longer. Stir in baking soda and vanilla until light and foamy. Spread thin on buttered tray. Let stand until cool. Break into serving pieces. Yield: 30 servings.

Approx Per Serving: Cal 71; Prot 1 g; Carbo 12 g; Fiber <1 g;
    T Fat 2 g; 30% Calories from Fat; Chol 0 mg; Sod 41 mg.

Cyndi Pratas, Lubbock

PEANUT BRITTLE

2 cups sugar
1 cup light corn syrup
2 to 3 cups raw peanuts

1 teaspoon vanilla extract
2 teaspoons baking soda

Bring sugar and corn syrup to a boil in large saucepan over medium heat. Add peanuts. Bring to a boil again. Cook to 300 to 310 degrees on candy thermometer, hard-crack stage. Remove from heat. Stir in vanilla and baking soda until light and foamy. Pour into 9x13-inch pan quickly. Cool. Break into serving pieces. Yield: 40 servings.

Approx Per Serving: Cal 125; Prot 3 g; Carbo 18 g; Fiber 1 g;
   T Fat 5 g; 36% Calories from Fat; Chol 0 mg; Sod 46 mg.

Alarah Russell, Lubbock

PEANUT PATTIES

2¹/₂ cups sugar
³/₄ cup light corn syrup
1 cup evaporated milk
3 cups raw peanuts

¹/₂ cup margarine
1 teaspoon vanilla extract
Several drops of red food coloring

Bring first 4 ingredients to a boil in saucepan over medium heat, stirring constantly. Cook to 244 to 248 degrees on candy thermometer, firm-ball stage. Combine with margarine, vanilla and food coloring in bowl. Beat for 45 minutes or until mixture is creamy and loses it luster. Drop by spoonfuls onto buttered waxed paper. Let stand until cool. Yield: 48 servings.

Approx Per Serving: Cal 131; Prot 3 g; Carbo 17 g; Fiber 1 g;
   T Fat 7 g; 44% Calories from Fat; Chol 2 mg; Sod 31 mg.

Wanda Murdock, Dimmitt

SUGARED PECANS

4¹/₂ cups pecans
2 cups sugar

1 cup water
¹/₂ teaspoon cinnamon

Combine all ingredients in heavy skillet. Cook over medium heat until water evaporates and pecans are sugar-coated. Spoon into 9x13-inch dish. Separate pecans using 2 forks. Cool. Store in airtight container. Yield: 36 servings.

Approx Per Serving: Cal 142; Prot 1 g; Carbo 14 g; Fiber 1 g;
   T Fat 10 g; 60% Calories from Fat; Chol 0 mg; Sod <1 mg.

Dahlia Hight, Lockney

BANANA-OATMEAL COOKIES

1 cup sugar
³/₄ cup shortening
1 egg, beaten
1¹/₂ cups flour
¹/₂ teaspoon baking soda
1 teaspoon salt

³/₄ teaspoon cinnamon
¹/₄ teaspoon nutmeg
1 cup mashed banana
1³/₄ cups quick-cooking rolled oats
¹/₂ cup chopped pecans

Cream sugar, shortening and egg in mixer bowl until light and fluffy. Add next 7 ingredients; mix well. Fold in pecans. Drop by spoonfuls onto greased cookie sheet. Bake at 350 degrees for 10 to 12 minutes or until light brown. Yield: 36 servings.

Approx Per Serving: Cal 112; Prot 2 g; Carbo 14 g; Fiber 1 g;
    T Fat 6 g; 46% Calories from Fat; Chol 6 mg; Sod 73 mg.

Myrtle Lee, Friona

BROWNIES

¹/₂ cup butter
1 cup sugar
2 eggs, beaten
1 teaspoon vanilla extract

²/₃ cup flour
¹/₄ cup baking cocoa
²/₃ cup chopped pecans

Cream butter, sugar, eggs and vanilla in mixer bowl until fluffy. Sift in flour and baking cocoa, mixing well. Fold in pecans. Pour into greased 8x8-inch baking pan. Bake at 350 degrees for 25 minutes. Cut into squares. Yield: 24 servings.

Approx Per Serving: Cal 109; Prot 1 g; Carbo 12 g; Fiber 1 g;
    T Fat 7 g; 53% Calories from Fat; Chol 28 mg; Sod 39 mg.

Holly Turner, Abernathy

BROWN SUGAR BROWNIES

¹/₄ cup butter, melted
1 cup packed brown sugar
1 egg, beaten
1 teaspoon vanilla extract

¹/₂ cup flour
1 teaspoon baking powder
¹/₂ cup chopped pecans

Combine butter and brown sugar, stirring until dissolved; cool. Beat in egg and vanilla. Stir in remaining ingredients. Pour into greased 9x9-inch baking pan. Bake at 350 degrees for 20 minutes. Cool; cut into bars. Yield: 16 servings.

Approx Per Serving: Cal 134; Prot 1 g; Carbo 20 g; Fiber <1 g;
    T Fat 6 g; 38% Calories from Fat; Chol 21 mg; Sod 57 mg.

Betty Parish, Earth

AUNT VIRGINIA'S BROWNIES

1/3 cup shortening
2 ounces unsweetened chocolate, melted
1 cup sugar
2 eggs, well beaten
3/4 cup cake flour
1/4 teaspoon salt
1/2 teaspoon baking powder

1/2 cup chopped walnuts
1 teaspoon vanilla extract
1/4 cup butter, softened
2 cups confectioners' sugar
1 tablespoon baking cocoa
2 egg yolks, beaten
1 teaspoon vanilla extract
2 tablespoons strong coffee

Mix shortening and chocolate in bowl. Beat sugar into eggs until foamy. Add to chocolate mixture, mixing well. Sift flour, salt and baking powder together. Add to chocolate mixture, beating until smooth. Stir in walnuts and 1 teaspoon vanilla. Pour into greased 8x8-inch baking pan. Bake at 350 degrees for 25 minutes; cool in pan. Cream butter in mixer bowl until light and fluffy. Sift in confectioners' sugar and baking cocoa, beating constantly. Add egg yolks and vanilla, stirring until thickened. Stir in coffee. Spread over cooled brownies; cut into squares. Yield: 18 servings.

Approx Per Serving: Cal 221; Prot 2 g; Carbo 30 g; Fiber 1 g;
    T Fat 11 g; 45% Calories from Fat; Chol 54 mg; Sod 70 mg.

Sue Haberer, Earth

CHOCOLATE BROWNIES

1 cup margarine
5 tablespoons (heaping) baking cocoa
2 cups sugar
4 eggs
2 cups (scant) flour
1 cup chopped walnuts
2 teaspoons vanilla extract

3 tablespoons margarine
3 tablespoons baking cocoa
1 1-pound package confectioners' sugar
1 teaspoon vanilla extract
6 to 7 tablespoons milk

Melt 1 cup margarine in saucepan; remove from heat. Add 5 tablespoons baking cocoa and sugar, mixing well. Add eggs 1 at a time, beating well after each addition. Stir in flour, walnuts and 2 teaspoons vanilla, mixing well. Pour into greased and floured 9x13-inch baking pan. Bake at 350 degrees for 30 minutes. Combine 3 tablespoons margarine and 3 tablespoons baking cocoa in saucepan. Heat until margarine is melted, stirring constantly; remove from heat. Add confectioners' sugar, vanilla and enough milk to make of spreading consistency. Spread over warm brownies; cut into squares. Yield: 24 servings.

Approx Per Serving: Cal 323; Prot 3 g; Carbo 49 g; Fiber 1 g;
    T Fat 14 g; 37% Calories from Fat; Chol 36 mg; Sod 121 mg.

Mern Lewis, Tahoka

CREAM CHEESE COOKIES

½ cup butter, softened
3 ounces cream cheese, softened
1 cup sugar

1 cup flour
½ cup chopped pecans

Beat butter and cream cheese in mixer bowl. Add sugar; beat well. Add flour; mix well. Fold in pecans. Shape into 1-inch balls. Arrange 2 inches apart on ungreased cookie sheet; flatten with glass dipped in water. Bake at 375 degrees for 12 minutes. Cool for 2 to 3 minutes; remove to wire rack. Yield: 30 servings.

Approx Per Serving: Cal 91; Prot 1 g; Carbo 10 g; Fiber <1 g;
    T Fat 5 g; 52% Calories from Fat; Chol 11 mg; Sod 35 mg.

Mickey Ann Miles, Slaton

CRUNCHY NUT COOKIES

1 cup sugar
1 cup packed brown sugar
½ cup shortening
2 eggs, beaten
1 teaspoon vanilla extract

3 cups flour
1 teaspoon baking soda
½ teaspoon salt
¼ cup milk
1 cup chopped pecans

Cream first 5 ingredients in mixer bowl until light and fluffy. Sift in flour, baking soda and salt; mix well. Stir in milk and pecans. Shape by teaspoonfuls into small balls. Place on ungreased cookie sheet; flatten with glass dipped in sugar. Bake at 375 degrees for 10 to 12 minutes or until light brown. Yield: 48 servings.

Approx Per Serving: Cal 105; Prot 1 g; Carbo 16 g; Fiber <1 g;
    T Fat 4 g; 35% Calories from Fat; Chol 9 mg; Sod 46 mg.

Carol Huggins, Lockney

EASY EASY COOKIES

1 2-layer package strawberry cake
    mix
1 cup whipped topping

2 eggs, beaten
½ cup chopped pecans
½ cup confectioners' sugar

Mix first 3 ingredients in bowl. Stir in pecans. Drop by teaspoonfuls into confectioners' sugar; shape into balls. Place 1 inch apart on ungreased cookie sheet. Bake at 350 degrees for 10 minutes. Cool. Yield: 36 servings.

Approx Per Serving: Cal 89; Prot 1 g; Carbo 14 g; Fiber <1 g;
    T Fat 3 g; 31% Calories from Fat; Chol 12 mg; Sod 92 mg.

Judy Pounds, Slaton

GRAHAM CRACKER COOKIES

10 graham crackers
1 cup butter
1/2 cup sugar

1 teaspoon light corn syrup
1 cup chopped pecans

Line cookie sheet with foil. Layer with graham crackers. Combine butter, sugar and corn syrup in saucepan. Bring to a boil for 2 minutes, stirring constantly. Pour over graham crackers; sprinkle with pecans. Bake at 350 degrees for 12 minutes; cool and break into pieces. Yield: 24 servings.

Approx Per Serving: Cal 130; Prot 1 g; Carbo 8 g; Fiber <1 g;
T Fat 11 g; 76% Calories from Fat; Chol 21 mg; Sod 83 mg.

Jan Wood, Slaton

HOLIDAY SCRAMBLE TREATS

3/4 cup packed brown sugar
2 eggs, beaten
1 cup chopped dates
1 cup chopped pecans

1 cup cornflakes
1 teaspoon vanilla extract
1/2 cup shredded coconut

Combine sugar, eggs and dates in skillet; mix well. Cook over medium heat until mixture pulls away from side of pan, stirring constantly; cool. Add pecans, cornflakes and vanilla; mix well. Shape into small balls; roll in coconut. Chill until firm. Yield: 32 servings.

Approx Per Serving: Cal 79; Prot 1 g; Carbo 12 g; Fiber 1 g;
T Fat 3 g; 37% Calories from Fat; Chol 13 mg; Sod 20 mg.

Linda Quarles, Lubbock

MOLDY MICE

1/2 cup butter, softened
1 tablespoon sugar
1 1/2 teaspoons vanilla extract

1 cup flour
1/2 cup finely chopped pecans
1/2 cup confectioners' sugar

Cream butter, sugar and vanilla in mixer bowl until light and fluffy. Toss flour and pecans in bowl; stir into creamed mixture. Shape into small 2-inch logs; place on cookie sheet. Bake at 425 degrees for 15 minutes or until light brown. Roll in confectioners' sugar while hot. Yield: 36 servings.

Approx Per Serving: Cal 54; Prot 1 g; Carbo 5 g; Fiber <1 g;
T Fat 4 g; 60% Calories from Fat; Chol 7 mg; Sod 22 mg.

Myra G. Burris, Lubbock

NICOLE'S GOBS

2 cups sugar
1 cup shortening
2 eggs, slightly beaten
1/2 cup baking cocoa
2 teaspoons baking soda
1 1/2 cups milk
2 teaspoons vanilla extract

4 cups flour
1 1/2 1-pound packages confectioners' sugar
1 1/2 cups shortening
1/2 cup butter, softened
1 egg, slightly beaten
3 tablespoons vanilla extract

Cream sugar, 1 cup shortening and eggs in mixer bowl until light and fluffy. Beat in baking cocoa, baking soda, milk, 2 teaspoons vanilla and flour until smooth. Drop by teaspoonfuls onto greased cookie sheet. Bake at 325 degrees for 5 to 10 minutes or until edges are light brown; cool. Cream confectioners' sugar with 1 1/2 cups shortening and butter in mixer bowl until light and fluffy. Add egg and vanilla, beating until creamy. Spread creamed mixture over half the cookies; top with remaining cookies to form sandwiches. Yield: 32 servings.

Approx Per Serving: Cal 392; Prot 3 g; Carbo 51 g; Fiber 1 g;
    T Fat 20 g; 46% Calories from Fat; Chol 29 mg; Sod 88 mg.

Nicole Parker, Lubbock

ORANGE-OATMEAL COOKIES

2 cups flour
1 teaspoon baking soda
3/4 teaspoon salt
1/2 teaspoon cinnamon
1/8 teaspoon allspice
1 cup shortening
1/2 cup sugar

1/2 cup packed light brown sugar
2 eggs
2 cups quick-cooking rolled oats
1/3 cup orange juice
1 cup raisins
1/2 cup chopped pecans
2 teaspoons grated orange rind

Sift flour, baking soda, salt, cinnamon and allspice together. Cream shortening, sugar and brown sugar in mixer bowl until smooth. Add eggs, beating until light and fluffy. Stir in oats. Add sifted dry ingredients alternately with orange juice, beating well after each addition. Stir in raisins, pecans and orange rind. Drop by teaspoonfuls onto greased cookie sheets. Bake at 350 degrees for 10 to 15 minutes or until golden brown. Yield: 48 servings.

Approx Per Serving: Cal 111; Prot 2 g; Carbo 14 g; Fiber 1 g;
    T Fat 6 g; 44% Calories from Fat; Chol 9 mg; Sod 55 mg.

*This was my mom's recipe. I don't know where she got it but
I've never tasted a better oatmeal cookie!*

Carol Tobias, Post

RAISIN-NUT COOKIES

½ cup margarine, softened
1 cup packed brown sugar
1 egg, beaten
1 teaspoon vanilla extract
½ cup milk
2 ounces unsweetened chocolate,
  melted

2 cups flour
2 teaspoons baking powder
½ teaspoon salt
1 teaspoon cinnamon
1 cup chopped pecans
1 cup raisins

Cream margarine, brown sugar, egg, vanilla and milk in mixer bowl until light and fluffy. Stir in melted chocolate until blended. Add flour, baking powder, salt and cinnamon, stirring well. Fold in pecans and raisins. Drop by spoonfuls onto nonstick cookie sheets. Bake at 400 degrees for 10 to 12 minutes or until golden brown. Yield: 36 servings.

Approx Per Serving: Cal 125; Prot 2 g; Carbo 18 g; Fiber 1 g;
  T Fat 6 g; 41% Calories from Fat; Chol 6 mg; Sod 85 mg.

Dianne Brown, Muleshoe

ENGLISH ROCKS

1 cup butter, softened
1½ cups packed light brown sugar
3 eggs, beaten
3 cups sifted flour
1 teaspoon baking soda
½ teaspoon salt
2 teaspoons cinnamon
½ teaspoon ground cloves

½ teaspoon allspice
½ cup buttermilk
6 cups pecan halves
16 ounces candied cherries
9 slices candied pineapple
2 cups chopped dates
9 tablespoons (about) brandy

Cream butter and brown sugar in mixer bowl until light and fluffy. Beat in eggs. Sift flour, baking soda, salt, cinnamon, cloves and allspice together. Add to creamed mixture alternately with buttermilk, beating well after each addition. Combine pecans, cherries, pineapple and dates in large bowl. Pour batter over fruits, mixing well. Drop by teaspoonfuls onto ungreased cookie sheet. Bake at 325 degrees for 20 to 25 minutes or until browned. Sprinkle warm cookies with brandy; cool. Store in airtight containers for up to 4 weeks. Yield: 108 servings.

Approx Per Serving: Cal 117; Prot 1 g; Carbo 16 g; Fiber 1 g;
  T Fat 6 g; 45% Calories from Fat; Chol 11 mg; Sod 37 mg.

*This is a family tradition. The cookies are always made in late November,
stored in a tin can and served during the holidays.*

JoAnn Cook, Wilson

Mary's Sugar Cookies

1½ cups sifted confectioners' sugar
1 cup butter, softened
1 egg, beaten
1 teaspoon vanilla extract

½ teaspoon almond extract
2½ cups flour
1 teaspoon baking soda
1 teaspoon cream of tartar

Cream confectioners' sugar and butter in mixer bowl until light and fluffy. Beat in egg, vanilla and almond extract. Combine flour, baking soda and cream of tartar together. Stir into creamed mixture. Chill dough for 2 to 3 hours. Divide dough into 2 equal portions, leaving half in refrigerator. Roll out to 3/16-inch thickness. Cut with favorite cookie cutters. Place on greased cookie sheet. Bake at 375 degrees for 7 to 8 minutes or until light brown. Repeat process with remaining dough. May sprinkle cooled cookies with confectioners' sugar or brush with mixture of 1 egg yolk beaten with ¼ teaspoon water and a few drops of food coloring. For different colors, divide egg mixture before adding food coloring. Yield: 48 servings.

Approx Per Serving: Cal 74; Prot 1 g; Carbo 9 g; Fiber <1 g;
    T Fat 4 g; 49% Calories from Fat; Chol 15 mg; Sod 51 mg.

This is one of Mary Blocker's recipes given to me years ago.

Joann Stewart, Lubbock

Tea Cookies

1 cup butter, softened
½ cup confectioners' sugar
2½ cups sifted flour
¼ teaspoon salt

1 teaspoon vanilla extract
¾ cup finely chopped pecans
2 cups confectioners' sugar

Cream butter and ½ cup confectioners' sugar in mixer bowl until light and fluffy. Stir in flour, salt, vanilla and pecans, mixing well. Shape into 1-inch balls; place on nonstick cookie sheet. Bake at 400 degrees for 15 minutes or until light brown. Shake warm cookies in paper bag with 2 cups confectioners' sugar until well coated. Let stand until cooled. Dust again with confectioners' sugar. Yield: 48 servings.

Approx Per Serving: Cal 92; Prot 1 g; Carbo 11 g; Fiber <1 g;
    T Fat 5 g; 49% Calories from Fat; Chol 10 mg; Sod 44 mg.

I have had this recipe for 40 years—it's always good.

Kate Beecher, Dimmitt

Pies

Lamb County

Thermal Hawks soar
over the dry bed of Illusion Lake,
the wind rustles the grasses over the dry bed
of Blackwater Draw.
At evening we are lulled by a Mourning Dove choir,
softly, like lamb's wool.

R.S.

APRICOT PIE

1 unbaked 10-inch deep-dish pie shell
1 8-ounce can apricots, drained
1 17-ounce can apricots, drained
1 cup sugar
3 tablespoons flour
1 cup whipping cream

Line pie shell with apricots. Mix sugar, flour and whipping cream together in bowl. Pour over apricots. Bake at 350 degrees for 50 minutes. Yield: 8 servings.

Approx Per Serving: Cal 402; Prot 3 g; Carbo 55 g; Fiber 2 g;
T Fat 20 g; 44% Calories from Fat; Chol 41 mg; Sod 182 mg.

Brenda Parker, Lubbock

BING CHERRY PIE

1 16-ounce can Bing cherries, drained, chopped
1 14-ounce can sweetened condensed milk
1 cup whipped topping
1 cup pecans, chopped
1/3 cup lemon juice
1 9-inch graham cracker pie shell

Combine first 4 ingredients in bowl; mix well. Stir in lemon juice. Spoon into pie shell. Chill until set. Yield: 8 servings.

Approx Per Serving: Cal 526; Prot 7 g; Carbo 66 g; Fiber 2 g;
T Fat 28 g; 46% Calories from Fat; Chol 17 mg; Sod 306 mg.

Shirley Tucker, Slaton

BLACK BOTTOM PIE

1/2 cup sugar
1/4 cup flour
1/8 teaspoon salt
2 cups milk
4 egg yolks, beaten
1 1/2 ounces unsweetened chocolate
1 baked 9-inch pie shell
1 envelope unflavored gelatin
1/4 cup water
4 egg whites, stiffly beaten
8 ounces whipped topping

Mix sugar, flour and salt in saucepan. Stir in mixture of milk and egg yolks. Cook over medium heat until thickened, stirring constantly. Spoon 1/2 into bowl. Add chocolate to saucepan. Heat until chocolate melts. Spoon into pie shell. Let stand for 30 minutes. Soften gelatin in water. Stir into remaining portion in bowl. Fold in egg whites gently. Spoon over cooled chocolate layer. Top with whipped topping. Chill overnight. Yield: 8 servings.

Approx Per Serving: Cal 373; Prot 8 g; Carbo 36 g; Fiber 2 g;
T Fat 23 g; 55% Calories from Fat; Chol 144 mg; Sod 231 mg.

Sharon Dykes, Wife of Texas Tech football coach Spike Dykes, Lubbock

CHOCOLATE PIE

1 cup sugar
1/4 cup flour
1/8 teaspoon salt
4 teaspoons baking cocoa
2 cups warm milk
3 egg yolks, slightly beaten
1 tablespoon butter

1 teaspoon vanilla extract
1 baked 9-inch pie shell
3 egg whites
1/2 teaspoon vanilla extract
1/4 teaspoon cream of tartar
6 tablespoons sugar

Sift 1 cup sugar, flour, salt and baking cocoa into saucepan. Stir in milk and egg yolks. Cook over medium heat until thickened, stirring constantly. Remove from heat. Stir in butter and 1 teaspoon vanilla until butter melts. Spoon into pie shell. Beat egg whites with 1/2 teaspoon vanilla and cream of tartar until soft peaks form. Add 6 tablespoons sugar gradually, beating until stiff peaks form. Spread over filling, sealing to edge. Bake at 350 degrees for 20 minutes or until golden brown. Yield: 8 servings.

Approx Per Serving: Cal 344; Prot 6 g; Carbo 51 g; Fiber 1 g;
    T Fat 13 g; 34% Calories from Fat; Chol 92 mg; Sod 231 mg.

This is an old recipe my grandmother, Zella Thomas, always made on our farm.

Jan Wood, Slaton

VIC'S CHOCOLATE PIE

1 cup sugar
3 tablespoons flour
2 tablespoons baking cocoa
2 cups milk
3 egg yolks, beaten
1/8 teaspoon salt

2 tablespoons butter
1 teaspoon vanilla extract
1 baked 9-inch pie shell
3 egg whites
6 tablespoons sugar

Mix 1 cup sugar, flour and baking cocoa in saucepan. Add milk, beaten egg yolks and salt; mix well. Cook over medium heat until thickened, stirring constantly. Remove from heat. Stir in butter and vanilla. Spoon into pie shell. Beat egg whites until soft peaks form. Add 6 tablespoons sugar, beating until stiff peaks form. Spread over filling, sealing to edge. Bake at 350 degrees for 15 minutes or until golden brown. Yield: 8 servings.

Approx Per Serving: Cal 353; Prot 6 g; Carbo 50 g; Fiber 1 g;
    T Fat 15 g; 37% Calories from Fat; Chol 96 mg; Sod 243 mg.

Debbie and Holly Wiles, Floydada

COCONUT CREAM PIE

1½ cups milk
¼ cup sugar
¼ teaspoon salt
3 tablespoons flour
1 egg yolk, beaten

1 tablespoon butter
½ teaspoon vanilla extract
1½ cups shredded coconut
1 baked 9-inch pie shell

Scald 1 cup milk in double boiler over hot water. Mix remaining milk, sugar, salt and flour in bowl. Stir into scalded milk. Cook until thickened, stirring constantly. Cook, covered, for 5 minutes longer. Stir in egg yolk. Cook for 1 minute. Stir in butter, vanilla and coconut. Spoon into pie shell. Let stand until cool. Chill until serving time. May prepare chocolate cream pie by substituting 1 ounce melted chocolate and 2 tablespoons sugar for coconut. Prepare banana cream pie by substituting 4 sliced bananas for coconut. Yield: 8 servings.

Approx Per Serving: Cal 284; Prot 4 g; Carbo 29 g; Fiber 2 g;
    T Fat 17 g; 54% Calories from Fat; Chol 37 mg; Sod 282 mg.

Betty Curry, Post

TEXAS CREAM PIES

1⅓ cups sugar
6 tablespoons cornstarch
¼ cup flour
1 teaspoon salt
6 egg yolks
1 cup cold milk

3 cups scalded milk
¼ cup butter
2 teaspoons vanilla extract
6 egg whites, stiffly beaten
4 baked pie 9-inch pie shells

Mix sugar, cornstarch, flour and salt in bowl. Beat egg yolks with 1 cup cold milk. Stir into dry mixture. Combine with 3 cups scalded milk in saucepan. Cook over medium heat until thickened, stirring constantly. Remove from heat. Stir in butter and vanilla until butter melts. Fold in stiffly beaten egg whites gently. Spoon into pie shells. Chill completely. Garnish with whipped cream and grated chocolate or toasted coconut. Store in refrigerator. Yield: 32 servings.

Approx Per Serving: Cal 201; Prot 3 g; Carbo 22 g; Fiber <1 g;
    T Fat 11 g; 49% Calories from Fat; Chol 48 mg; Sod 240 mg.

Myrtle Lee, Friona

EASY FUDGE PIE

½ cup melted margarine	½ cup flour
2 tablespoons (heaping) baking cocoa	2 eggs
1 cup sugar	1 teaspoon vanilla extract

Mix margarine, baking cocoa, sugar and flour in bowl. Stir in eggs and vanilla. Spoon into greased 8-inch pie plate. Bake at 350 degrees for 30 minutes. May serve hot with ice cream, drizzling chocolate syrup over top. Yield: 6 servings.

Approx Per Serving: Cal 335; Prot 4 g; Carbo 43 g; Fiber 1 g;
    T Fat 18 g; 46% Calories from Fat; Chol 71 mg; Sod 203 mg.

Kathy J. Carr, Springlake

TRIED AND TRUE LEMON CHESS PIE

4 eggs	1½ tablespoons cornmeal
2 cups sugar	1 tablespoon vanilla extract
½ cup melted butter	¼ teaspoon salt
¼ cup whipping cream	1 unbaked 9-inch pie shell
¼ cup lemon juice	

Beat eggs slightly in bowl. Add sugar, butter, whipping cream, lemon juice, cornmeal, vanilla and salt; mix well. Do not beat. Spoon into pie shell. Bake at 325 degrees for 1 hour. Yield: 8 servings.

Approx Per Serving: Cal 485; Prot 5 g; Carbo 63 g; Fiber 1 g;
    T Fat 25 g; 45% Calories from Fat; Chol 148 mg; Sod 339 mg.

Kate Beecher, Dimmitt

LEMON CHESS PIE

1 cup butter	2 teaspoons lemon extract
3 cups sugar	8 eggs
¼ cup lemon juice	2 unbaked 9-inch pie shells

Cut butter into sugar in mixer bowl. Add lemon juice, lemon extract and eggs; mix well. Spoon into pie shells. Bake at 400 degrees for 10 minutes. Reduce oven temperature to 300 degrees. Bake until pies are set. Yield: 16 servings.

Approx Per Serving: Cal 401; Prot 5 g; Carbo 48 g; Fiber <1 g;
    T Fat 22 g; 48% Calories from Fat; Chol 138 mg; Sod 270 mg.

This recipe is from the kitchen of Circle G B.B.Q., Dickens, Texas.

Guy H. Goen, Dickens

MERINGUE PIE

³/₄ cup sugar
2¹/₄ cups water

2 eggs, separated
1 baked 9-inch pie shell

Mix ¹/₂ cup sugar, ¹/₄ cup water and egg yolks in saucepan. Stir in 2 cups water. Bring to a boil over medium heat, stirring constantly. Spoon into pie shell. Beat egg whites until soft peaks form. Add ¹/₄ cup sugar gradually, beating until stiff peaks form. Spread over filling, sealing to edge. Bake at 425 degrees for 5 minutes or until golden brown. Chill for 4 hours. Yield: 8 servings.

Approx Per Serving: Cal 204; Prot 3 g; Carbo 29 g; Fiber <1 g;
    T Fat 9 g; 39% Calories from Fat; Chol 53 mg; Sod 152 mg.

Tina Ramos, Abernathy

OATMEAL PIE

2 eggs
³/₄ cup each dark corn syrup and milk
¹/₂ cup melted butter
¹/₂ teaspoon rum or brandy extract
1 teaspoon vanilla extract

¹/₂ cup sugar
¹/₂ cup packed brown sugar
³/₄ cup oats
¹/₂ cup each coconut and pecans
2 unbaked 9-inch deep-dish pie shells

Mix first 6 ingredients in bowl. Add sugar and brown sugar; mix well. Stir in oats, coconut and pecans. Spoon into pie shells. Bake at 375 degrees for 35 minutes or until set near center. Let stand until cool. Yield: 16 servings.

Approx Per Serving: Cal 343; Prot 4 g; Carbo 42 g; Fiber 1 g;
    T Fat 19 g; 48% Calories from Fat; Chol 44 mg; Sod 228 mg.

Gail Threet, Lubbock

TOLL HOUSE PIE

2 eggs, beaten
¹/₂ cup flour
¹/₂ cup sugar
¹/₂ cup packed brown sugar

1 cup melted butter, cooled
1 cup semisweet chocolate chips
1 cup chopped walnuts
1 unbaked 9-inch pie shell

Beat first 4 ingredients in mixer bowl until smooth. Beat in butter. Stir in chocolate chips and walnuts. Spoon into pie shell. Bake at 325 degrees for 1 hour. Yield: 8 servings.

Approx Per Serving: Cal 680; Prot 7 g; Carbo 60 g; Fiber 2 g;
    T Fat 49 g; 62% Calories from Fat; Chol 115 mg; Sod 361 mg.

Marlana Tharp, Lockney

GRANNY GRUNT'S PECAN PIE

3 tablespoons flour
1 cup sugar
1 cup light corn syrup
1/2 cup evaporated milk

1/2 teaspoon vanilla extract
2 eggs, slightly beaten
1 unbaked 9-inch pie shell
1 1/2 cups chopped pecans

Mix flour and sugar in bowl. Add corn syrup, evaporated milk, vanilla and eggs; mix well. Spoon into pie shell. Sprinkle pecans over top. Press down using a spatula until pecans are coated with filling. Bake at 325 degrees for 50 minutes. Yield: 8 servings.

Approx Per Serving: Cal 524; Prot 6 g; Carbo 74 g; Fiber 2 g;
    T Fat 25 g; 42% Calories from Fat; Chol 58 mg; Sod 191 mg.

TyAnn Nichols, Lubbock

BROWN SUGAR PECAN PIE

1 cup light corn syrup
1 cup packed dark brown sugar
1/3 cup melted butter
1 cup (heaping) pecans

3 eggs
1 teaspoon vanilla extract
1/8 teaspoon salt
1 unbaked 9-inch pie shell

Combine light corn syrup, brown sugar, butter, pecans, eggs, vanilla and salt in bowl; mix well. Spoon into pie shell. Bake at 350 degrees for 45 to 50 minutes or until set. Yield: 8 servings.

Approx Per Serving: Cal 552; Prot 5 g; Carbo 77 g; Fiber 1 g;
    T Fat 27 g; 43% Calories from Fat; Chol 100 mg; Sod 294 mg.

Phyllis Geissler, Earth

PECAN PIE

1/4 cup butter, softened
1 cup sugar
4 eggs, beaten
2 cups light corn syrup

2 tablespoons flour
2 teaspoons vanilla extract
1 cup pecans
2 unbaked 9-inch pie shells

Cream butter and sugar in mixer bowl until light and fluffy. Stir in eggs. Add corn syrup, flour, vanilla and pecans; mix well. Spoon into pie shells. Bake at 300 degrees for 45 to 60 minutes or until set. Yield: 16 servings.

Approx Per Serving: Cal 375; Prot 4 g; Carbo 56 g; Fiber 1 g;
    T Fat 17 g; 39% Calories from Fat; Chol 61 mg; Sod 198 mg.

Jenna Parish, Springlake

PINEAPPLE PIE

1 8-ounce can crushed pineapple
1 8-ounce can water
3 cups sugar
6 tablespoons flour

1 recipe 2-crust pie pastry
1 tablespoon melted butter
1 tablespoon sugar

Combine pineapple, water, sugar and flour in saucepan; mix well. Cook over medium heat until thickened, stirring constantly. Spoon into pastry-lined 9-inch pie plate. Cut remaining pastry into strips; arrange lattice-fashion on top. Bake at 350 degrees for 20 minutes or until brown. Brush with butter; sprinkle with 1 tablespoon sugar. Yield: 8 servings.

Approx Per Serving: Cal 553; Prot 3 g; Carbo 104 g; Fiber 1 g;
    T Fat 15 g; 24% Calories from Fat; Chol 4 mg; Sod 290 mg.

Lana Banks, Springlake

PUMPKIN PIE

3 cups sugar
6 medium eggs
1/2 cup butter, softened
6 tablespoons flour
1 1/2 teaspoons vanilla extract
1 1/2 teaspoons cinnamon

3/4 teaspoon nutmeg
3/4 teaspoon allspice
1/2 teaspoon ground cloves
1 1/2 cups evaporated milk
1 cup mashed cooked pumpkin
2 unbaked 9-inch pie shells

Beat sugar and eggs in mixer bowl until light and fluffy. Add butter, flour, vanilla and spices; mix well. Fold in evaporated milk and pumpkin gently. Spoon into pie shells. Bake at 300 degrees for 1 hour. Do not overbake. Yield: 16 servings.

Approx Per Serving: Cal 386; Prot 6 g; Carbo 53 g; Fiber 1 g;
    T Fat 17 g; 40% Calories from Fat; Chol 102 mg; Sod 239 mg.

Barbara June Jones, Slaton

Pumpkin-Pecan Pie

4 eggs, slightly beaten
2 cups canned pumpkin
1 cup sugar
1/2 cup dark corn syrup
1 teaspoon vanilla extract

1/2 teaspoon cinnamon
1/4 teaspoon salt
1 unbaked 9-inch pie shell
1 cup chopped pecans

Combine first 7 ingredients in bowl; mix well. Spoon into pie shell. Sprinkle with pecans. Bake at 350 degrees for 40 minutes or until set. Yield: 8 servings.

Approx Per Serving: Cal 429; Prot 6 g; Carbo 58 g; Fiber 3 g;
    T Fat 21 g; 42% Calories from Fat; Chol 106 mg; Sod 256 mg.

Former First Lady Nancy Reagan

Old-Fashioned Raisin Pie

1 1/2 cups seedless raisins, rinsed
1 1/2 cups boiling water
1 tablespoon flour
1 cup sugar

1/2 cup walnuts
1 tablespoon lemon juice
Grated rind of 1 lemon
1 recipe 2-crust pie pastry

Cook raisins in water in saucepan over medium heat until plump. Stir in mixture of flour and sugar. Cook until thickened, stirring constantly. Stir in walnuts, lemon juice and lemon rind. Spoon into pastry-lined pie plate. Cut remaining pastry into strips; arrange lattice-fashion on top. Bake at 450 degrees for 35 to 40 minutes. Reduce temperature to 350 degrees. Bake for 10 minutes. Yield: 8 servings.

Approx Per Serving: Cal 444; Prot 5 g; Carbo 70 g; Fiber 3 g;
    T Fat 18 g; 36% Calories from Fat; Chol 0 mg; Sod 280 mg.

Joanne Flusche, Idalou

Sugar Pie

5 eggs
2 1/2 cups sugar
2 tablespoons flour
Salt to taste

2 teaspoons vanilla extract
1 1/2 cups evaporated milk
1/2 cup melted margarine
2 unbaked 9-inch pie shells

Beat eggs in mixer bowl. Add next 6 ingredients; mix well. Spoon into pie shells. Bake at 400 degrees for 10 minutes. Reduce oven temperature to 325 degrees. Bake for 20 minutes longer or until set. Yield: 16 servings.

Approx Per Serving: Cal 346; Prot 5 g; Carbo 45 g; Fiber <1 g;
    T Fat 17 g; 43% Calories from Fat; Chol 74 mg; Sod 252 mg.

Hazel Donovan, Matador

Janet Harris' Wonder Recipe

1½ cups warm milk	1 teaspoon vanilla extract
1½ cups sugar	1 baked 9-inch pie shell
¼ cup flour	2 egg whites
2 egg yolks	¼ cup sugar
½ cup milk	

Mix 1½ cups warm milk, 1½ cups sugar and flour in glass bowl. Microwave on High for 5 minutes. Blend egg yolks and ½ cup milk in small bowl. Stir into warm milk mixture. Microwave for 4 to 5 minutes or until mixture is thickened, stirring after each minute. Stir in vanilla. Let stand until cool. Spoon into pie shell. Beat egg whites until soft peaks form. Add ¼ cup sugar gradually, beating until stiff peaks form. Spread over top of pie, sealing to edge. Bake at 325 degrees for 15 minutes or until light brown. Yield: 8 servings.

Approx Per Serving: Cal 354; Prot 5 g; Carbo 60 g; Fiber 1 g;
   T Fat 11 g; 28% Calories from Fat; Chol 62 mg; Sod 179 mg.

This is the easiest and best cream pie recipe ever! And it never fails!

Lynn Buxkemper, Slaton

Yummy Pie

1 cup whipping cream	1 8-ounce can crushed pineapple
1 14-ounce can sweetened	½ cup coconut
condensed milk	¼ cup lemon juice
1 cup pecans, chopped	1 9-inch graham cracker pie shell

Beat whipping cream in mixer bowl until soft peaks form. Add condensed milk, pecans, pineapple, coconut and lemon juice; mix well. Spoon into pie shell. Chill completely. Yield: 8 servings.

Approx Per Serving: Cal 611; Prot 8 g; Carbo 64 g; Fiber 2 g;
   T Fat 38 g; 54% Calories from Fat; Chol 58 mg; Sod 314 mg.

Lee Ruth Krieg, Lubbock

Eating Healthy

Garza County

The Double Mountain Fork of the Brazos River
falls for a thousand feet
from the walls of the Caprock Cathedral.
Post, Garza County, Texas.
In the wind you can hear the snap of the whip
and the call of the wagoneer pushing his rig to the top.

R.S.

FRUIT SALAD WITH HONEY DRESSING

1 11-ounce can mandarin oranges	¼ cup each orange juice and oil
1 apple, chopped	⅓ cup (or less) honey
1 banana, sliced	½ teaspoon lemon juice
1 avocado, chopped	½ tablespoon poppy seed
1 20-ounce can pineapple chunks	¼ teaspoon salt
¼ cup each raisins and chopped pecans	¼ teaspoon prepared mustard

Combine drained mandarin oranges and next 6 ingredients in bowl; mix well. Mix orange juice and next 6 ingredients in jar. Shake, covered, until blended. Pour over fruit salad; toss gently. Chill for 2 hours before serving. Yield: 8 servings.

Approx Per Serving: Cal 289; Prot 2 g; Carbo 45 g; Fiber 5 g;
T Fat 13 g; 39% Calories from Fat; Chol 0 mg; Sod 76 mg.

Betty Anne Kyle, Lubbock

PINEAPPLE FANTASY

1 large pineapple	1 cup sliced banana
1 cup grapes	½ cup coconut
1 cup strawberries	½ cup chopped pecans

Cut pineapple into halves through fruit and leaves. Scoop out fruit, leaving ¼ inch to form shell. Cut removed pineapple into chunks. Combine pineapple chunks with remaining ingredients in large bowl; mix well. Spoon into pineapple shells. Yield: 6 servings.

Approx Per Serving: Cal 195; Prot 2 g; Carbo 30 g; Fiber 4 g;
T Fat 10 g; 41% Calories from Fat; Chol 0 mg; Sod 4 mg.

Patsy Vessels, Slaton

YOGURT

4 cups milk	¼ cup plain yogurt

Pour milk into heavy 3-quart enameled pan with tight-fitting lid. Heat over low heat to 180 degrees, stirring constantly. Cool to 110 degrees. Stir in yogurt immediately. Place lid on pan. Wrap top and side of pan with towel. Place in warm draft-free spot. Let stand for 6 hours or until slightly set. Chill for 4 hours or until firm. May use ¼ cup of the mixture for starter for next batch of yogurt. Yield: 8 servings.

Approx Per Serving: Cal 79; Prot 4 g; Carbo 6 g; Fiber 0 g;
T Fat 4 g; 48% Calories from Fat; Chol 17 mg; Sod 54 mg.

Jan Kennedy, Lubbock

STUFFED CHICKEN BREASTS

6 chicken breast filets
4 to 6 large mushrooms, chopped
2 large carrots, shredded
2 stalks celery, chopped
1/2 medium green bell pepper,
   chopped

1/2 medium onion, chopped
1/4 cup chopped fresh parsley
Mrs. Dash seasoning to taste
Pepper to taste
1/4 teaspoon basil
2 tablespoons grated Parmesan cheese

Rinse chicken; pat dry. Tenderize with meat mallet. Combine mushrooms, carrots, celery, green pepper, onion, parsley, seasonings and Parmesan cheese in bowl; mix well. Divide vegetable mixture into six portions. Place 1 portion in center of each filet. Fold up to enclose filling; secure with wooden pick. Arrange in 8x11-inch baking dish coated with nonstick cooking spray. Bake at 325 degrees for 45 minutes or until chicken tests done. Yield: 6 servings.

Approx Per Serving: Cal 172; Prot 28 g; Carbo 5 g; Fiber 2 g;
    T Fat 4 g; 20% Calories from Fat; Chol 74 mg; Sod 117 mg.

Kathy Hunt, Lubbock

PINEAPPLE CHICKEN

1 whole chicken, cut up
3 to 4 tablespoons butter
Salt and pepper to taste
Poultry seasoning to taste

1   15-ounce can sliced pineapple
3/4 cup packed brown sugar
2 cups cooked rice

Remove skin from chicken. Rinse chicken; pat dry. Brown chicken in butter in skillet. Add salt, pepper and poultry seasoning. Arrange pineapple slices on top of chicken. Cover pineapple slices with brown sugar. Bake, covered, at 300 degrees for 1 hour. Serve with hot cooked rice. May adjust amount of brown sugar to suit personal taste. Yield: 6 servings.

Approx Per Serving: Cal 453; Prot 21 g; Carbo 64 g; Fiber 1 g;
    T Fat 13 g; 25% Calories from Fat; Chol 80 mg; Sod 138 mg.

Lyn Vandiver, Muleshoe

Turkey Hominy

1 pound ground turkey
3 tablespoons margarine
1 tablespoon flour
1/2 cup sliced green onions
1/2 teaspoon thyme

1/4 teaspoon pepper
1   16-ounce can hominy
1 cup chicken broth
2 tablespoons soy sauce
1 carrot, shredded

Brown turkey in margarine in skillet, stirring until crumbly; drain. Stir in flour. Add green onions, thyme and pepper. Cook for 2 minutes, stirring constantly. Add hominy, chicken broth and soy sauce. Cook until slightly thickened, stirring constantly. Simmer, covered, for 10 minutes. Stir in shredded carrot. Serve in bowls. Yield: 4 servings.

Approx Per Serving: Cal 360; Prot 26 g; Carbo 18 g; Fiber 1 g;
    T Fat 20 g; 51% Calories from Fat; Chol 72 mg; Sod 1242 mg.

Dell Jones, Idalou

Cheesy Lasagna Roll-Ups

12 lasagna noodles
3/4 cup chopped onion
2 tablespoons butter
1   10-ounce package frozen chopped
    broccoli
1 1/4 cups cottage cheese
1 1/4 cups shredded Cheddar cheese

1/8 teaspoon garlic powder
1/4 teaspoon seasoned salt
1/8 teaspoon pepper
1/2 cup grated Parmesan cheese
1 tablespoon flour
2   8-ounce cans pizza sauce
1/4 cup shredded Cheddar cheese

Cook noodles using package directions. Place cooked noodles in cold water. Sauté onion in butter in skillet. Cook broccoli using package directions; drain. Beat cottage cheese in bowl until smooth. Add 1 1/4 cups Cheddar cheese; mix well. Add sautéed onion, broccoli, seasonings, Parmesan cheese and flour; mix well. Drain noodles; pat dry. Spread 1/4 cup cottage cheese mixture on each noodle. Roll up. Spread a small amount of pizza sauce in bottom of 2-quart shallow baking dish. Arrange roll-ups seam side down in sauce. Cover with remaining sauce. Bake at 350 degrees for 30 minutes. Sprinkle with remaining 1/4 cup Cheddar cheese. Bake until cheese melts. Yield: 12 servings.

Approx Per Serving: Cal 251; Prot 13 g; Carbo 27 g; Fiber 1 g;
    T Fat 10 g; 36% Calories from Fat; Chol 26 mg; Sod 430 mg.

Suzanne Hatch, York, Pennsylvania

LATTICE-TOPPED VEGETABLE PIE

1 pound potatoes, peeled, thinly
　sliced
1　16-ounce package carrots, thinly
　sliced
1 small bunch broccoli, coarsely
　chopped
3 tablespoons margarine
1/4 teaspoon pepper
3 tablespoons flour
1 1/2 teaspoons salt

1 3/4 cups milk
1 cup shredded lowfat mozzarella
　cheese
2 cups flour
1/2 teaspoon salt
1/3 cup chopped parsley
3/4 cup shortening
5 to 6 tablespoons cold water
3 tablespoons chopped parsley

Cook potatoes with enough water to cover in 3-quart saucepan until tender. Remove potatoes to large bowl using slotted spoon. Cook carrots in potato water until tender. Remove carrots to separate bowl using slotted spoon. Cook broccoli in same water until tender. Remove broccoli to separate bowl using slotted spoon. Melt margarine in 2-quart saucepan over medium heat. Stir in pepper, 3 tablespoons flour and 1 1/2 teaspoons salt. Cook for 1 minute. Add milk gradually, stirring constantly. Cook until mixture thickens, stirring constantly. Reduce heat to low. Add cheese, stirring until cheese melts. Remove from heat. Set aside. Mix 2 cups flour, 1/2 teaspoon salt and 1/3 cup parsley in bowl. Cut in shortening until crumbly. Add cold water 1 tablespoon at a time, mixing with fork until mixture forms ball. Divide dough into 2 portions with 1 slightly larger than the other. Roll larger portion into circle 2 1/2 inches larger than pie plate on lightly floured surface. Fit pastry into pie plate. Spoon potatoes into prepared pie plate. Spoon 1/3 of the cheese mixture sauce over potatoes. Layer carrots, half the remaining sauce and broccoli over potato layer. Top with remaining sauce. Roll remaining pastry into 12-inch circle. Cut into strips; arrange lattice-fashion on top. Bake at 425 degrees for 35 to 40 minutes or until filling bubbles and crust is golden. Sprinkle with remaining 3 tablespoons parsley before serving. Yield: 8 servings.

Approx Per Serving: Cal 485; Prot 12 g; Carbo 48 g; Fiber 5 g;
　T Fat 28 g; 52% Calories from Fat; Chol 15 mg; Sod 705 mg.

Light: Omit the pie pastry for the lattice top.

Approx Per Serving: Cal 342; Prot 10 g; Carbo 36 g; Fiber 4 g;
　T Fat 18 g; 48% Calories from Fat; Chol 15 mg; Sod 638 mg.

Lighter: Omit all pie pastry and top pie with 8 baking mix biscuits.

Approx Per Serving: Cal 310; Prot 10 g; Carbo 40 g; Fiber 4 g;
　T Fat 13 g; 36% Calories from Fat; Chol 17 mg; Sod 873 mg.

Lightest: Bake pie as casserole, omitting all pastry and topping.

Approx Per Serving: Cal 200; Prot 8 g; Carbo 24 g; Fiber 4 g;
　T Fat 9 g; 38% Calories from Fat; Chol 15 mg; Sod 570 mg.

Ann Owens, Littlefield

SPINACH-RICOTTA PIE

1/3 cup cold butter
1 cup flour
3 tablespoons cold buttermilk
8 ounces chopped spinach
1 small onion, chopped
1 tablespoon butter
1/2 teaspoon basil
1/2 teaspoon salt

Pepper to taste
16 ounces ricotta cheese
1/2 cup grated Parmesan cheese
3 tablespoons flour
3 eggs, beaten
Nutmeg to taste
1 cup yogurt
Paprika to taste

Cut 1/3 cup butter into flour until crumbly. Add buttermilk, stirring just until mixture forms a ball. Chill for 1 hour. Press into bottom and side of pie plate. Sauté spinach and onion in 1 tablespoon butter in skillet. Season with basil, salt and pepper. Combine spinach mixture, cheese, flour, eggs and nutmeg in mixer bowl; mix well. Spoon into prepared pie plate. Top with yogurt, sealing to edge. Sprinkle with paprika. Bake at 375 degrees for 40 to 45 minutes or until set. Yield: 8 servings.

Approx Per Serving: Cal 330; Prot 15 g; Carbo 21 g; Fiber 2 g;
    T Fat 21 g; 58% Calories from Fat; Chol 141 mg; Sod 445 mg.

Light: Use margarine, lowfat ricotta cheese, Parmesan cheese and liquid egg substitute.

Approx Per Serving: Cal 262; Prot 17 g; Carbo 22 g; Fiber 2 g;
    T Fat 12 g; 41% Calories from Fat; Chol 23 mg; Sod 558 mg.

Cathy Amen, Portland, Oregon

HONEY-WHOLE WHEAT BREAD

2 envelopes dry yeast
1/2 cup warm water
1/2 cup honey
1/4 cup shortening
1 tablespoon salt

1 3/4 cups warm water
3 cups whole wheat flour
3 to 4 cups all-purpose flour
1 tablespoon melted butter

Dissolve yeast in 1/2 cup warm water in large bowl. Stir in honey, shortening, salt and 1 3/4 cups water. Stir in whole wheat flour and enough all-purpose flour to make soft dough. Knead on floured surface until smooth and elastic. Place in greased bowl, turning to grease surface. Let rise for 1 hour. Punch dough down. Knead again. Shape dough into 2 loaves. Let rise until doubled in bulk. Bake at 375 degrees for 40 minutes. Brush hot bread with melted butter. Yield: 24 servings.

Approx Per Serving: Cal 172; Prot 4 g; Carbo 33 g; Fiber 3 g;
    T Fat 3 g; 16% Calories from Fat; Chol 1 mg; Sod 272 mg.

Dahlia Hight, Lockney

No-Knead Whole Wheat Bread

1½ cups whole wheat flour
¼ cup sugar
1 tablespoon salt
2 envelopes dry yeast
1 cup water

1 cup milk
¼ cup oil
1 egg
2½ to 3 cups all-purpose flour
1 tablespoon melted butter

Combine whole wheat flour, sugar, salt and yeast in large bowl; mix well. Combine water, milk and oil in saucepan. Cook over low heat until very warm. Add warm liquid and egg to flour mixture. Beat at low speed until moist. Beat at medium speed for 3 minutes. Stir in enough remaining flour to make stiff dough. Let rise, covered, for 50 minutes. Punch dough down. Spoon into two 4x8-inch pans. Bake at 375 degrees for 30 to 35 minutes or until bread tests done. Let stand until cool. Brush with melted butter. Yield: 24 servings.

Approx Per Serving: Cal 125; Prot 3 g; Carbo 20 g; Fiber 2 g;
    T Fat 4 g; 26% Calories from Fat; Chol 12 mg; Sod 279 mg.

Jan Kennedy, Lubbock

Whole Wheat-Banana Biscuits

1 cup all-purpose flour
1 cup whole wheat flour
2 teaspoons sugar
2 teaspoons baking powder
¼ teaspoon baking soda
¼ teaspoon cinnamon

⅛ teaspoon nutmeg
3 tablespoons margarine, softened
½ cup mashed banana
¼ cup vanilla low-fat yogurt
2 tablespoons skim milk
2 tablespoons all-purpose flour

Combine 1 cup all-purpose flour, whole wheat flour, sugar, baking powder, baking soda, cinnamon and nutmeg in bowl; mix well. Cut in margarine until crumbly. Stir in banana and yogurt. Add milk, stirring just until moistened. Let dough rest on floured surface for 5 minutes. Knead dough 4 times, adding enough remaining flour to prevent dough from sticking to hands. Roll dough ½ inch thick. Cut with 2-inch biscuit cutter. Place on baking sheet coated with nonstick cooking spray. Bake at 450 degrees for 8 minutes or until golden brown. Yield: 16 servings.

Approx Per Serving: Cal 89; Prot 2 g; Carbo 15 g; Fiber 1 g;
    T Fat 2 g; 24% Calories from Fat; Chol <1 mg; Sod 83 mg.

Susan McDonald, Ransom Canyon

HEALTHY MEXICAN CORN BREAD

1 cup plus 3 tablespoons cornmeal
1/2 teaspoon baking soda
1 teaspoon salt
1 cup egg substitute
2 tablespoons canola oil
1 cup skim milk
1   17-ounce can cream-style corn

1 teaspoon cornmeal
1 cup chopped onion
1 pound cooked very lean ground beef
12 ounces low-fat longhorn cheese,
   shredded
1/2 cup chopped jalapeño peppers

Combine cornmeal, baking soda, salt, egg substitute, oil, milk and corn in large bowl; mix well. Sprinkle 1 teaspoon cornmeal in hot oiled cast-iron skillet. Pour half the cornmeal mixture into skillet. Layer with onion, cooked ground beef, cheese and jalapeño peppers. Pour remaining half of batter over top. Bake at 350 degrees for 45 to 50 minutes or until browned. Yield: 12 servings.

Approx Per Serving: Cal 303; Prot 20 g; Carbo 22 g; Fiber 3 g;
   T Fat 15 g; 45% Calories from Fat; Chol 41 mg; Sod 634 mg.

Kathy J. Carr, Springlake

BRAN MUFFINS

3/4 cup raisins
2 1/2 cups All-Bran cereal
2 cups skim milk
1/2 cup canola oil
5 eggs, beaten
1 cup honey
2 teaspoons vanilla extract
2 1/2 cups whole wheat flour
1 1/4 teaspoons salt

2 tablespoons sugar
1 tablespoon baking powder
1 cup chopped pecans or walnuts
2 cups shredded carrots
1 cup drained crushed pineapple
2 apples, coarsely chopped
3/4 cup chopped dates
12 prunes, chopped

Soak raisins and cereal in milk in large bowl for 15 minutes. Stir in mixture of oil, eggs, honey and vanilla. Mix whole wheat flour, salt, sugar, baking powder, pecans, carrots, pineapple, apples, dates and prunes in bowl. Add to bran mixture. Stir just until moistened. Fill greased muffin cups 2/3 full. Bake at 350 degrees for 30 minutes. May use equivalent amount of egg substitute in place of eggs to reduce cholesterol. Yield: 36 servings.

Approx Per Serving: Cal 178; Prot 4 g; Carbo 30 g; Fiber 4 g;
   T Fat 7 g; 35% Calories from Fat; Chol 30 mg; Sod 189 mg.

First Lady Barbara Bush

HEALTH MUFFINS

2¹/₂ cups whole wheat flour
2¹/₂ cups all-purpose flour
5 teaspoons baking soda
1 teaspoon salt
2 cups All-Bran cereal
2 cups 40% bran flakes cereal
2 cups wheat germ

2 cups chopped pecans
2 cups raisins or chopped dates
4 eggs
1 cup oil
1 cup honey
2 cups water
4 cups buttermilk

Combine flours, baking soda, salt, cereals, wheat germ, pecans and raisins in very large bowl; mix well. Mix eggs, oil, honey, water and buttermilk in large bowl. Add to dry ingredients; mix well. Store in airtight container in refrigerator for up to 6 weeks, using as needed. Fill muffin cups with batter. Bake at 400 degrees for 20 minutes. Note: It is now recommended that batter be prepared and baked at once in order to reduce the risk of salmonella contamination. Freeze extra muffins, reheating as needed. Yield: 60 servings.

Approx Per Serving: Cal 160; Prot 4 g; Carbo 22 g; Fiber 3 g;
T Fat 7 g; 39% Calories from Fat; Chol 15 mg; Sod 171 mg.

Rhonda Bentley, Friona

BEST-EVER ORANGE CAKE

1³/₄ cups sifted flour
¹/₂ teaspoon salt
6 egg whites, at room temperature
¹/₂ cup sugar
6 egg yolks

1 cup sugar
6 tablespoons orange juice
1 tablespoon grated orange rind
¹/₂ cup confectioners' sugar

Sift flour and salt together. Beat egg whites in mixer bowl until soft peaks form. Add ¹/₂ cup sugar gradually, beating constantly until stiff peaks form. Beat egg yolks in mixer bowl for 3 minutes. Add 1 cup sugar gradually, beating constantly at low speed until smooth. Add flour mixture and orange juice alternately, beginning and ending with flour mixture. Beat well after each addition. Stir in orange rind. Fold egg yolk mixture into egg whites gently using a whisk. Spoon into ungreased tube pan without removable bottom. Bake at 350 degrees for 30 to 40 minutes. Invert on funnel to cool completely. Loosen cake from side of pan. Invert onto cake plate. Sprinkle with confectioners' sugar. Yield: 16 servings.

Approx Per Serving: Cal 165; Prot 4 g; Carbo 33 g; Fiber <1 g;
T Fat 2 g; 12% Calories from Fat; Chol 80 mg; Sod 89 mg.

Cathy Amen, Portland, Oregon

PEACH FROZEN YOGURT

1/2 cup sugar
1 teaspoon unflavored gelatin
1/8 teaspoon ground nutmeg
1/2 cup skim milk
2 tablespoons light corn syrup

1 1/2 pounds peeled peaches, cut into
   quarters
1 cup plain low-fat yogurt
1/2 teaspoon vanilla extract

Combine sugar, gelatin and nutmeg in saucepan. Stir in milk. Let stand for 1 minute. Cook over low heat for 5 minutes or until gelatin dissolves, stirring constantly. Remove from heat. Stir in corn syrup. Let stand until cool. Process peaches in food processor until smooth. Combine peach purée, gelatin mixture, yogurt and vanilla in large bowl; mix well. Chill, covered, for 8 hours. Pour mixture into freezer can of ice cream maker. Freeze using manufacturer's instructions. Allow to ripen for 1 hour in freezer can. Yield: 10 servings.

Approx Per Serving: Cal 99; Prot 2 g; Carbo 23 g; Fiber 1 g;
   T Fat <1 g; 4% Calories from Fat; Chol 2 mg; Sod 25 mg.

Susan McDonald, Ransom Canyon

BANANA SMOOTHIE

1 peeled banana, frozen
1 apple, cut into chunks

1 cup 2% milk
1/2 cup plain lowfat yogurt

Combine all ingredients in blender container. Process until smooth. Yield: 2 servings.

Approx Per Serving: Cal 185; Prot 8 g; Carbo 33 g; Fiber 3 g;
   T Fat 4 g; 17% Calories from Fat; Chol 15 mg; Sod 101 mg.

Stella Urrutia, Lubbock

365-DAY STRAWBERRY DRINK

1   16-ounce package frozen
   unsweetened strawberries, thawed
1   12-ounce can diet Sprite or 7-Up

5 packets artificial sweetener
1 1/2 cups orange juice

Purée all ingredients in blender. Pour into glass. Garnish with strawberry fan or orange slice. Yield: 5 servings.

Approx Per Serving: Cal 65; Prot 1 g; Carbo 16 g; Fiber 3 g;
   T Fat <1 g; 3% Calories from Fat; Chol 0 mg; Sod 9 mg.

Good all year around!

Lisa Cook, Wilson

Kids Cooking & Fun

Lynn County

New Home, Lynn County, Texas.

Where was the old home?

Was it a set-jaw, no-nonsense work to be done New Home?

Or, was it joyous, new start, safe haven New Home?

It was a new place,

calling a challenge to the best.

R.S.

CHARLIE BROWN CHEESE BALLS

1 cup (heaping) shredded Cheddar
  cheese

½ cup flour
2 tablespoons butter

Combine cheese, flour and butter in bowl. Add enough water to form a stiff dough. Shape into balls; place on baking sheet. Bake at 400 degrees for 15 minutes or until light brown. Remove to wire rack to cool. Yield: 24 servings.

Approx Per Serving: Cal 37; Prot 1 g; Carbo 2 g; Fiber <1 g;
  T Fat 3 g; 62% Calories from Fat; Chol 8 mg; Sod 37 mg.

Mickey Ann Miles, Slaton

PIGS IN-A-BLANKET

1　10-count can biscuits

10 miniature sausages

Separate biscuits. Place 1 sausage on each biscuit. Fold biscuits over to enclose sausage; pinch edges to seal. Place on baking sheet. Bake at 450 degrees for 10 minutes. Yield: 10 servings.

Approx Per Serving: Cal 95; Prot 3 g; Carbo 10 g; Fiber <1 g;
  T Fat 5 g; 45% Calories from Fat; Chol 1 mg; Sod 341 mg.

You can eat more than one of these.

Vanessa Gonzalez, Lubbock

FRANKS AND BEANS

1　1-pound package Wrangler franks
2　15-ounce cans pork and beans
¼ cup packed brown sugar

½ cup barbecue sauce
1 small onion, chopped

Cut franks into thin slices. Combine with beans in saucepan. Cook over medium heat until heated through. Stir in brown sugar, barbecue sauce and onion; mix well. Simmer for 10 minutes. Yield: 6 servings.

Approx Per Serving: Cal 464; Prot 17 g; Carbo 46 g; Fiber 8 g;
  T Fat 25 g; 47% Calories from Fat; Chol 48 mg; Sod 1498 mg.

This is my husband's recipe. The Wrangler franks give it the unique flavor.

Beth Mims, Muleshoe

Honey-Marmalade Bubble Loaf

1 can biscuits
2 tablespoons butter
3 tablespoons honey

¼ cup orange marmalade
½ cup chopped pecans

Cut each biscuit into 4 pieces. Place in greased 8-inch baking pan. Melt butter in saucepan. Stir in honey and marmalade. Pour over biscuit pieces; sprinkle with pecans. Bake at 375 degrees for 20 to 25 minutes or until golden brown. Garnish with sliced oranges. Serve hot or cool. Yield: 5 servings.

Approx Per Serving: Cal 331; Prot 4 g; Carbo 43 g; Fiber 2 g;
   T Fat 17 g; 45% Calories from Fat; Chol 14 mg; Sod 541 mg.

Sara Lewis, Springlake

Dirt for Dessert

1   6-ounce package vanilla instant
   pudding mix
2½ cups milk

1 cup vanilla wafer crumbs
8 gummy worms

Combine pudding mix and milk in bowl; mix until smooth. Spoon into serving dish. Top with cookie crumbs and gummy worms. Chill. Yield: 8 servings.

Approx Per Serving: Cal 189; Prot 3 g; Carbo 34 g; Fiber <1 g;
   T Fat 5 g; 22% Calories from Fat; Chol 17 mg; Sod 217 mg.

Sylvia Gonzalez, Lubbock

Fruit Pizza

1 roll refrigerator sugar cookie dough
8 ounces cream cheese, softened
½ cup sugar
1   8-ounce can crushed pineapple,
   drained

Sections of 2 mandarin oranges
2 bananas, sliced
4 cups strawberries
2 kiwifruit, sliced

Slice cookie dough using package directions. Line pizza pan with slices. Bake at 350 degrees for 10 to 15 minutes or until light brown. Cool to room temperature. Beat cream cheese and ½ cup sugar in saucepan until light. Heat until melted. Spread over cookie layer. Top with fruits. Chill until serving time. Cut into wedges to serve. Yield: 8 servings.

Approx Per Serving: Cal 659; Prot 9 g; Carbo 612 g; Fiber 4 g;
   T Fat 28 g; 9% Calories from Fat; Chol 31 mg; Sod 489 mg.

Monda Daniel, Earth

Ice Cream and Pretzel Menagerie

Ice Cream   Raisins
Pretzel nuggets, sticks and rings

Place 1 scoop ice cream on each child's plate. Furnish pretzel nuggets, pretzel sticks, pretzel rings, raisins and time to create as the imagination dictates. **Cat:** use pretzel sticks as whiskers, eyes, nose and ears. **Turtle:** Use pretzel nuggets for feet and head; use stick for tail. **Porcupine:** Stud all over with pretzel sticks for quills; use nugget for nose. **Funny Faces:** Use pretzel sticks for hair, pretzel rings for ears, raisins for eyes and sticks for mouth.

Nutritional information for this recipe is not available.

Lee Ruth Krieg, Lubbock

Summer Pops

2 12-ounce cans lemon-lime soda   1 14-ounce can sweetened
¼ cup lemon juice   condensed milk

Combine all ingredients in bowl; mix until smooth. Spoon into ten 5-ounce paper cups. Cover with foil. Insert wooden stick through foil into each pop. Freeze for 4 to 6 hours or until firm. Remove paper and foil. Yield: 10 servings.

Approx Per Serving: Cal 156; Prot 3 g; Carbo 29 g; Fiber <1 g;
    T Fat 3 g; 19% Calories from Fat; Chol 14 mg; Sod 58 mg.

Stella Urrutia, Lubbock

Desert Storm Cake

1 2-layer package yellow cake mix   4 1-ounce Skor candy bars, crushed
1 8-ounce jar caramel topping   16 ounces whipped topping
1 6-ounce package vanilla instant   1 cup chopped pecans
   pudding mix, prepared

Prepare and bake cake mix using package directions for 9x13-inch cake pan. Pierce warm cake with handle of wooden spoon. Pour caramel topping over cake; cool. Spread chilled pudding over cake. Sprinkle with candy. Spread whipped topping over top; sprinkle with pecans. Store in refrigerator. Yield: 15 servings.

Approx Per Serving: Cal 523; Prot 6 g; Carbo 71 g; Fiber 1 g;
    T Fat 26 g; 43% Calories from Fat; Chol 8 mg; Sod 369 mg.

Shonda Bentley, Friona

POPCORN CAKE

10 cups popped popcorn
1¹/₂ cups cocktail peanuts
2¹/₂ cups miniature marshmallows
¹/₄ cup butter

20 caramels
1¹/₂ cups oil
2 cups "M & M's" Chocolate Candies

Mix popcorn and peanuts in large bowl. Melt marshmallows, butter and caramels with oil in saucepan, stirring to mix well. Add to popcorn mixture; mix well. Stir in candies. Press into greased bundt pan. Invert onto waxed paper. Let stand, covered, for 12 hours before serving. Yield: 12 servings.

Approx Per Serving: Cal 596; Prot 8 g; Carbo 43 g; Fiber 3 g;
    T Fat 46 g; 67% Calories from Fat; Chol 11 mg; Sod 96 mg.

Judy Bowman, Littlefield

CRACKER JACK POPCORN

1 cup margarine
2 cups packed brown sugar
1 cup corn syrup
1¹/₂ cups chopped pecans

1 teaspoon vanilla extract
¹/₂ teaspoon baking soda
24 cups popped popcorn

Combine first 4 ingredients in saucepan. Bring to a boil. Boil for 5 minutes; remove from heat. Stir in mixture of vanilla and baking soda. Pour over popcorn in large bowl; mix well. Spread on 3 greased baking sheets. Bake at 225 degrees for 1 hour, stirring every 20 minutes. Cool to room temperature. Break into bite-sized pieces. Store in airtight container. Yield: 24 servings.

Approx Per Serving: Cal 271; Prot 2 g; Carbo 40 g; Fiber 2 g;
    T Fat 13 g; 41% Calories from Fat; Chol 0 mg; Sod 123 mg.

Pat Moses, Slaton

EASY MARSHMALLOW COOKIES

10 tablespoons peanut butter
30 butter crackers

30 marshmallows

Spread peanut butter on crackers; place 1 marshmallow on each. Place on baking sheet. Bake at 350 degrees just until marshmallows start to brown.
Yield: 30 servings.

Approx Per Serving: Cal 69; Prot 2 g; Carbo 9 g; Fiber <1 g;
    T Fat 4 g; 44% Calories from Fat; Chol 0 mg; Sod 58 mg.

Tabatha, Angel and Camille Blevins, Post

HAMBURGER COOKIES

1/2 cup coconut	12 mints
Green food coloring	Sesame seed
24 vanilla wafers	

Tint coconut green with food coloring in small bowl. Place 12 vanilla wafers rounded side down on serving plate. Top each with 1 mint, coconut and remaining wafers, rounded side up. Sprinkle with sesame seed. Yield: 12 servings.

Approx Per Serving: Cal 106; Prot 1 g; Carbo 20 g; Fiber <1 g;
    T Fat 2 g; 21% Calories from Fat; Chol 5 mg; Sod 36 mg.

Jan Kennedy, Lubbock

HOLLY WREATHS

1/2 cup margarine	11/2 teaspoons green food coloring
30 large marshmallows	31/2 cups cornflakes
1/2 teaspoon vanilla extract	1 ounce red hot cinnamon candies

Melt margarine with marshmallows in saucepan, stirring to mix well; remove from heat. Stir in vanilla and food coloring. Add cornflakes; mix gently with wooden spoon. Drop by teaspoonfuls onto waxed paper; shape into wreaths with greased fingers. Press candies onto wreaths while still warm. Let stand for several hours or until cool. Yield: 24 servings.

Approx Per Serving: Cal 80; Prot <1 g; Carbo 11 g; Fiber <1 g;
    T Fat 4 g; 42% Calories from Fat; Chol 0 mg; Sod 94 mg.

Jan Kennedy, Lubbock

SCOTCHIES

2 cups butterscotch chips	1 13-ounce can chow mein noodles
1/2 cup peanuts	

Microwave butterscotch chips, covered, in medium glass bowl on High for 2 minutes or until melted. Stir in peanuts and noodles. Drop by teaspoonfuls onto waxed paper. Let stand until cool. Yield: 30 servings.

Approx Per Serving: Cal 114; Prot 3 g; Carbo 12 g; Fiber 1 g;
    T Fat 6 g; 48% Calories from Fat; Chol 1 mg; Sod 142 mg.

Shonda Bentley, Friona

BANANA-CHOCOLATE SHAKE

8 bananas, sliced
6 cups cold milk
1 cup chocolate instant drink mix

1 teaspoon vanilla extract
1½ pints vanilla ice cream

Combine bananas, cold milk, drink mix and vanilla ⅓ at a time in blender container. Process until smooth. Spoon into glasses. Top with scoops of ice cream. Yield: 8 servings.

Approx Per Serving: Cal 370; Prot 11 g; Carbo 59 g; Fiber 2 g;
    T Fat 13 g; 29% Calories from Fat; Chol 47 mg; Sod 190 mg.

Sylvia Gonzalez, Lubbock

MOUNTAIN BERRY SLUSH

2 packages mountain berry drink mix
2 cups sugar

4 cups cold water
4 liters ginger ale, chilled

Combine drink mix, sugar, water and 3 liters ginger ale in 1 gallon container; mix well. Freeze until slushy. Combine with remaining 1 liter ginger ale in punch bowl or large pitcher. May substitute lemon-lime soda for ginger ale. Yield: 24 servings.

Approx Per Serving: Cal 118; Prot <1 g; Carbo 31 g; Fiber 0 g;
    T Fat 0 g; 0% Calories from Fat; Chol 0 mg; Sod 11 mg.

Shelia Duckworth, Olton

ORANGE JULIUS

1 6-ounce can frozen orange juice
   concentrate
1 cup milk
½ cup honey

1 cup water
1½ teaspoons vanilla extract
12 ice cubes

Combine orange juice concentrate, milk, honey, water, vanilla and ice cubes in blender container; process for 30 seconds or until smooth. Pour into glasses. Yield: 4 servings.

Approx Per Serving: Cal 234; Prot 3 g; Carbo 54 g; Fiber <1 g;
    T Fat 2 g; 8% Calories from Fat; Chol 8 mg; Sod 29 mg.

Angela Quarles, Lubbock

MODELING CLAY

1 cup cornstarch	**2 cups salt**
2/3 cup water	**2/3 cup water**

Mix cornstarch with 2/3 cup water in bowl. Combine salt and 2/3 cup water in saucepan. Bring to a boil. Add to cornstarch mixture; mix with wooden spoon until smooth and pliable. Store in airtight container. May dry modeled objects at room temperature. May tint clay with food coloring. Yield: 3 cups.

Lee Ruth Krieg, Lubbock

PLAY DOUGH

1 cup flour	**1 tablespoon oil**
1/2 cup salt	**2 teaspoons cream of tartar**
1 cup water	**Food coloring (optional)**

Combine flour, salt, water, oil and cream of tartar in saucepan; mix well. Cook over medium heat until mixture forms ball. Knead on work surface, adding food coloring if desired. Store in airtight container; do not store in refrigerator. May double oil for smoother dough that is softer for the hands. Yield: 2 cups.

Joan Johnston, Lubbock

PLAY CLAY

1/2 cup salt	**2 tablespoons oil**
2 cups water	**2 cups flour**
Food coloring	**2 tablespoons powdered alum**

Mix salt and water in saucepan. Heat just until salt dissolves; remove from heat. Add food coloring and oil; mix well. Add flour and alum; mix well. Let stand until cool enough to handle. Knead for several minutes. Store in airtight container. May add a few drops of peppermint, lemon or orange extract for scented dough. Yield: 3 cups.

Lee Ruth Krieg, Lubbock

SILLY PUTTY

3 tablespoons (generous) liquid starch   **¼ cup white liquid glue**

Combine starch and glue in small bowl; mix for 5 minutes. Knead on work surface, working out any excess moisture. Store in airtight container in refrigerator. May add food coloring if desired. Yield: ½ cup.

Lee Ruth Krieg, Lubbock

CRYSTAL GARDEN

¼ cup salt
2 tablespoons water
2 tablespoons ammonia

2 tablespoons laundry bluing
Lumps of coal
Food coloring

Combine salt, water, ammonia and bluing in bowl; mix well. Pour over coal in flat glass dish. Sprinkle with food coloring. Let stand for several days for crystals to begin to grow and spread. May add additional food coloring to formations as they grow.

The coal for this project usually can be found in hardware stores.

Lee Ruth Krieg, Lubbock

INTERNATIONAL FRIENDSHIP SOUFFLÉ

1 cup greetings
1½ cups smiles
1 large handshake

4 cups love
2 teaspoons sympathy
2 cups hospitality

Cream greetings and smiles together well. Add handshake. Blend in love gradually. Sift sympathy and hospitality together. Fold in carefully. Bake in moderate oven. Serve to everyone you meet.

Joni Lynch Wilson, Lubbock

INDEX

Mail Order Form

Name _____

Address _____

City/State/Zip _____

Number of copies _____

   x Cost ($12.95 per book) _____

Shipping & Handling at _____ per book _____

Tax at 8.25% _____

Total _____

Make checks payable to:

Caprock Girl Scout Council
Gatherings
2567 74th Street
Lubbock, Texas 79423
(806) 745-2855

- -

I would like the following individual to receive information on *GATHERINGS*.

Name _____

Address _____

City/State/Zip _____

- -

I would like to see *GATHERINGS* in the following stores in my area.

Name _____

Address _____

City/State/Zip _____

- -

I would like the following individual to receive information on *GATHERINGS*.

Name _____

Address _____

City/State/Zip _____

- -

I would like to see *GATHERINGS* in the following stores in my area.

Name _____

Address _____

City/State/Zip _____

- -